EVERYTHING IS FINE UNTIL IT ISN'T

EVERYTHING IS FINE UNTIL IT ISN'T

LISA KARTUS

© 2015 Lisa G. Kartus Living Trust

This is a work of fiction. Names, characters, businesses, locales and events are products of the author's imagination, except in the case of historical figures or actual locations, which are used fictitiously. Yale University's Beinecke Rare Book and Manuscript Library does exist in all its wonder, and bibliophiles may even rate its magical presence stronger than I've described. The character of Constance Cordrey is not based on any Beinecke librarian, but she is surely inspired by the kindness, courtesy and competence of those who helped me.

Acknowledgements

Every book has a story behind the story. Mine began when I observed relationship after relationship where a parasitic man took over a strong woman. And the occasional parasitic woman living off a strong man. The parasite could be emotionally abusive, physically abusive, or both, but always manipulative. This is real, not fiction. It takes place behind the doors in your neighborhood.

Then the most wonderful thing happened: one of those doors opened wide. Sam Bowen, the most lady-like of women, read my book and cried. This, she confided, happened to her. Thank you, Sam. To say she helped strengthen my story is an understatement.

Also behind every novelist is a lot of love.

Emily Monk, honorary daughter, served as brilliant reader and editor, not only catching proofreading errors but also what can only be termed generational differences. Not to mention that she knows more about cars and farming than I ever will.

Paula Haglund read the book not once but twice and caught errors that everyone else missed.

A few years back, my BFF Mary Beth Woodall and honorary daughter Veronika accompanied me on a look-and-see trip. We drove the semi-antique Woodall Mercedes from where MB then lived in Guilford, CT, to Yale and its Beinecke Rare Book and Manuscript Library, and from there to Lenox, MA and Edith Wharton's estate, The Mount. We had a number of adventures that we still laugh about. MB has always been my creative enabler. I hope I sometimes return the favor.

Why Edith Wharton? Because I've been a huge fan forever. Because her life is equally as interesting as her books. Because she survived a manipulative mother and parasitic husband to build her own life her own way. That she wrote for Henry James is my fiction —let's be clear on that. However, if you haven't read her books, including her autobiography, do so now. She had a very clear idea of the economic basis of marriage which holds true in our era for relationships, married or not. She was a strong woman with the courage to open those doors around her and reveal what was behind them.

Wharton is a role model. I hope you have the courage to open those doors for yourself. Women caught in abusive, parasitic relationships find it nearly impossible to talk about their situations. If such a friend lets you see a glimpse of her life, don't back away. If you've been hiding behind that closed door, think about reaching out. This book is about what amazing things can happen when women help women.

Finally, first and always to Jesse, who defines the supportive husband.

Lisa Kartus
2015

Prologue

"I could have stopped him so many times," Constance said. "When I said yes to a date. Or after he walked two miles to bring me a single rose, his mouth still numb from having his wisdom teeth pulled.

"Or when I told a college classmate what he had done and she asked, her voice filled with a level of awe I can still hear, 'And you believed him? That he'd walked miles to bring you a rose after dental surgery? Sure he didn't take a bus? I mean, we're talking Manhattan here, right?' Instead of considering her skepticism sufficiently valid to think over, I registered it as unfair criticism of a romantic gesture.

"Yes, I believed him. We will believe, women like us. Until we don't. What was I thinking?"

Lily said, "Here I sit, living proof that thinking doesn't enter into it. Which, may I remind you, had to be pointed out to me before it was too late."

Cara, the youngest of the trio by nearly a decade and far more skeptical than Constance's long-ago classmate, said, "Wow, Constance, you must have been a completely different person back then, buying into that crap. A red rose? I mean, he couldn't be more inventive? How about a tea rose? Or maybe something that showed he understood you."

"For example?" Constance asked.

"Like a book. An old book. Hell, any book." Cara shook her head. "It's like these men cast us in the movie of their lives, write the whole script, then we recite the lines they assign us. We don't know it's not a performance until the pain begins."

"I married him." Constance seemed to be reminding herself. "His script was exactly what I had been brought up to do and be. Until the script changed."

Lily said, "We play by their rules. Until we don't. It just takes some of us longer to begin to write our own rules."

Chapter 1

March

The worn oak flooring creaked with each of Lily's steps. Her first thought was that she had to lose weight. Her second thought was that even if she did, the floor would still complain. Everything in Prairie Shores College's Old Stanley Hall complained. She slid into one of the student seats, parking her pile of grading before shrugging out of her black coat. For a moment she had the room to herself. That she was always a few minutes early proved that she'd never run on academic time. One panel of the room's blackboard was lined for music, treble clef over bass clef, a few notes sketched in. Down the hall a pianist repeated an opening of what could have been Bach, while from another direction she heard an oboe. She wondered what it would have been like to take another direction in her own life, to have tried music or art. Her imagination placed her in the front line of the woodwind section of a symphony orchestra, voicing the song of the oboe down the hall. She could hear the silk of her concert skirt rustle softly, lending an aura of richness to the experience.

Lost in her orchestral daydreaming, Lily failed to notice when the English department chair walked in to set up for the meeting. It took Jane Hardy saying "That's a sizable grant application you've submitted" to snap Lily back to reality. "Any chance of getting it? That's not like that teaching award—grants are hard to come by."

So are teaching awards, Lily thought. For a fact, Jane had never won such an award. "You know the adage," Lily said, "nothing ventured, nothing gained." She couldn't remember the last time Jane had bothered to make small talk with her. This might be the first time. One of her uncle's sayings was something about beware of people who change, or maybe it was people whose habits suddenly change. That they were up to something. Probably because Lily tended to let people reveal themselves to her gradually, her mother regarded her as a lousy judge of character. Lily had known Jane Hardy for five years, though, and the woman remained opaque.

"With $50,000, you could go anywhere you want to." Jane's round face and flattened features lent her a stern look, as did her straight-cut gray hair and angular body. She favored slinky knit outfits which accentuated an impressive cleavage.

Jane came over to lean against an adjacent desk, her feet nudging Lily's.

Lily pulled away, feeling invaded. She wished the other professors would come in and distract this woman. "So when do you expect word?"

"June."

"That late?"

Before Lily could ask why that was late, some of the wished-for faculty wandered into the room.

Jane turned to the rest of her flock. Lily had once heard her say that she thought the metaphor appropriate. Jane wasn't so much the kind shepherd as the efficient rancher. She'd gather the flock and cull the herd as necessary.

The department settled in for another session planning the new class progression for undergraduate literature majors. They'd been discussing these changes since Lily's first department meeting here five years ago. She didn't understand why they didn't just decide. Looking at the pile of freshman composition journal entries under her hand, she began reading.

The top paper looked as if grape jelly had been blotted off of it. "Coach says that we only play our own game, not the other side's game, that we make the other side play our game."

Without thinking, she wrote in the margin of her student's paper, "Why? What does he mean?"

"My high school coach said the same thing, then gave us all the plays, like we couldn't think for ourselves."

It never ceased to surprise her what a tight community the athletes were, with rules repeated to them from the time they first donned a helmet or picked up a bat. Specific rules that everybody knew. Her world was equally closed, rules equally rigid, but never specified, unless someone who failed to receive tenure forced the university to explain why. She glanced at Jane, who caught the glance on one of her regular sweeps of the room. The chair looked pointedly at Lily's red pen. Lily ignored her. She was so tired of being the good girl, the obedient sheep.

Lily straightened her back, one hand going automatically to shield her abdomen before she remembered. It was the first week of the spring term, the end of March. Outside it was snowing, one of those spring snows that Lake Michigan favored: big wet flakes that piled up in a hurry, bringing out students to build snow forts and pitch snowball fights as if they were in elementary school. She sniffed, but instead of overheated air she caught a whiff of freedom.

Lily looked with interest to see what her athlete had to say. "But Coach Ford assigned us some defense strategy, says we have to know how to plan these things, that if we work out the plans ourselves then what he tell us on game night make sense." She circled his verb and spelling errors, admiring how few he'd made so far. Not bad. She ought to get to know Coach Ford—the thought brought on a laugh, which she quickly squelched. As if she could get to know a campus star, which in her world meant anyone who brought in outside money to the college. In theory, if her grants came in, including the ones the department chair didn't know about, Lily could be a campus star. In theory. Still, a coach who insisted his team think for themselves was someone she'd like to meet. In the margin, she wrote, "How does it feel constructing strategy? What's it like? Consider using simile or metaphor: is it like working a math equation?" She read to the end of the journal, another paragraph, then added "Want to rewrite this? Grade for now: C-."

She shuffled the football player to the bottom of the pile. Next were pages from Cara Lynne Stanley. Cara Lynne. Lily silently pulled the dark green grade book out of her book bag and opened it to this Comp I section. Ignoring her boss didn't require being openly rude. Voices around her were being raised in enthusiastic debate. "Stanley, Caroline" was what she'd neatly copied from the computerized registration list yesterday morning after class. She tried to bring the girl to mind but couldn't. It was too early in the term. Cara Lynne wrote, "I've been trying to determine what is spousal abuse."

That brought Lily up short. The department meeting faded. Spousal abuse? Was this an eighteen-year-old?

> Though I'm not married, but live with my boyfriend, so maybe what I am talking about is spousal abuse or maybe not. I don't even know why I'm writing about this, except that you said to write what was on our mind, and to analyze it, not just to report what was happening as if we were writing in a datebook or phone calendar. Well, this is what's on my mind. I have no external bruises. My boyfriend, I'll call him Angel but that's not his real name to protect the innocent and all that, doesn't hit me, probably couldn't hit me, not physically.

In the margin, Lily automatically scribbled, "run-on sentence—rewrite this into two sentences."

"We live in a one-bedroom apartment in Rogers Park," the northeastern-most Chicago neighborhood.

"Angel ought to be a film director. He's got lots of experience directing my life. Get out from behind that bar and go to college, he says. So hear I am, 25 years old, surrounded by adolescants." Lily circled the misspellings absently. Sometimes comp students wrote to her as if she were their therapist. Therapist or confidante, either was a dangerous role for a professor to assume. There had to be boundaries set between student and teacher. "But I think I know what I want to do when I grow up unlike Jamie in the next seat."

Lily stifled another giggle. Jamie was one of those fey boys, lock of hair over one eye, with an air of the perpetually dreaming. Yesterday morning, during introductions, she'd stepped behind him, removed his earbuds and handed them to him, saying, "Someone is paying over $40,000 a year for you to be here. Listen. See if it's worth it." He smiled, nodded, and stashed his iPod.

Cara Lynne wrote conversationally,

> But here's the thing. Yesterday Angel took my cat to the vet and had him put down. I loved Charlie. He just had a urinary infection is all. He was peeing outside the box. Angel was supposed to get him medicine. When he told me what he'd done, he said no cat was worth $400 in medical care. I don't know where he got the $400 number from. Last time the pills cost $10. I've been crying ever since yesterday. Angel killed Charlie. Angel killed Charlie. I've known Angel for two years, Charlie for seven. Angel killed Charlie. He acts like that was his right, that he could determine life and death. In my life.

Lily wrote, "Be scared," then told herself to cross it out. The correct thing to do would be guide Cara Lynne into the proper teacher/student relationship. Still she looked at the words, red inked on the right side of the page. The oboe down the hall moaned. At the front of the room, Jane asked the assembled faculty if there was any news to share with the department. A few professors proudly told of papers accepted for publication. An old-timer announced that he was considering retirement, but didn't mention when. Jane and several others made discouraging noises while nodding their heads. The room fell silent. Jane looked expectantly at Lily.

But Lily was looking at Cara Lynne's cleanly-printed paper. "Angel killed Charlie." Lily tucked her hands underneath her thighs to still their trembling.

"Lily, do join us," Jane called.

Startled, Lily looked up to see some twenty faces peering at her. For many of them, it was the first time they'd noticed her, which had always been fine with Lily. She sniffed again, felt that hint of freedom, like fresh air. "Well, I've applied for a National Endowment for the Humanities grant to finish my search for documents concerning Edith Wharton and Henry James."

"She says she requested $50,000," Jane added, "which will undoubtedly scare off the NEH, even if they do get the paperwork."

The pianist down the hall tried out a few major chords. The oboist in the opposite direction blew flat notes, causing a few of the English professors to cringe. "Of course, sometimes it's necessary to take risks," Jane said. Lily didn't think it was a risk—grant applications took so long, you might as well ask for the moon. That didn't mean the NEH would give her the whole moon, but neither did it mean they would deny her a taste of green cheese. Jane's attention shifted to another member of her flock, and Lily's eyes returned to the student journal on the top of the pile.

"But here's the strange thing," Cara Lynne wrote. "The apartment seems empty. I'm here, Angel will be back in a few minutes, but the place seems, I don't know, abandoned. Like one of those science fiction movies or Star Trek where the spaceship finds a city where everyone just vanished in the middle of what they were doing. Or am I thinking of Pompay?"

Lily stopped herself from marking "sp" by that last word.

"Charlie's dishes are still on the floor. His cat box is next to the back door, his favorite catnip toy by the chair I study in. I can see it right now. It's blue, and when he'd take it in his mouth it made a nice rattling noise. Oh, shit, I'm crying and I can hear Angel on the stairs."

That was the end of the journal entry except for a note written in a neat square hand: "Dr. Atwood, this is as far as I got last night. I'll bring more by later today or tomorrow. I need to write this on campus. Thanks. Cara Lynne." Then there was a P.S. "Angel isn't a student here. Or anywhere. He owns the bar I worked at. CL"

Lily looked up to find the meeting had adjourned, leaving her once again alone in the room. She supposed she should be thankful that no one had turned off the lights.

"Angel killed Charlie," Cara Lynne had written. But instead of marking out her own words, "Be scared," Lily drew a red arrow from them to "Angel killed Charlie." Then added, "What happened when you confronted him?"

That note of freedom played again, this time by the oboe.

Chapter 2

God how she hated teaching in University Hall. Every midwestern college she'd ever been to had one, the oldest building on campus, faced in some rough-cut native stone, boiler dating from the changeover from coal to oil. The ceilings were so high that the buzzing fluorescent lights hung from pipes. What bothered her was the heat. They could have been in a steam room and were all overdressed for the experience. The twenty students in her second comp section, scattered toward the back of the room, had stripped down to tee shirts and jeans.

Lily kept on her suit jacket. She'd discovered during her first year as a graduate teaching assistant, when she was no more than four years older than her students, that a black suit helped establish her authority. At a couple of inches over five feet, she was too short for students to take her seriously if she dressed like them. Her older male colleagues got away with jeans and tee shirts, but she figured she'd have gray hair before she could pull that off. She put her black hair up in a ballerina knot on top of her head for the same reason: it made her look formal. And it was a bit cooler. Still she sweltered. Maybe she'd get to know the registrar and charm him into moving her into a building with a heating system installed in the last couple of decades. Sure, Lily, she told herself, you could charm him, that'd be a first, then threw open the window closest to the front of the room. "If you begin to drip icicles, let me know," she said, before writing on the blackboard "Dr. Lily Atwood. English 101 — Academic Writing." A pair of large males read what she'd written, rose, nodded at her and left. "Anyone else?" Lily asked the remaining students. "If you're not here for English 101, one of us is in the wrong room."

No one moved. "In that case, let's look over the syllabus." She passed out copies. After the students realized that they'd be writing three essays in nine weeks, two more large males departed, probably to fish for a teacher with a reputation for lounging through the term. The English Department hired adjunct freshman composition teachers by the truckload, several of whom would be guaranteed to offer easy A's. Not Assistant Professor Lily Atwood, on the tenure track and who usually taught graduate courses. But she bet the students would find those other comp classes already filled by athletes and girls from sororities that kept lists of the easy teachers. The pair would be back, somewhat chagrined. Some of her students in a previous year had shown her one sorority's write-up about her: "tough but fair, you'll learn a lot. Worth the work." The kiss of death in a review that secretly pleased her.

In theory at least they were there for an education. She chuckled, then tested the theory.

"Take out your book of readings."

The first thing she taught freshmen was how to read. When she'd told Jonas that, when they'd met during her first year of doctoral study, he'd pointed out that students must know how to read if they'd been accepted to college. "Yes, but they believe everything they see in print."

"Makes them nice and manageable," Jonas had replied. They had been sitting in one of the cheap pizza joints that populated Lakeland near the campus of Lakeland University. This one was dark and yeasty-smelling, filled with loud undergraduates drinking too much beer on a school night.

"But boring," Lily said. "I can manage them, but dread being bored by them. If college isn't the place to develop your own ideas, where, then?"

That years-ago night, Jonas had tossed his long silky brown hair behind his shoulders. He hadn't cut it until right before his first job interview. That night it was almost as long as her black hair. She knew the other female grad students thought him sexy. He projected sexual electricity. At first she hadn't responded to it. His mien reminded her of a cat who only rubs up against you when he wants something. To her surprise, her lack of interest attracted him. In the dark restaurant, she could tell he wasn't really listening to her. He played with her hand, tracing the life lines on her palm, putting her fingers into his mouth. His moves excited her but at the same time she wished he'd listen to her words. Maybe men couldn't do two things at once. She didn't know, since Jonas was her first real boyfriend. She didn't quite know what to do with Jonas.

And here she was eleven years later, married to Jonas. Until the previous June, they'd both been at Prairie Shores. He'd begun there as a tenure-track psychology professor, but a few years before had moved into development, i.e., alumni fundraising, then moved the previous summer to the much more prestigious and therefore better-paying Lakeland University as a vice president of development. She'd stayed at Prairie Shores, where she had been contented enough.

Now, when she looked out at her students, winnowed down to nine women and seven men, she wondered which of them was going through that first-boyfriend stage. Thirty minutes later, the class had worked through the first seven paragraphs of an essay comparing the driving habits of men and women. She'd chosen the piece because it contained so many "everybody knows it's true" comments, and there was nothing like *ad populum* arguments to move an adolescent firmly into the defense or offense position. Once she'd roused their hearts, then she had access to their minds, to begin to teach them to question everything. Before they could write anything interesting, they had to question. Otherwise they'd parrot parents, high school teachers, or whatever the latest was on the internet or social media. The parroting, the lack of imagination, was what she found boring.

It was in the midst of one particularly rousing session about men refusing to ask for directions, with the boys insisting on offering anecdotal evidence against, that Lily said, "But think. Picture the moment you're describing. Is that what really happened? Or are you leaving out some crucial detail? Before you can read critically you have to be honest with yourself and not suppress some inconvenient bit of data."

During the silence that followed, her words played back through Lily's mind: "'Be honest with yourself.'" Well, honestly, last night Jonas was in top form, she thought. Her husband hadn't devoted that much attention to her in months.

Be honest. Had she missed it? Her hand protected her midsection.

She looked out at her students, who were looking back at her expectantly. For a brief moment she thought she might have spoken her thoughts aloud. Consciously she put both hands at her waist. "Well, what have you come up with?"

The young men looked at one another, silently daring each other to be the first to break ranks. There was a titter from one of the women, tall and blonde and too perfect who wore a Tri Delt sorority sweatshirt. Lily could have sworn the boys clustered closer together.

She awaited their decision.

Jonas' attention: did she miss it? Yes and no. His constant need to overpower her with his sexuality: did she miss it? Ditto. She'd actually briefly considered faking orgasm last night so Jonas would go away. Then didn't have to. She never did.

Her skin felt hot and she'd turned away from the class toward the blackboard when one of the more mature-looking boys spoke up. "I never ask for directions, but I never get lost. My dad says I must have been born with a compass installed." He looked smugly at the blonde from the safety of the opposite side of the room.

"If you've never gotten lost, it means you've never ventured out of your comfortable little environment," the blonde said, chin raised, looking down her perky nose at the young man.

He reddened. "I can read a map."

"Not everything's on a map," put in another girl, emboldened by her classmate's comments.

"Or did your daddy buy you a phone with a GPS system?" asked the blonde.

The young man straightened. "My father delivers your father's mail."

The sorority girl looked at him with interest. Lily understood that look, that fascination with someone outside of the girl's experience. The fascination arrived in Lily's life, in the form of Jonas, when she was older and should have known better. Stop it, she chided herself. It was time to bring the class discussion and her thoughts back on track. Lily asked the Tri Delt, "Have you ever stopped to ask for directions?"

The blonde thought about Lily's question. She glanced at the mailman's son and confessed, "My phone has GPS which my car broadcasts, but it's only as good as the information I key in. Same with Google maps and that. I've gotten lost and had to ask for directions, especially last summer when Mandy and I drove to the Ann Arbor art fair. We found the town, no problem, but had to ask our way to the fair."

"You could have searched out another map on your phone," pointed out a nondescript boy.

Mandy, a stunning sepia copy of her blonde friend, said, "We could have. But it was easier to ask."

"Why?" put in Lily at the same time that several students, male and female, made disagreeing noises. Now they'd gotten to where Lily wanted them: it might be easier to ask, but only if you're not afraid to show your ignorance. It took some students years to learn to ask what they needed to know, to find out that everything wasn't out there in the ether of internet, and sometimes they learned the lesson too late.

Chapter 3

Lily stopped back at her University Hall office. She found Cara Lynne's second journal entry sealed in an envelope pushed under her office door, plus a third that the student had left in Lily's English department mail slot. The first sentence of the new entry said, "This morning when I woke up, Angel was gone. So were Charlie's things, his bowl and his cat box and his toys. As if I'd forget him like that, like he'd been erased."

Lily's gut clenched, leaving her with that unanchored feeling of driving over black ice. Taking deep breaths, she placed the typed pages on the desk. She looked out the window at the gray sky and graying snow plowed away from campus sidewalks. It's a student journal, she told herself. What's so different about this one? Lily Miller Atwood knew herself well enough to understand when she was out of her depth. Usually her solution was to dig herself out with facts, facts and more facts. But in-depth facts about real people, especially students, were hard to come by. Read, she told herself. See what Cara Lynne wants to tell you. Then worry about why.

Lily closed the office door and sat down with Cara Lynne's journal entries. The pages had been slipped into a manila envelope with Lily's name typed neatly on a white label. Typed, not printed by a computer. That was one fact. Where would the girl find an actual typewriter? With her fingertip, Lily traced the indentations left by typewriter keys in the letters of her name and title. The pages, though, had been printed. Probably the student had made use of the computers available in the library or student union or even the writing center. That also meant she was writing someplace away from the eyes of Angel. Another fact.

"As if I'd forget him like that, like he'd been erased," Lily read again. It was that word "erased" that seemed to punch her right below her breasts. Sure, it was a powerful word not normally used by students, who were more likely to hit the delete button than erase anything. Why did "erase" hurt Lily personally? She knew but didn't want to know. Instead, she read on.

> How did I end up sharing an apartment with a man who understands me so little? No, that's not it. It's not that he doesn't understand me. It's that it doesn't occur to him to try. I'm still circling around the truth here, but it's not because I'm avoiding it. It's because I'm trying to figure it out. If you don't want to read this, Dr. Atwood, that's

OK. But I need to write this for me, and I know I won't do this unless it's aimed at a reader. So you're stuck. Sorry.

Lily wrote, "I'm honored" in the margin, in black ink. She caught herself and started to cross it out, then stopped. Boundaries between professor and student should be clearly demarcated. Yes, but not this time. Lily wanted to know why the girl had gotten to her, just as the student was analyzing toward her own 'why.' She added "by your trust" and kept reading.

I've been doing a lot of thinking in the last few days, thinking I probably should have done a few years ago. But you know how life takes over? I'm trying to figure out how I got here. No, truth time again: I know how I got here. What I'm trying to understand is why. I'm 25. I've been supporting myself since I was 18. In 7 years you'd think I could have figured things out.

But maybe lives, like decent whiskey, have to age first. The cheap stuff at the bar smells raw. I don't know how those guys who come in for a beer and a shot can even get it down, their throats must be like leather. But the good stuff, the stuff that says on the label that it's been aged for whatever number of years, smells good. Mellow. Smooth. It's also like ten times as expensive as the cheap stuff. Not many guys who can afford it come into Angel's bar — it's way on the north side almost to Howard Street. He'd have to really redo the place to rate the folks who'd buy the aged stuff regularly.

So how did Angel rate me?

I left home as soon as I could. Well, almost as soon. I wanted to graduate from high school first. But believe me when I say I thought about leaving before that, when I could work legally, so at 16. My father—well, he's not a drunk or violent—well, angry all the time, but yelling and screaming and slapping, not punching or stuff like that — but he always has to be in charge. Of everything. My mom likes to be told what to do. It took me a while to figure that out. It makes her comfortable that Dad's in charge. That way she doesn't have to think for herself. Nothing's ever her fault, either, you know? My little brother doesn't pay any attention to Dad, which for some reason doesn't bother Dad. But me, from the time I can remember I had to jump when he said to. I can't remember when I didn't dread his coming home at night, waiting to see what I'd forgotten to do, waiting to be slapped or yelled at. I try to remember if he ever complimented me or said thank you for anything, but honestly, I can't. He must have. But if he did it got lost in all the noise. His noise. All the time. When I think of my father that's what comes into my head, loud noise, like jackhammers they use to drill pavement.

So I moved out the day I graduated high school. I'd been working after school and on weekends for two years, saving every penny. Those girls I went to high school with — this was on the northwest side of Chicago, in a sort of middle-class neighborhood, where no one's poor but no one drives a Porsche, either — spent their money on clothes. I wore jeans and sneakers that my mom bought for me. I cut my own hair. My make-up was from the Walgreens. I was saving every cent I could, and I knew damn well what the money was for. I was buying my way out. Two weeks before graduation I put down a security deposit on a studio apartment in Rogers Park. I think I may have been the only person in my new building that spoke English. But the place was mine. The day after graduation I moved in. I slept on the floor until I got a mattress from someone who'd advertised in the Reader. Then I went to downtown Chicago to the Anti-Cruelty Society and found Charlie.

He was a tiny little black kitten. He had long hair and these bright gold eyes. He hung back in the back of his cage when the other people went by. But I could tell he was watching me. When I went over, he marched right up to the front and put his paws through the wire, like he wanted to shake hands. I remember I opened the cage without the assistant's OK and took him out. Charlie tucked his head under my chin and purred. That was it. I paid the fee and signed the contract that said I'd bring him back to be neutered. That night he slept on my neck. It was quiet in the apartment. The door was double-locked and chained. I was the only one with the key. I think that was the first night in my whole life that I really slept. It was like I dreamed about sleeping.

• • •

Lily looked up from Cara Lynne's pages. Sometimes when she read, the world contained within the pages was more real than the world around her. To break that spell she went over to the window. The snow had stopped. There was a low sun, red and pink rays breaking through thin overcast. She put her hand on the window, fingers spread, feeling the cold. This was real.

Without intending to, she found herself back reading her student's pages. This was more real.

> How did I end up living with a guy who killed my Charlie? Sure Charlie was a cat. But he was seven years of me, too. He was the person I, Caroline who renamed herself Cara Lynne, chose to live with. I was his person. He was my comfort, my Charlie.
>
> Here's the picture in my head: I'm tied down by both feet and one hand. The only hand free is the one I'm writing with.
>
> I've got to think about this. Because I have this terrible feeling that I'm back where I started. Suffocated by the noise.

Lily put the pages back in their envelope. She put the envelope in her desk drawer and locked it. Then she put her long black coat on, carefully locked her office door and headed downstairs. Cara's story ran in her head like a movie. Lily wasn't paying any attention to her surroundings. Distantly she heard a few students greet her. She was on autopilot until she reached the Student Finance office. There she went past the reception counter and two workers and walked right into Iris Sowerby's office. "Dean Sowerby, I need a student loan application, the one for an independent student. Plus a work-study application. Please."

The dean looked stunned. "Who are you?"

Lily felt her entire body go limp. "I'm Dr. Lily Atwood from the English Department."

"Well, then these forms aren't for you."

"They're for a student. I want to give her options."

"That's not your job."

Lily looked the woman in the eye. The dean was in her forties, plump, with dyed red hair. She didn't look like the keeper of the money gates, Lily thought, but then what should such keeper look like? Scrooge? "Believe me when I say I know that." Lily sat down in the chair that bumped right up against Sowerby's desk. "I'd like to attach the forms to a journal entry I'll be returning in a day or two."

The dean leaned forward to ask, "Freshman comp student?"

Lily nodded.

"Information that you don't feel right about sharing?"

"Exactly."

"But that worries you?"

"Very much."

The dean took out a pad of paper with her name printed across the top. She scribbled a note. Without a word she got up and went into the outer office. A moment later she returned with the forms Lily had requested, stapled to a note that said, "Feel free to drop in any time. Dr. Atwood has vouched for you. She also hasn't passed on any other information."

Lily looked at the dean for a long moment. She felt as though she were going to cry. It wasn't within Lily's experience that women helped each other. She stood up and held out her hand. The dean clasped it in her own large, warm and dry hand.

Chapter 4

Returning to her office, she heard the commotion before she'd reached the second-floor landing outside of the department secretary's office. A man's tenor voice, harsh, insistent, just that much too loud, "Where's this Atwood person? How do I find her? No, you find her, because let me tell you she's going to talk to me."

"Please tell me your name, sir," said Dorcas, the unflappable secretary, "so I can leave her a message. I'm sure she'll call you as soon as she gets back for office hours."

"My name? Angelis. Frank Angelis. I pay a shitload of tuition at this place and she sure as hell better call me." The voice pronounced Angelis as "angel iz"—Lily was listening to Cara Lynne's Angel. She hid the manila envelope with Cara's name in her mail slot before quickly writing "Dorcas, call campus security immediately" on a pink phone call slip. Coat still on, she strode into the English department's front office, handed the folded note to Dorcas, saying, "I couldn't help but overhear. I'm Dr. Atwood."

Angelis turned on her. At first he smiled because he was looking down at a woman. Not that tall himself, with thinning mouse-brown hair brushed back from a high forehead, he looked like the losing side before a shoot-out in an old Wild West movie. His cowboy boots were polished, his jeans ironed with a crease. A disguise hiding the real person, Lily thought. When he moved into her personal space, spitting out, "Where's Cara Lynne? She come crawling to you?" in a voice still too loud, she stood her ground but pivoted slightly, forcing Angel to move into the doorway without realizing it. Behind her, Lily heard Dorcas punch in the security-needed-now code.

Lily pivoted a bit more. Angelis found himself with his knees backed against the wall bench. "What are you doing, bitch? Trying to push me over? Well, I'm no pushover." He reached out to shove her chest. She moved aside. He almost lost his balance, then pulled back to regard her.

"Mr. Angelis, is that your name? Shall we begin this meeting again?" Lily heard her classroom voice ring crisply. Years of dealing with students, particularly the occasional angry young man, had come to her aid.

When his eyes darted next to her, Lily became aware that campus security had arrived. "You threatening me?" Angelis demanded.

"Looks like you're threatening Dr. Atwood," said Tim, Lily's favorite hulking campus cop. He'd walked her to the faculty parking lot after night classes many times over the past five years; Lily knew all about how he was working his way through college so he could become something besides what he called a fake cop. They'd last discussed whether he should apply to the Chicago Police Academy or the FBI, protect his community or fight terrorism. Big considerations, but Tim was a big man with a big mind.

"Tim, would you join Mr. Angelis and me in the outer office?" No way Lily would allow this man into her private office. His anger burned so hot it would leave a foul odor.

Responding to a man's voice—Tim's was a nice baritone—Angelis' shoulders straightened and his eyes hooded. Lily waited until Angelis was seated; she remained standing. Tim stood behind the man. "Now, tell me what it is that you wanted to talk about." Lily smiled at him. "Then I'll tell you whether I want to talk about it."

Angelis frowned. "I'm paying the bills here. You owe me."

Tim glanced at Lily, who shook her head. "Mr. Angelis, would you clarify what you mean by 'here'?"

"This college, Prairie Shores."

"You are paying for what here?"

"I wrote a honking tuition check for Cara Lynne."

"I see. And who is Cara Lynne?"

"Hell, lady, she's been writing stuff to you for days. Don't you read? She claimed it was homework."

"What did the stuff say?" Lily asked.

"No idea. Not interested. Until she left and took everything with her. But I remembered your name." He cocked his head, a gotcha grin deepening wrinkles that ran from nose to mouth. He was at least 40, Lily guessed, probably closer to fifty. He's done this before, she understood at that moment, owned a young girl.

But he didn't know what Cara Lynne had written. Lily did. "Does Cara Lynne have a last name?"

"Stanley." Still grinning.

"Let me check my grade book. Tim, would you wait here with Mr. Angelis?"

In her office, Lily looked out the window for a moment. Never before had she been capable, emotionally or physically, of going on the offensive. Confrontation? Lily avoided it. Until now. There was an entire book's worth of what she didn't know about what was going on here, but what she did know she knew with complete clarity: this Frank Angelis was dangerous. A threat to Cara Lynne/ Caroline.

The other question, of course, was what Cara Lynne or the idea of Cara Lynne was to Lily.

Returning to the two men, Lily said, "I'm sorry, I don't have anyone by that name in any of my classes." Which in fact she didn't. Caroline Stanley, not Cara Lynne. Lily smiled sweetly.

"You're lying, cunt." Angelis was on his feet but Tim was faster. He took Angelis' arm and escorted him toward the stairs. When the man swiveled on his slick-soled boots to shout, "Where is she? I own her," Tim pulled his arm high so that one of those boots swung above the carpeting.

Dorcas came to Lily's side. "You all right?"

"Oddly, yes. Hope Tim doesn't hurt him."

"As if that guy would notice. You know, I didn't realize men his age used the word 'cunt.'" Both women looked at the blessedly empty stairway. "Dr. Atwood?"

"Lily."

"Right. Lily. Um, I didn't know you could handle a guy like that."

"An educational few minutes," Lily agreed. She could feel the reaction headache gathering at the base of her skull. Why was it that though before she had always avoided confrontation, lately she seemed to be courting it? She could have slipped out and avoided Frank Angelis. Dorcas and Tim would have taken care of the situation. There was a catalyst here. Cara Lynne, who had left behind her childhood self Caroline Stanley. The student—her student—was eight years younger than Lily. But Lily had been there. The choices she'd made at the time or, more precisely, allowed someone else to make for her were billowing out now like sails in a brisk wind on Lake Michigan. Cara Lynne appeared to have more common sense than Lily had at the same age, since Cara had cut away from Angelis.

What no one had shown Lily was that there were options. Other options besides the old ways.

Chapter 5

Back in her office, after swallowing a migraine pill, Lily took out Cara Lynne's journal. At the bottom of the last page, she wrote, "You're still working toward answering how A. rated you. This is a good beginning. No, an incredible beginning. Please keep going. Come see me during office hours tomorrow afternoon." She would have to tell Cara Lynne about Angelis' visit. Information being power and all that. She clipped the financial aid forms to the pages. But before slipping it all back into the manila envelope, she added, "Cara, I have to put something in the grade book. Unless I tell you otherwise, assume you'll get an A for journal entries. I look forward to the next installment." She scribbled her initials. Once again she carefully locked the envelope in her desk drawer and made sure she locked her office door. She'd stop by in the morning before class to retrieve the envelope.

Where was Cara Lynne sleeping tonight? That thought stopped her. Homeless? Another problem to solve.

Maternal instinct kicking in so late? Lily was thirty-three. No, she decided, something else. Something to examine.

The sun had set. The weather was cold and crisp. Jonas hadn't said anything about what time he'd be home that evening. She stood on the University Hall portico, enjoying the clean feel of the air. There was no answer at his office or on his cell phone. She left a message saying she'd see him later. Maybe when he got home he'd tell her where he'd been. Or, more likely, he would act as though he'd told her and she'd simply forgotten. What he didn't know was that she'd taken to noting down when and what he'd told her about his plans. He had accused her of not paying attention so many times since he'd left Prairie Shores that she wanted to see if he was right. So far, he'd been right once. It was as if she were running her own behavioral research project, she thought, putting on her gloves. It should have been funny. Maybe her husband was cheating on her. Sitting down on a porch bench, Lily considered that possibility. Her gut clenched. Another confrontation coming? But when?

…

The next morning in the ten o'clock class—Cara's class—Lily returned graded journal entries. The first time she handed back graded work, Lily told the class that since she'd taken the time to write comments, they owed her the time to read them. While they at least pretended to consider her comments, most of them fast-forwarded to the grade written at the end of the journal Lily took particular note of Cara Lynne, whose expression remained calm as she read the pages from the envelope.

Cara Lynne wore the same jeans and tee shirt as the rest of the class, but her jeans were worn to pale softness. They didn't have the trendy ripped look of some of the other students' jeans. Her tee shirt had been washed so often that its logo had faded to white blotches. A large plain clip pulled back and secured her dark brown hair. Over the course of the class, Lily discerned that Cara Lynne was sure of herself physically. She didn't hunch over her desk or cover her mouth in embarrassment or constantly fuss with her hair like other female students. Her long legs stretched out into the aisle, ankles crossed, feet in relatively-new sneakers, her blue eyes following Lily. Perhaps, Lily thought, it's Cara's high cheekbones or pointed chin that seem to give her flair, even that morning when she looked tired, her face clean of makeup. Lily wondered what the young woman's smile might be like. At the end of class, Cara Lynne handed in another envelope without looking at her.

Lily returned to her basement office. The bench outside her door was empty of waiting students.

It was warm in the office. Lily hung up coat and suit jacket. Since the coat tree was by the office door, she again checked for students. Sometimes they parked themselves on the bench when her door was closed, assuming that she was busy with someone else. The hallway was quiet. Lily locked the door, sat down at her desk and took out Cara Lynne Stanley's next journal entry.

There was a note handwritten across the top of the first page: "Dr. Atwood: I'll understand if you don't want to read this. CLS"

Lily looked at that note for a long while before calling the office of the Dean of Students. Having met Angelis, she was after independent facts on Cara. Lily was a literary researcher by training, profession and nature. Jonas accused her of blocking out the world behind a wall of research. Well, she thought, somehow he's missed the part where research shines light on a problem.

Was Caroline Stanley, freshman, on scholarship? No, a Dean's office assistant told Lily, she was paying full tuition. Lily asked whether it would be possible to know when she graduated from high school. "Sure," the assistant said, "that will be in her file." After a pause, she got back to Lily, saying that she had checked Caroline's application and then double-checked her high school transcript. "Your student graduated seven years ago, with a 3.97 GPA. Smart girl. Could have come here right away. Wonder why she didn't apply for one of our scholarships?"

Lily realized that she had a newbie on the line who hadn't taken any of the required seminars on student privacy laws. It was like running into a small cache of gold, such as an Edith Wharton letter that hadn't been accessioned properly, like the one Lily had discovered during her previous summer's research. "Maybe her family has money. Who signs her tuition checks?"

"Hmm," the Dean's assistant said. "Frank Angelis. Oh, good heavens, the name on the check is the Angel Bar. How odd."

Lily pushed her luck. "What other classes has she registered for?" Science and math. It appeared that Caroline Stanley could be pre-med.

She thanked the assistant and clicked off. Lily took up the student's journal pages once again, her fingers covering the warning in its neat handwriting.

I was reading my history assignment in bed last night when Angel got home. He was hours early. Without a word he took off his clothes and took my book away. Or tried to. I held onto it. He just shook his head. "No, my girl."

"What's going on? What are you doing home so early?"

"Jimmy's closing for me."

"Jimmy can't count the fingers on his hands and toes." Jimmy's the bar back. He was probably drinking the expensive stuff and under-charging for what he served. Angel knows that better than me.

"I can afford it."

I was holding that book to my chest, you know, both arms around it. I don't have any idea what Angel can afford. From the time I went to work for him a couple of years ago, he's kept his eye on the money. When he's around, if one of the waitresses rings up too little for a drink, he takes it out of their tips.

I told Angel that I had to finish reading the history assignment because I had to write about it for class the next day. There he is, lying next to me, naked. He smelled like the bar, like cigarette smoke from the guys who stand outside and stale beer. His breath smelled like pretzels. Angel doesn't believe in drinking his profits but he doesn't mind eating them. Anyway, when he leaned over to kiss me, I leaned away. "Give me half and hour," I said.

Without a word, he yanked the book out of my arms and tossed it on the floor. When I turned to reach over the side of the bed for it, he grabbed me by the ankle with one hand and pulled me onto the bed. The other hand tore off my panties.

> I'm writing this in the library. I keep looking around me to make sure no one's close enough to read the screen. I keep having to type stuff over and over because my hands are shaking.
>
> You're married, Dr. Atwood. You wear a wedding ring. So you know about men and sex and stuff.

Man, Lily thought. One man and sex. And stuff? Maybe. Book stuff, mostly. On a run-of-the-mill student journal, she would have written "never assume."

"Well, here it is. He held me face down and fucked me from behind, no foreplay. I still hurt."

Unless I'm very much mistaken, Lily thought, the correct verb is rape. Angelis raped this young woman.

> How does Angel rate me? He doesn't. Because last night, when he was all done with me, he had this creepy smile. He said something that keeps playing in my head. He said, "Now, my girl, I've got you all to myself."
>
> Is that why he killed Charlie?
>
> When I left, I took all my school stuff and all my identification, my checkbook. I won't go back there, even if I have to sleep in my car.
>
> When I opened the door to leave, Angel called to me from the bedroom. He'd been sound asleep until then, I swear. He said, "You're mine, Cara." Just before I closed the apartment door, I swear he said, "I own you."

He said it, Lily thought. I heard him. He said it with pride.

> So I'm in the library, trying to figure out how I ended up here. The physical pain will go away. I don't care about that. But here's the thing: I'm the only one who owns me. I, Caroline Stanley.

So, Lily thought, what happened to Cara Lynne? Has she been knocked back so far that she's Caroline again? Or were there no remaining tatters of innocence to make her think changing her name changed anything substantial.

In any case, this was one tough young woman. Did she realize how tough? Or was it a persona she was projecting?

Chapter 6

There was a single knock on Lily's office door, then silence. When Lily opened it, Cara Lynne was turning to go. She turned back to Lily hesitantly, as if it had taken all of her courage to knock that once. Lily gestured her inside.

Cara Lynne prowled the bookcases. She pulled out a copy of Edith Wharton's *House of Mirth*. "Feel free to borrow any of those books," Lily said.

Her student whirled back, startled. "But they all have your writing in them."

"Guilty," Lily laughed. "I write in my books. It's always been like I'm having a conversation with the writers that way, you know? The rule in our house, when I was growing up, was that I could write in my own books. My parents' books and library books were out of bounds. So guess what I spent my money on? Though I found out about used books pretty early." She pointed to the chair. "Did you want to sit down?"

Cara Lynne didn't seem to hear the question. She reached for another book, this one Wharton's *The Age of Innocence*. "I saw the movie of this. Daniel Day-Lewis seemed like such a wimp, or anyway the guy he played. Why didn't he stand up for himself?" This afternoon, the student's hair was pulled back into a ponytail, so when the back of her neck reddened, Lily could see it.

Lily said firmly, "Take off your coat and sit down, Cara Lynne."

She did both in one fluid motion. With her inherent gracefulness, the young woman could have been a dancer, Lily thought. Lily sat back, hands resting on the arms of her chair. She wanted to present a relaxed image to Cara so that the student might also relax. That Cara was wound in knots was obvious, despite her graceful movements. There were tiny lines next to her mouth, and her eyes squinted, as if the overhead light hurt them. Without thinking, Lily said, "You have a headache."

Cara Lynne's mouth twisted. "I didn't sleep last night."

"Do you prefer tea or coffee?"

"No thanks, I'm fine."

"We both need some caffeine. Tea all right?"

"Uh, sure, I guess."

Lily popped out into the hallway and around the corner to the common room. She grabbed two tea bags, filling two of the clean mugs sitting next to the hot water urn. Carefully she brought them to her office. Back at her desk, she put a tea bag in each mug, pushing one across the desk to Cara. "Let it cool a bit," she advised. "The common room urn is kept at boiling, probably so we don't all poison ourselves. Do you want sugar?"

Cara shook her head, wincing.

Lily fished in her drawer for a bottle of aspirin. "Here. Take this with your tea."

For the first time, Cara Lynne smiled, though wryly. "Well, I know I'm not in high school. No way a teacher would hand out drugs there."

"Aspirin and caffeine together will help your head. I'm the world expert on headaches. I suppose we could walk over to the infirmary, but it seems like a waste of time." Now Lily leaned forward. "Cara, tell me why you wrote to me."

The young woman sat back as if Lily had struck her. Her face froze. Damn, Lily thought, why is it I don't seem to be able to do anything but come right to the point? Cara was obviously petrified and using up all her energy to keep going.

"I'm sorry, Cara Lynne. I shouldn't have been so blunt. I'm worried about you. I'm honored that you've chosen to confide in me. It would help me enormously if you would tell me why." Lily took the Lipton's bag out of her cup and dropped it in the wastebasket. While Cara considered her answer, Lily found an empty mug on the shelf behind her and placed it next to Cara's mug. Cara dropped the used tea bag in it and cautiously sipped tea. She shook two aspirins out of the bottle and popped them into her mouth, swallowed them dry, then drank tea. When she looked up, Lily was grinning at her.

"What?" she said.

"Anyone who can swallow aspirins dry is tough, whether she knows it or not."

Cara's mouth pursed, and Lily couldn't tell whether it was from the aspirin or whether she was going to laugh or cry. Her student laughed. Taking a tissue from the box Lily held out, Cara wiped her eyes. "Can you take them dry?"

"Not on your life. I'd gag." Lily sipped her own tea. "I speak from experience." She pointed at Cara. "Now, tell me."

Cara sat back, tea mug cradled in her hands. "I wrote to you the first time because you said to write what was on your mind. I thought for sure that you'd tell someone or read it to the class or something and that I'd regret it, but I took the chance. But you didn't tell. You talked to me on my journals like, well, like I guess you talk to Edith Wharton." She bent her head toward the two books she'd put on the corner of the desk. "It was like you were listening. That was, well, that was different."

"Different?"

"Maybe paying attention to what I was thinking is what I mean. That's, uh, an experience unique to, well, college." She looked down at her tea, then up again at Lily.

Could Lily be the first person to ever have actually listened to Caroline Stanley? Sad but commonplace. The luck of the draw. That Lily's uncle, Nate Miller, knew his niece inside out was sheer luck that Lily had come to appreciate more and more the older she got.

"What haven't you told me?" Lily's words were soft.

Caroline raised her head. "Not much. I mean, what happened between leaving home and meeting Angel, sure. But that seems, oh, old history, somehow."

"Is Angel the first man you lived with?"

She nodded. "Not the first I slept with, just the first I allowed into my life. Huge mistake." She clunked the tea mug onto the desk, then quickly leaned over to wipe up a tiny spill with the side of her hand. She dried her hand on her jeans.

"Whose idea was it to move in together?"

"Oh, his. I was still living in my little studio in Rogers Park." She looked wistful. "Why did I ever leave? It was my own place."

"How did Angel sell you on the idea of moving in with him?"

"Great big apartment, I was spending all my time there anyway, it would save on rent, help pay for college, blah blah blah. All good arguments." She looked away.

"Did you trust him?"

At the question, Cara set her mug down and walked to the window. Since Lily's basement office only offered small windows high enough up to catch the sidewalk-level view, Cara stood on tiptoe, as Lily always did. Lily drank her tea. She waited the way that Nate had always waited for her, until she'd worked out the answer. He never hurried her. Too bad Lily hadn't always taken seriously the answers she came to when she was Cara's age.

When Cara returned to her chair, she looked straight at Lily. "Dr. Atwood, I don't think I know what that means. I mean really know. I guess I'm trying to say that I don't think I've ever trusted anyone."

"But you trust yourself?" Lily asked.

"Until last night. No, until he killed Charlie. I mean, how can I trust my own thinking when it all came out so wrong?"

Lily again handed her the tissue box. This time Cara clasped it in her lap.

"He fooled you. The next man won't."

"But Charlie paid with his life."

There wasn't anything Lily could say to that. "Where are you going to sleep tonight?"

"What?"

"You wrote that you'd essentially moved out. Where are you going to stay?"

She reddened again. "My car."

"That's a short-term solution."

"All I can afford, unless I quit school. I don't want to do that. I feel like I've grown up more here in the last few weeks than I did in the years since leaving home. So I'm filling out all those financial aid forms you got for me. I'll make sure that Angel's tuition check is paid back as soon as money comes through."

Lily put up her hand. "Here's the deal." Cara opened her mouth, but Lily shook her head. "You can't bring Charlie back." Tears came to Cara Lynne's eyes and she pulled another tissue from the box. "But you owe it to him to learn from your mistakes." Lily tightened the pressure on this young woman. "Here's what I think. You need a place to stay for a few days while the college finds you a room. Do you want me to help you with that?"

The student nodded, still wiping tears. "Would you? I mean, could you?"

"We'll see. Hang tight while I make some phone calls."

Lily's first call was to the college's housing office. No, they didn't have emergency housing. Yes, they might be able to find something for Caroline Stanley, freshman, but it would take a few days or a week. Where could Housing reach Caroline? "Cara Lynne, do you have a cell phone?" She nodded. "Give me the number." Cara recited it and Lily repeated it to the housing office. Then she explained to Cara about the delay.

"Do you have any friends you can stay with?"

Her student shook her head. "There were some girls I used to hang with but Angel drove them away. I'd be embarrassed to call them now."

"They might understand," Lily said.

"Not a chance. They won't have anything to do with me. They're afraid of Angel. He made sure of that." She sipped tea, thinking. "I have just enough money to pay for a motel room for a few days. Maybe a week if it's cheap. I have to get a job, anyway."

"A woman without any money is a woman at risk," Lily said. "Edith Wharton knew that before she started writing." She pointed to the two books next to Cara Lynne. "Both of those books warn of just that." Lily knew what she wanted to do but needed to consider if it was the right thing to do. Oh, what the hell, she thought, just put it on the table.

"There are distinct boundaries between teachers and their students." Cara started to stand up. Lily said, "Sit. Those boundaries have a purpose. I teach writing. I frequently know what's going on in my students' lives because they write about it. But I'm not a psychologist or a doctor or a parent. That's the usual boundary." She held up her hand as Cara started to interrupt. "But you know, I'm tired of paying attention to the rules, even if they're my own rules. Let me make a second call." She clicked her phone; it rang for awhile, as was usual when calling Nate. She stepped outside the office and told him about Cara and Angel.

When she opened the door to the office, Cara was back at the bookcases. "There might be another option, Cara. I want to introduce you to my Uncle Nate. He's a cabinet-maker. His studio isn't far from here."

Cara was shaking her head.

"You'd be okay with this if it was my aunt and not my uncle?"

Cara stilled. "Yes."

Angelis had raped this young woman. Stupid, stupid, Lily screamed silently at herself. She needs help. More help than just a place to stay.

"Would you like to talk to a counselor? They're pretty good here, or so my advisees have told me."

Cara put a book on the desk, then wrapped her arms around herself. Tight. She rocked in the chair, looking so much like a little girl trying not to cry that it was all Lily could do not to go around the desk and hold her. She sensed that Cara wasn't ready for that. Trust was only built brick by heavy brick.

Lily waited, finishing her now lukewarm tea. "I'll be right back." She picked up the mugs and took them down the hall, closing the office door behind her. When she returned, Cara was wiping her eyes.

"I can't do this alone." Cara swallowed hard, wiping the back of her hand across her eyes. "Wow that's hard to admit. I've always done everything alone until Angel took over. Maybe that's why I let him. It was sort of a relief to let someone else make the decisions, you know?"

"Perhaps not your fault if it was the wrong decision?" Lily suggested.

"Maybe. I've been an adult for as long as I can remember. If relying only on yourself is what adult means."

Good question, Lily thought. Very good question.

"So let me try the counselor thing. How do we get that started?"

Lily pointed at the desk phone and looked questioningly at her student. She nodded. Lily made the call, then handed the phone to Cara.

When Cara hung up the phone, Lily asked, "Do you want to be called Cara Lynne or Caroline?"

"That's a heavy question." The young woman looked at Lily for a few seconds before wandering the office. As her eyes scanned the dozens of copies of Edith Wharton books, she asked, "Did Wharton have a nickname?"

Lily closed her eyes and massaged them. When she opened them, Cara Lynne/ Caroline was peering at her from across the desk. "What did I say? Is something wrong?"

"No, no. It's just that, well, one of Edith Wharton's nicknames was Lily."

"Are you named after her?"

"No, after a long-dead great-aunt. It's just one of life's ironic coincidences that Edith Wharton is the focus of my research."

"That is so cool."

"It is? I always thought it was embarrassing."

"Who told you that?"

"My husband." Lily answered before censoring the thought.

"You want to come to counseling with me?" Cara asked, smiling. The child actually smiled.

"When's your appointment?"

"Now. Then I've got history class."

"All right, meet me here after your class. I'll take you to meet Nate, then we'll head to Lakeland if necessary." And Jonas. That ought to be interesting.

"Dr. Atwood? Call me Cara for now, okay?"

Chapter 7

Nate Miller's woodworking studio was in the town of Prairie Shores. Like most towns hugging this part of the shore of Lake Michigan, it began as a group of summer houses built by affluent Chicagoans, with smaller houses built for the help, all connected to Chicago by the railroad. Now it was one of the smallest commuter towns furthest north from Chicago's Loop. A tiny train station stood in the center of town. A few streets, some with original brick paving, spiralled away from the station. There was a bakery, a diner, a butcher shop, a pet shop, a little grocery store, a yarn shop, a dress shop, all within a handful of blocks. "What's weird is there's no McDonald's or Starbucks," Cara said from the passenger seat of Lily's car.

"Thank the zoning laws," Lily said.

"Is that a real hardware store?" Cara pointed at a long plate-glass window where gardening tools, wheelbarrows and spring flowers were on display.

"The real deal. My uncle and the owner are old friends. They have breakfast at that diner across the street every morning."

"This place is like something out of television. I didn't even know there was a town of Prairie Shores. Just the college, you know?"

"The town came first, then the college."

Nate's shop was down a short alley from Main Street. There was no front window nor a sign over the door. All of his clients came to him via word-of-mouth, driving down the alley and into the little parking lot behind, itself hidden behind evergreen trees. The front door faced the parking area, as did a loading dock at the corner of the building.

Lily drove into the lot. Cara got out and looked around. "This is like a secret place. Like, you know, the Hogwarts Express that only appears to students like Harry Potter."

"Or Three Pines, which doesn't appear on any maps," said Lily. At Cara's confused look, she said, "A fictional town in Quebec, beautiful and full of people you really want to know."

"Oh." But Cara's interest was held by the old red-brick building. "Do you need a special password to get in?"

The door—Cara had never seen such a door, made of some dark wood polished so that it shone like glass—opened and Nate Miller appeared.

He wore a faded flannel shirt and carpenter jeans. "Just say 'friend of Lily.' That'll do it." Lily came up and stepped into his arms. Nate held her close for a moment. Cara noticed Lily's uncle had her same straight black hair, though his showed gray at the temples. But he was tall and lean compared to Lily's slightly plump, slightly short. When Lily stepped back, Nate bent down to brush sawdust off her coat and the top of her head.

"Uncle Nate, this is Cara Stanley. She's my student and she needs our help."

He turned to greet Cara, taking her hand in both of his. He smelled like fresh wood and cinnamon. She felt like he guessed what kind of help she needed, but how could he?

"I'm about ready to knock off for the day. Come on in and look around while I tidy up." He led them through the amazing door, gesturing for them to explore.

"Can I touch stuff?" Cara asked.

"Sure. That's what it's all for, being used. No smoking, though."

"Duh," said Cara, then quickly, "Sorry."

"'Duh' is right," said Nate, heading toward the back of the shop, where late-day sunlight fell over his workbench and hand tools.

The cabinetry shop was organized by groupings of deceptively simple-looking furniture. Cara moved to the nearest tall dresser built of deep-red wood with drawers so flush their openings were almost invisible. When she ran her hand across the flat top, a latch clicked and a mirror appeared at just the right height for her to see her face. "Oh," she breathed.

"Now pat it on the side," Lily said from behind her.

Cara did, and the mirror slid silently away. "Magic."

Lily had always thought so. She hadn't gotten to know her uncle until she was in high school. In fact, she didn't know she had an uncle until then. Her father and grandparents never mentioned him; her mother and father were the sort of tight couple that excluded everyone else, including their only daughter. They treated information as if everything was a secret.

Lily read in her grandfather's obituary that he had two sons, her father and Nathan. Her father's response when she asked him if that was a mistake in the obit was, "Oh, him. He's nothing. Younger. Left home early." That of course intrigued teen-age Lily. She promptly tracked down Nathan Miller who, according to the obit, lived in Prairie Shores. One day she took the Metra train north from Lakeland, alighted in the little Prairie Shores downtown, and asked her way to Nate's shop. When he opened the hidden door, he found a niece he didn't know he had but was delighted to meet. From the beginning he answered all of her questions, including why he hadn't gone to his father's and her grandfather's funeral. His answers made sense.

Now Cara was sitting in a chair that matched the dresser. "This looks like it should be as uncomfortable as a school chair but it's soft. How can wood be soft? Or is it because of the shape?" She got out of the chair to kneel next to it and run her hands over the seat, arms and back. Then she sat back down. "It's shaped like me."

"So is the customer." Nate showed up in the grouping with a tray of mugs, tea bags and a big teapot. "She was a little surprised when I asked her if she'd mind me taking some measurements and they turned out to be be of her, uh, what do you all call tush these days?"

"Booty?" suggested Cara.

Nate laughed. Lily loved his laugh, how it was the real thing, not something put on to charm or get along. He laughed when something tickled him. "Booty. I like that. Well, luckily her husband was along and he owns a couple of my chairs so he knew I wasn't making a pass at his wife. Once I'd taken the measurements, his wife said that now she understood why her husband loved his own chairs."

"She's getting the dresser and the chairs?" Cara asked.

"This table, too. All goes into their bedroom."

"Are they rich?"

Nate just looked at her. Cara sat down in one of his chairs and looked at her lap. "Uh, inappropriate question?"

"No such thing," he said. "But to quote you, the answer is 'duh.'"

"It's kind of a given around here," explained Lily.

"Got it."

Nate sat cross-legged on the floor in front of the low table and offered tea. His preference was Constant Comment—he'd told Lily once that he didn't care if it was in or out of fashion, it tasted good at the end of a dusty day. In the summer he poured it over ice. All year round, there were ginger snaps to go with the tea. Lily and Cara both had what he was having.

"You both addicted to tea?" Cara asked. Lily laughed and told Nate that this was their second round today.

"There are worse addictions," Nate said. "All right, Cara, tell me what's going on. You're the first student Lily has brought here, so there must be a story. Tell me."

"That's what Dr. Atwood says, 'tell me.'"

"Now you know where she picked it up." Nate dunked a cookie into his tea and popped it into his mouth before it could disintegrate.

Cara looked at Lily, then down at her tea and dissolved into tears.

Nate looked at Lily, who nodded at him. "Well, let me see if I can tell your story." In a soft voice, he went on, "If I go off the track, just let me know.

You're up against the wall. Lily knows about it because you wrote something she read and thought it serious enough to bring you here. Someone has hurt you. Probably a man. Probably a man who has or had some control over you."

Cara nodded. She wiped her eyes with the sleeve of her sweatshirt. Nate silently handed her a blue bandana from his back pocket. From behind it she said, "Thanks. I don't know why it's so hard to talk about this." She turned to Lily. "Did you bring what I wrote?"

"Do you want Nate to read your journal entries?" That would be a huge step across a vast boundary. One that Lily found intimidating even if the decision was Cara's.

Cara closed her eyes and stretched her neck, chin pointed toward the ceiling. Then, lips tight and eyes clenched, she nodded. "Yes," she said. "Yes, I think so. Do you think he should?" she asked Lily.

"Completely your decision."

"Could I think about it?"

"Of course. Tell you what, let's cut to the chase. Nate, Cara needs a place to stay for a few days. The source of her trouble lives where she lived until last night."

"You're thinking of the place upstairs here?" Nate asked. "Nobody has lived there for awhile. We'll have to go up and see if Cara here wants to take it on."

Cara looked up at him. "You don't live here?"

"Used to. Got myself a little house a few blocks away, oh, maybe five years ago. Couldn't resist all that wood to mess with, floors and stairs and built-in bookcases."

"When he got married. There are also kitchen cabinets to mess with," added Lily.

"Those, too. Since moving out I installed a fancy security system, so it's probably safe enough for Cara here. Want to see the place?"

Cara gave Lily a long look. "Is this why you brought me here?"

"Partly."

"What's the other part?"

This time it was Lily's turn to contemplate her tea.

"Lily's parents aren't all that reliable," Nate prompted.

Lily snorted. "That's one way to put it. Let's just say I never could trust them. Every time I did they'd fool me and I'd berate myself for being an idiot to believe them yet again. I just wanted to believe my parents. A truth that society regards as a given is, in my experience, not. Who knew that the only person I've learned to trust would be a master woodworker?"

"You're married, right?" Cara asked Lily.

"Yes."

"Oh. Okay. But wait," she said to Nate. "Where's your wife?"

"Right about now, in Hong Kong. I'm hoping she stays out of the Middle East, but that's not my call. Eleanor is a photographer. Freelance, but mostly news. Does video, too. Anyway, whenever she feels the need for a little sawdust, she's here. Works for both of us." Nate stood up. "Ready for the grand tour?"

Cara followed him upstairs. When Nate returned alone, Lily told him about Frank Angelis' threatening visit to the English Department. "You need to take that into consideration before agreeing to let her stay here. He's so focused on pulling Cara back under his control that he's out of control of himself. I don't want to put all this beauty," she gestured around the workshop, "into jeopardy."

Ten minutes later Cara bounced down the stairs like a happy teenager. "There's a bed and dresser and a full bathroom and all the furniture is handmade and this is unbelievable. Yesterday Angel …" Her words stopped as she slumped down on one of the stairs. She chewed the inside of her cheek. Then she straightened her back, squared her shoulders, looking as if she were going into battle. "Dr. Atwood, you'd better give your uncle what I wrote. He needs to know what he's getting into."

Chapter 8

Cara could feel the quiet surround her. She could almost reach out and touch it, draw it closer, swirl it, like the most malleable cloud. She turned around next to the bed, her bed now, feeling the quiet above Nate Miller's workshop. Alone. Alone was not lonely—she had forgotten that after going to live with Angel. She had herself. Time to think. When she'd moved into her studio apartment just after high school she'd looked up the meaning of the word "introspection" and liked it. She'd had time to look into her life, into her mind.

Sitting down at the cherry-wood desk that, if not hidden up here, would have been at home in a museum of American design, Cara dug in her backpack for a notebook. She tore out three sheets of paper and lined them up on the silken surface. On one sheet she wrote "Then." On another she wrote "From now on." On a third she wrote "In between," then added "transition." On the second she added "What I want." She stood and looked at all three sheets before grabbing them and sitting on the floor. On top of the pile was "Then."

"A good place to start," she told the silence. Under the heading she wrote:

"The past.

"Noise. No more noise. No more noise from people I don't want in my life.

"From my father and my mother. From Angel."

She stopped. Though she would never mention it to an actual person, she still hurt from Angel's dry thrusts the previous night. She'd found blood in her panties when she'd gone to the college library bathroom afterwards, causing her to spend a precious fifty cents on a sanitary pad from the machine there. No place to wash and she only had one change of clothes. That's all she'd dared grab before fleeing Angel's apartment while he slept.

"Noise includes physical noise. I'm trying to remember why I had sex with Angel the first time. I wasn't drunk. I never am. I don't like the way it makes me feel. Drunks are so stupid, the stuff they say and do." Bartenders, especially female ones like her, heard it all. After bartending she never wanted to be a therapist, even if she could charge millions of dollars for her time.

"Quit procrastinating. Why did I have sex with Angel?

"What it wasn't: desire, love."

She wrote:

I was tired. I'd been supporting myself for five years. Angel took on some of that responsibility. He let me lean on him. That felt good. Then he started talking me into going to college. I didn't have that kind of money; even community college would cost lost wages. No problem, he kept saying, I'll pay for it. You're a great bartender but you're too smart for that.

Why did I believe him?

The question she wrote flashed at her, black words on white notebook paper.

"Because I wanted to believe him. Because when he took charge, I didn't have to be.

"Because I am my mother's daughter."

Cara threw down the pen and pushed away from those words. Tears threatened again but she wouldn't have them. "Stop it," she heard herself say. But she was talking to her mother, telling her to stop letting her father make all the decisions.

It was her father who decided that his daughter was nothing but a servant. Her mother carried out his dictates. Cara washed the day's dirty dishes each night. Trash night was her responsibility. Changing the bedding. Washing the floors. Vacuuming. Her mother liked mending and cooking. When the daughter, whom Cara thought of as Caroline, rebelled, it was her father who was the enforcer. Cara had written in her journal for Dr. Atwood that her father wasn't physically abusive but that wasn't quite the truth. Frank Stanley—had she ever noticed that her father's name was the same as Angel's real first name?—liked using his belt. What he didn't like doing was explaining why he was belting his daughter. He's just say, "You know what you did." He'd stopped before Caroline hit puberty. She'd always figured it was because she'd stopped arguing. By then she had an escape plan and followed it.

"I had sex with Angel because it was the easiest thing to do," she wrote.

"I am my mother's daughter but I am not her.

"My choice." Cara looked at the two words. Then carefully crossed them out and added them to the second and third sheets of paper. It would be her choice from now on.

"Forgive myself." For being an idiot, she didn't write. She thought she was so grown up. Not.

"But forgiving doesn't mean forgetting."

There would be more to add under "Then." But now she turned to the "What I want" heading.

"I want not to rely on a man.

"I want to learn how to figure out if I can trust a person.

"I want to get a cat." At this she smiled. Charlie had taught her more about love than any human had. That Angel had killed Charlie was so sick, sicker even than last night. Angel made her bleed but killing Charlie—that made her hurt inside. Like a clenched fist.

"I want to be a veterinarian."

Well, in order to not rely on a man and get to be a vet, she'd better be first in line at the financial aid office in the morning. Plus she had to get a job. She added these to the sheet titled "Transitions."

Planning felt good. She was good at planning.

On the same sheet of paper, she wrote, "Ask Nate how he feels about cats."

In the distance a train whistle didn't so much break the quiet as emphasize it.

Cara pulled out her homework. That she had a plan gave her energy. She remembered how her escape plan during high school seemed to stretch the hours in a day, allowing her to excel in school while holding a job and serving as the Stanley family maid. But this time she could focus her energy. She opened her biology book after writing "resilience" on the "Transitions" sheet.

・・・

By April, Cara and Nate decided that her living in his workshop apartment improved both of their lives. It gave Cara a home and time around a man who actually conversed rather than just giving orders—new to her. Scary at first, but she got to like it. That the apartment was being loved appealed to Nate. Though there were some hurdles.

When Cara approached him after the first week to timidly ask if he would consider letting her rent the apartment, Nate had to think about the ramifications. First he asked the Prairie Shores mayor, another of his breakfast companions, if it was legal. Then he had to contemplate rent. Cara said she could afford $400 a month, which he doubted. Market rent on such an apartment was well over $1000 a month, more if he threw in utilities. He'd never intended to rent the place. When he moved out his idea was to maybe expand the workshop upstairs at some point or use it as storage space.

He and Cara sat down one Saturday morning and drew up a budget for her. How much she needed for tuition after scholarships (not much), books, food, gas, car insurance, cell phone service. How much her job as receptionist and helper at an emergency veterinary practice brought in. How much more she'd earn when she'd have the required two years of college to work as a vet tech in the practice. Nate wanted to just let the child live upstairs for free but understood that Cara desperately needed to be independent. When he suggested paying her for watching over the place after hours she refused, citing the workshop security system. Instead, they worked out a sliding scale for rent, based on her earnings. Then she brought up the cat issue.

"Sorry, no, cat claws wreck woodwork. Can't happen."

Cara blinked away tears, looking around the shop that had become her haven. "Then I guess I'll have to find another place. I really want another cat, Nate. I need to atone for Charlie. I need to show that a cat can trust me to protect him and keep him alive and healthy."

That was a lot of emotion to put on one cat. Still, Nate found it interesting that she called the cat "him." Cara must have found her cat already. "Who is the cat?"

She smiled. "His name is Izzy and he's about a year old and huge because he's a Maine Coon cat." Her words all ran together as if Izzy already lived with her in her imagination. "And his front claws have been removed so he can't really scratch like, you know, a scratching post. He's really, really smart. Maine Coons are, they're like the smartest cats around."

"Where'd such a breed name come from?"

"Maybe because he has long hair that looks like a raccoon? Brown with really dark brown stripes, like tiger stripes. Kind of a face mask, like a movie bandit. Green eyes, well, greenish gold."

"Where did you meet this feline paragon?"

She hugged herself. "Someone left him where I work. We've been hanging together while the vets try to find a place for him. I've nicknamed him Velcro because of how he sticks to me. He's chosen me. Like Charlie chose me."

"Cara, this might not work." Nate stood up to search through his pockets. "There are still those back claws. Any cat spray or peeing would ruin my work."

Her face lit up. "He's fixed, neutered, so no spraying." She jumped up when Nate pulled out his van keys. "You mean there's a chance? You want to come and meet Izzy?"

"How do you know his name is Izzy?"

"It's on his collar."

"Never heard of a cat wearing a collar."

"Well, Izzy does. When I took it off one time he kept bringing it to me and dropping it in my lap or on the desk until I got the message. So I put it back on him. He kind of nodded at me as if to say, thanks."

Chapter 9

June

On a perfect June morning Lily tripped on worn steps, dropped her book bag, and caught herself against the rough limestone blocks of the Prairie Shores College administration building. She squeezed her stinging palms before looking at them. Superficial scratches, no blood this time. "Ever the picture of grace," she muttered. "Slow down, Lily. You're finished for the semester." Leaning over, she patted the warm wall of the building, inevitably named Old Main, like every other original structure at small midwestern liberal arts colleges. "Not your fault."

It was 10:55. Final grades were due at the registrar's office by 11:00. Lily doubted that anything horrible would happen if she were a few minutes late, but she did try to be prompt. Besides, if she made the deadline, she'd have a whole half hour of solitude before meeting with the English department chair. Jane Hardy's secretary had called Lily that morning to make the appointment. Lily didn't have any idea what the woman wanted; maybe something about the NEH grant; couldn't be the other grants, since Jane didn't know about them. No one knew, not even Jonas. She bent down, picked up the book bag, and stepped carefully over the high stone threshold.

Air conditioning hit her along with that faintly medicinal smell emitted by new carpeting. Old Main had been renovated during the past year, creating a presidential office suite more befitting the chief of a multinational corporation than the head of a five-thousand-student college. The building housed some smaller offices for the lesser mortals who actually ran the school, as well as the campus post office. This was the first time she'd been to the redone registrar's office, and when she arrived at the counter, she saw two men about her age admiring the renovation. "Not bad," one said to her. "When do you suppose they'll update the science building?"

Lily laughed. "Years before the English and foreign languages building."

The second man chuckled. "If you all would just start doing stuff that the rest of us could understand."

Lily shrugged. "Don't look at me. My field's literary research—you know, tracking down original documents." Then she grinned again. "I actually write using concrete verbs."

"Uh, oh," said the first professor, wagging an index finger at her. "Maybe you don't want to brag about that here."

She held out her hand. "I'm Lily Atwood." She winced at the pressure of the handshakes.

They chatted about the sciences' attitude toward English and vice versa until the registrar's assistants took their grade sheets and shooed them out of the office.

Lily checked her watch, a gold one that had belonged to her grandfather and hung loosely from her wrist. Just enough time. She walked with care down Old Main's steps and took a small detour towards Lake Michigan. The day was cool, the scent of the water offering childhood memories of playing on the beach in Lakeland. She wondered how her students would spend their summer.

Spring term she had taught introduction to literature for non-majors. One of her students, a bright blonde freshman named Bethany, from a high school in a rural town halfway between Chicago and the Mississippi River, seemed to have blossomed in the class. She'd come to Prairie Shores high school valedictorian, homecoming queen, cheerleader, all that stuff. When Lily had interviewed her for a scholarship, Bethany offered canned responses drilled into her by parents and teachers. She'd gotten that scholarship, even though Lily hadn't recommended her. In the early part of the term, the girl was incapable of thinking for herself. Essay questions stumped Bethany, who had been taught in the culture of the multiple choice test. But the possibility that her precious grade point average would dive because of a required course forced her to think, to take notes as she read, to drop into Lily's office to talk about the short stories and novels they were covering, to begin to argue in class.

Lily wondered if Bethany had been as timid when she'd learned to drive, taking only known roads, until perhaps someone had taught her to use a map to discover the seductive joy of independence. Because that's what she'd discovered in lit class. She'd turned in a creative final project, a staging of key scenes from James Joyce's *Portrait of the Artist as a Young Man*. One of the grades Lily had just turned in was Bethany's A-, which the registrar would round up to an A. Lily was proud of her for taking chances. She just hoped that over the summer Bethany wouldn't regress to mindlessness again. Lily had seen that too often: brilliant young women turning into either arm candy during their first summer home from college or getting pregnant and returning to college married to young men possessed of nowhere near their intelligence.

Lily was pleased when Bethany had asked if she could email Lily over the summer. "I'll look forward to hearing what you're up to," she'd said.

"Lifeguard at the town pool." Bethany looked embarrassed.

"Sounds like it will give you a lot of time for reading," Lily observed.

Bethany perked up. "I'll tell them it's for school."

"Them?"

"My parents, my boyfriend." She looked down at her feet. "They're not readers, or not very much. I don't want to make them feel left out."

A sweet child, Lily thought.

She was still contemplating Bethany's chances of continuing to mature over the summer when she arrived in the building that housed the English department. Unlike Old Main, the place was run down. Cast-off couches sat in the communal space on one of the stair landings. In many places you could see where a coat of paint had been slapped on over black mold.

When she saw Jane Hardy, Lily felt underdressed in her jeans, sandals and Prairie Shores tee shirt. Jane wore a navy skirt and jacket out of something drapey over a shell of the same material. Whatever the fabric was, it had become the uniform of administrative women and faculty aiming for higher positions in the pecking order at the college.

Lily looked over Jane and thought she herself would prefer not to wear a uniform, then thought, well, uniforms are convenient because you know what you have to wear, it's just a given. Not that she'd put any thought into what she wore today, putting on the first pair of clean jeans and shirt she'd come across in the bedroom that morning.

Lily's mind always wandered when she was meeting with Jane Hardy. Jane never said what she meant, approaching every subject crab-like. She was careful not to make a definitive declaration on one side or another of any topic. More protective coloration, Lily thought. She tried to tune into Jane's words and heard academic euphemisms. "You've had a challenging year." "Challenging" could mean successful or trying. Or nothing at all. What it never meant was "challenging."

Lily tried to respond in similar euphemisms, that one class was a special challenge, how the English majors were handling required coursework by "rising to the challenges and presenting us with what could be graduate-level coursework." Jane smiled approvingly at this. Lily was exaggerating. No grad school would consider the old-fashioned Prairie Shores English department service courses anything but what they were, dull requirements.

Suddenly Jane launched into a series of unfamiliar euphemisms and the novelty finally caught Lily's attention. "New opportunities." Though she loved to pry the meaning from the words people strung together, Lily wasn't particularly good at doing this while people were talking. Her forte was the printed page, whether by Edith Wharton or Cara or Bethany. Lily felt as if she were trapped in a cartoon, where everyone else could read the dialogue bubbles except her. She frowned, caught herself, and smiled and nodded at her boss.

The department chair asked, "What are your plans for the fall?"

Her uncharacteristically direct question threw Lily off. She paused, unsure how to respond, and Jane said, "Well?"

Lily went for an equally simple response, "Teach Bibliography 510, a freshman comp section, a section of intro to lit and a grad section of nineteenth century American lit."

"Those classes have been assigned to our new faculty." Jane's head tilted slightly, her eyebrows raised, as though she were discussing something completely unsurprising. Then she straightened the navy skirt. She took her reading glasses off, reached into a desk drawer, pulled out a cloth and polished the glasses.

Lily could read the comic strip now, but the story didn't make sense. She looked at Jane, whose eyes were on her glasses. She looked out the window at the campus, freshly-mowed grass a brilliant green, corner gardens everywhere filled with annuals, petunias and impatiens tumbling over each other. It reminded her of the classic short story about ritual sacrifice on a beautiful summer morning, a story that had shocked Bethany's class. Lily muttered, "The Lottery," and Jane's head snapped up, surprise on her face. Her features instantly rearranged themselves into academic blandness, but not before she said, "Ah, you understand, then."

"Why?" Lily asked.

"You know there have been budget cuts, especially in the non-science departments."

"What if my grant application comes through?"

"It won't. That was a long shot and you knew it, even if you did finally send in the paperwork."

"Of course I sent in the paperwork." None of this made sense. "Why cut me?"

"Last hired, first fired." Jane's shoulders delicately rose and fell, shrugging away a distasteful task.

"What did I do wrong?" Lily asked. Another mistake. Showing weakness here was the human equivalent of prey turning its neck to the hunter for the death blow.

"I'm so sorry, my dear." Jane looked at her watch. She was apologizing for having to leave, not for booting Lily. "If you have any questions, do let me know." She tried to escort Lily to the door.

Lily stayed where she was. "You have no idea whether I'll get a $50,000 grant. You're willing to risk losing the administrative fees the college and department would receive for that to replace me. To recap, you wait until after I've turned in final term grades to tell me. Too late for me to have applied for tenure-track jobs elsewhere. I may not play your administrative games, Janie, but it seems like you're taking a huge risk for little gain."

"I don't take risks. That's why you're out of here." Jane's face flamed.

Lily briefly pitied her that she blushed when angry. Briefly. "What's also interesting is that you never consulted with me about any of this. Yet you're absolutely certain of your information. You haven't contacted the NEH or they would have told me. So it's someone else."

"Please leave my office." The department chair pulled the door open too hard and it slammed against the wall. A bit of paint cracked off the wall and fell to the floor.

"You know, I never liked nor disliked you," Lily said as she gathered her belongings. "But I never took you for a fool until now."

• • •

It was only when Lily stood in the hall that she analyzed the words Jane used. "If you have any questions, let me know," the chair had said, not that she'd be happy to answer them. And what about "last hired, first fired"? The English department had hired two new professors that year, making them five years newer than Lily. Lily had been part of the search committee for one of them. Had Jane known that Lily was investing time interviewing her replacement? In the dark hallway, she seemed to have walked into freezing air. Goose bumps rose above her elbows; she wrapped her arms around her chest, bowed her head and hurried downstairs to the front door.

The building that housed the English department had but a single note of elegance, a covered brick porch that remained from its previous life as a North Shore mansion. Lily found her way to one of the old wicker chairs in a corner and collapsed.

At first she didn't see beyond the porch, but the warmth of the day finally reached her. The flower beds in front were in perfect order, some in graduated shades of red, some in shades of purple—the school colors. The young woman who had been hired as a full-time landscaper for the small campus rode nearby on her golf cart. Lily had heard somewhere that the budget for landscaping was several hundred thousand dollars a year, the equivalent of perhaps five professorial salaries.

There weren't any budget cuts at Prairie Shores.

Lily had landed the job out of grad school then helped Jonas follow her here. Jonas had moved on to Lakeland University, a few miles further south along the Lake Michigan shoreline, at the beginning of the academic year, leaving Lily on her own. It was one of the reasons she'd had more time to spend with her students.

The college wasn't even going to allow her to continue long enough to apply for tenure. What happened?

What about money? The chills returned. Jonas earned a good salary at LU, but they relied on her salary to make ends meet. Had Jane Hardy given Lily fair warning at the end of the fall term instead of ambushing her now, Lily might have had a chance at a position at another college, a chance to visit the hiring market at the annual Modern Language Association convention in December. But not now, not in June. The hiring season was over. Jane had trapped Lily, but not without toying with her first. How did Lily miss all the signs of things going wrong? She could hear her mother sighing, "Real life doesn't take place in your books. Look up occasionally, learn to read what's going on around you."

Pushing herself out of the tattered chair was hard. Her legs felt heavy. Her feet were numb. She bent slowly, like an old woman, to massage her feet. Outside, the campus looked remote, untouchable. Lily stood up carefully and turned to go indoors.

Bethany. She'd promised Bethany email conversations. A few minutes later, at her computer, Lily forwarded her personal email address to her student, hoping she wouldn't ask any questions that Lily couldn't answer.

That she could no longer be reached via her Prairie Shores electronic address made it all seem real, not some bad dream that had happened to a character in one of the novels she taught Bethany and her classmates. Real. Now. Four years of college, four years of graduate school, several years of research and publishing, five years of teaching at Prairie Shores toward this, THE END. It was like finding the denouement of the story missing, the pages ripped out.

Chapter 10

Cara found Lily back on the building's front steps. "Dr. Atwood?" Lily looked at her as if she hadn't the faintest idea who she was. "Lily?" Cara ran up the steps and took Lily's hand, dragging her into one of the porch chairs. "What's wrong? Are you all right?"

Lily's black hair had slipped from its mooring on top of her head. She pulled out hairpins and covered elastic and automatically redid the knot. But her eyes seemed unfocused to Cara. "Dr. Atwood? It's me, Cara."

Slowly her mentor's eyes shifted from the horizon to her. In a voice that sounded old, she said, "She fired me."

"Fired you? Who fired you? Who could fire you? I thought you were tenured."

Lily shook her head so hard her hair loosened again. This time she ignored it. Didn't matter anymore. "Tenure track. I would have applied next year. They got rid of me before I could even apply."

"But that doesn't make sense. You've won teaching awards. You're published. I mean, I haven't been around here that long, but isn't that what colleges want from teachers? What am I missing?"

Lily sat so still for so long that Cara thought she'd lost her again. Then Lily said, "It's like I'm living in a parallel universe."

"*Star Trek*? I mean, like that old episode where the crew discovers there's a universe that's the mirror image of the one they're in?"

Lily nodded. "Where white is black and black is white. It's like I know what I am, but what they see is someone completely different. How did I do that?"

"But you're the one who came to my rescue." Cara realized her voice sounded shrill, but it seemed to catch Lily's attention.

"How couldn't I not?" Lily laughed. "I don't sound like an English teacher, do I?"

Cara had never thought of Lily Atwood as an English teacher, one of those people who correct grammar and count the paragraphs students write. "You're not an English teacher."

"Not anymore, for a fact." Her laugh chilled Cara.

"No, I mean. Shit." She thought before she spoke next. Cara had her own suspicions about who and what had created that parallel universe for Lily. Now that the student had lived over Nate's woodworking shop for three months and had talked with him at length, she'd gotten to know about some of the players in Lily's life, although, as she knew perfectly well, entirely from Nate's biased-for-Lily point of view. From what little he let drop, Cara could connect the dots. "You teach us to think. To analyze. To work through problems. To look objectively at ourselves, our assumptions about ideas. About people." Cara hoped Lily would understand.

Lily looked right at Cara. Yes, now Cara had her complete attention. Then her teacher smiled ruefully. "Teacher teach thyself," she said. Her voice was brisk. "Excuse me, Cara. I must go tell my husband that he's the sole breadwinner."

That, thought Cara, would be an interesting conversation to eavesdrop on. "After that, please come find me."

Lily turned to look at her in surprise. "For what?"

Cara grinned, hoping that Lily couldn't tell that she was faking the smile. "Lunch. My treat. I'm learning to cook."

Lily shook her head. "Don't know."

Cara stepped forward and hugged her. "Now that you're not my professor, may I call you Lily?"

"What? Sure, I guess." Then Lily really looked at Cara. "Of course you can. I'm not sure why I didn't offer before."

"Boundaries," Cara reminded her.

Lily nodded. "Something else that used to be important." She trudged down the steps.

• • •

Cara watched her go before heading inside to see another student, one who worked in the English department office. She had a little research project of her own in mind.

Upstairs, the department office enjoyed end-of-term quiet. Cara managed to catch Steph before she shut down her computer. "Hey, Steph, you up for a little detective work?"

"Cara? What are you doing here?"

"Anybody in there?" She pointed to the department chair's office.

"Like she ran out of here after Dr. Atwood left."

Cara plopped down on the chair next to Steph's desk. She knew the other student from helping her with biology and math homework. Steph was an English geek through and through, able to analyze text and talk authors with enthusiasm. When it came to required Gen Ed science courses she was a head-scratcher. So, yes, she owed Cara. "You know what Hardy did to Atwood?"

Steph scooted her chair closer to Cara. "What?" she whispered.

After hearing how the department chair had pulled the rug out from under Lily's career, Steph said, "Wow. She really is a fool."

"Dr. Atwood?" Cara asked sharply.

The other student shook her head. "No, Hardy. I heard Atwood tell her she was a fool."

"No way," Cara breathed.

Steph nodded enthusiastically. "Way. I could hear because Hardy had already opened the door for Atwood to leave. 'Cause you know what? I think Atwood may have gotten that grant."

"Tell," demanded Cara.

"You know one of my jobs is to put their mail into the professors' boxes?" She pointed to the beaten-up open wood-slatted squares that held faculty mail. Cara nodded. "Well, there was a letter from the National Endowment for the Humanities yesterday. A fat letter, not the little 'sorry you bothered' thing. Atwood must have picked it up after meeting with Hardy."

"What's that endowment thing?"

Steph shook her head sadly. "You are such a science nerd. NEH is one of the biggest moneybags for the kind of research Atwood does. I typed Hardy's reference letter for the application. Did you know she'd applied for fifty thou? That's more than she makes here, I bet, or almost anyway. Other granting organizations like to wait and see if NEH comes through then they'll like throw more money in the pot."

"No shit." Cara sat back and thought for a moment. "Okay, like, why did Hardy dump Dr. Atwood if there was that kind of money heading her way?"

"Wanna know what I think?" Steph didn't wait for an answer. "I think old Jane's getting a little on the side."

The two young women, one tall and graceful, the other medium in height and coloring, both in the bloom of youth, shook their heads in disgust at the thought. "So who's the guy? What's the connection?" Cara asked.

"Not sure who he is but I get the feeling he worked here before this year. He was no stranger to Hardy, that's for sure."

"Steph, can I show you a photo on your computer?" Steph vacated the computer chair. Cara sat while Steph looked over her shoulder. Cara Googled Lakeland University then clicked on the development office staff. "Any of those guys look familiar?"

"It's him," Steph said excitedly. She pointed at a photo of Jonas Atwood.

"Holy crap," Cara said. "I was right." They traded places again. "Steph, when did this guy show up to, you know, with Jane?"

"I think it was, like, about the time I took the work-study job. So last September. At first he'd come around once a week or so, then every month or so, but lately more often, back to every week or few days."

Cara nodded. "Makes sense. He hooked her, then strung her along after she was hooked."

"Then came back when she said yes to whatever it was he wanted," Steph said. "So guys don't change even when they're old, huh?"

"Only the ones you want to stay clear of. Or so I've learned. The question is, why does Dr. Atwood's husband want her so badly to fail?"

"You mean that he'd hook up with old Jane? Yeah, that's some strong wanting. Pretty old-time, too."

"How?" Cara asked.

"It's like he's operating in an era out of last century, before women had the vote and stuff."

"Steph, not sure I agree with you there. Some things really don't change, you know?"

Her fingers drummed the desktop. "How can we find out more? Him just being here isn't enough. How can we find out if they hooked up?"

Steph checked the time on her computer screen. "Okay, it's after one o'clock. Usually the guy comes around at the end of the workday, but there's no work since the term is over today."

"Wait, you're saying he might come around again?" Steph nodded. Cara thought Lily probably was talking to her husband right about now. After that, if he was the guy, maybe he'd want to to talk to Hardy. Maybe thank her. In person. In fact, she might be able to find out exactly when. She texted Lily, "Let me know when you're done talking to your husband. I have news." To Steph, she said, "I think we have time for lunch. My treat if we go cheap."

Chapter 11

His wife halted in front of Jonas' desk, where he was absorbed in the Bradens' tax returns. He'd determined what they could actually afford to give to the university, an unimpressive figure. It wouldn't do him any good and it wasn't enough to get the Bradens the kind of recognition they craved from their alma mater. Jonas had developed his own interpretation of charitable giving rules and was about to apply it to the Bradens' situation when Lily burst into his office.

The knot in her hair had slipped sideways and her face was shiny. When he looked closer, he realized the sheen was from perspiration. He wrinkled his nose, but Lily didn't seem to notice.

"I..." She stopped. She tried to catch her breath. "Jane..." She stopped again.

Jonas strode around the desk, put an arm across her shoulders and led her to the corner of his office. A lowly vice president, but the title meant a lot to him. He pushed her down onto one of the soft chairs where he met with university donors. He remained standing, looking down at her, waiting, arms crossed, white shirt crisp, cuffs turned back just so to reveal ropy muscles in his forearms. "Jane what?" His face rarely showed extreme emotion. Even now it betrayed no more than slight interest. Lily tried to remember the last time she had found that composure comforting. He prompted, "Jane, your department chair?"

Lily filled her lungs and exhaled while nodding. Jonas glanced toward his desk. Lights flashed on the phone. "Jane Hardy. She fired me."

"Fired you? How?" He sat down on the far end of the sofa, facing her. "You signed a contract last spring, didn't you?"

She squinted at her husband. "I signed it. The college never sent me the copy with the vice president's signature."

"Damn it, Lily."

Hands held palms toward him, as if to fend him off, she said, "I never get contracts until just before classes start in the fall. Neither did you when you were there. This time didn't seem any different."

He reached over and patted her knee, changing quickly to stroking. "Don't worry."

Lily jerked her knee away. "Jonas, we need my salary."

"We'll figure something out. I'm making plenty of money." He gestured at his office. It didn't rate a window, but it was much bigger than his accommodations at Prairie Shores. A look of complacency passed briefly over his even features. He glanced at his new suit jacket, draped on a mahogany hanger hooked to the back of the office door. The look became one of satisfaction. The jacket was part of a charcoal silk and wool summer suit he'd had tailored to his thirty-eight regular frame.

Lily followed his gaze and winced. That suit had swallowed a month of her college salary. Worse, she'd not known Jonas had bought it until it turned up on their credit card statement. "Who knows," he said, "now maybe you can do something that brings in more money. You're worth so much more than that podunk college was paying you."

Lily got up and walked past his desk to lean out of the open doorway. She watched the comings and goings in the Development Office. Her back to Jonas, she asked, "What did you have in mind? There's not much an English Ph.D. can do except be a professor."

"Of course not, darling." He came over and put his arms around her, turning her to face him. The phone in her pocket vibrated. "Ignore that."

She leaned out of his arms. He looked over her shoulder into the hall. "Eleven years down the drain," she said.

"You have your research. More important," he looked down at her, smiling slowly, "you have me."

"Research," she spit. "What good is it without a college backing me? No one will take me seriously."

"I do." He pulled the pins out of her hair, causing it to fall heavily down her neck and back.

"Stop that. It's hot."

"Yes, it is." He continued running his hands through her hair.

"Jonas, cut it out." She pulled away from him again. "What are we going to do?"

He held her by her hair. "We? We're going to be fine. We'll live on my salary until you find something to do."

"We'll live on your salary?" She tugged his hand away, but a few hairs remained in his grasp. She yelped when the hairs yanked from her scalp. He put a hand over her mouth. His private life was no business of the rest of the office.

She pulled away. "You know, I'm the only one in my graduate school group who got a tenure-track job. The rest went to work for foundations or became writers or something unrelated."

Jonas raised his eyebrows. Once after they'd married she'd caught him in front of a mirror practicing raising one eyebrow, but he didn't seem to have mastered the trick. "My point exactly. They're all perfectly happy."

"They're all jealous of me," Lily said.

His office phone buzzed. He held up a finger to her, crossed to his desk and answered, "Atwood." He listened. "Would you ask them to wait for a moment? I'll be right out. Thanks." He put down the receiver, then came back to Lily and placed his hands on her shoulders. "This is a good thing."

He whipped around from behind the desk to spin his wife through the office. Jonas didn't know whether he'd distracted Lily, but he wasn't making up his own exuberance. It delighted him that she was out of Prairie Shores. Lately he'd worried that perhaps the timetable he'd set in motion had been way off the mark.

When Lily pulled away from him and asked, "Do you think there could be some reason I don't know about why Prairie fired me?" Jonas returned to his desk chair.

"They didn't fire you. Budget cuts." He propped his chin on his hands, watching his wife. Amazing and reassuring that she didn't suspect. She looked at the book titles on his shelves, the pictures on the walls. "No tenure, you go," he added. "Could happen to anyone." He tried not to smile, gave up and transformed his features into a comforting expression.

Lily wasn't paying attention. "It happened to me. Why? What could stop it from happening again?"

"Don't waste your time on it. You've got the summer off. Enjoy it." She turned toward him. "You can sleep in, go to the beach, get a little exercise." He pinched her waist when she drew within reach. "Getting a little heavy there."

She slapped his hand away.

"What the hell was that for?" he demanded. Lily always submitted to his suggestions for her appearance. It was one of the things that had drawn him to her back in graduate school. Now he looked at her with a critical eye. She looked rumpled, without makeup. "Did you put on make-up this morning?"

She turned slowly, eyes traveling over him, his monogrammed shirt, tie. She stepped back to see what pants he was wearing, then reached with purpose to see what jacket was hanging on the back of the door. Always buy the best, he'd told her. The best, she'd learned, meant for Jonas, not his wife.

"Are you trying to change the subject," she asked, "or is how I look what's really important to you right this very moment?"

Sometimes Jonas forgot how smart Lily was when she paid attention to details. "I'm sorry, that came out wrong."

She nodded, and he relaxed. She leaned against the door jamb, arms crossed. "I'm missing something about this whole firing thing," she said. One foot tapped. "I left there in such a hurry. I think I'll go back this afternoon, talk to Denise and Len, maybe the math chair. She always tells me what's going on."

Jonas waved his hands as if to brush away a cloud of gnats. "Don't bother. What's over is over. Just clear out of there." He expected her to agree, as usual. Instead, she walked up to him, stood toe to toe and peered down at him. He felt like one of those bits of Wharton text she was always examining, which made him angry. He'd learned as a child not to show his anger, that doing so was dangerous. "This is so much better for you."

"How can you be so sure?" One-third of her life shot, gone, devoted to teaching students who wouldn't remember either her name or what she'd taught. If she had started her research without going for the doctorate, then she'd be much further along, probably have several books to her credit rather than one measly dissertation and a bunch of articles published in journals no one read. The race for tenure now seemed so futile, such a waste of time, of her life.

"Trust me."

She'd wanted to trust him, back when. Oh, how she'd wanted to. She'd tried. He was her husband. Like she wanted to trust her parents when she was a child.

He stood up, put his hand on her back to guide her to the door. "I've got the Bradens waiting for me," he told her. "They think they're millionaires."

Momentarily distracted, she asked, "Why?"

"Because I told them they are."

"Does that work?"

"Always. Now enjoy the day. We'll be fine."

She wondered how the Bradens could be so gullible.

Jonas walked her to the department lobby, past a couple he greeted although he didn't stop to introduce her to the potential donors. Probably he was embarrassed that this red-eyed sloppy woman was his wife. Wouldn't have been the first time.

The phone. Checking, she saw Cara's text. "On my way home," she wrote in response. "Rain check for lunch?"

She wandered outside and sat on the brick steps facing the sorority quadrangle. Students were packing up cars for their end-of-the-year trip home. Nate had always driven her to and from university at the beginning and end of school years, before she'd returned to Lakeland for grad school. She watched the older students tote boxes and suitcases to their cars. All the women were tall, toned, hair perfect, though they wore the rattiest clothes possible. Their cars were newer models of Audi A4, Land Rover, Toyota Prius or Chevrolet Volt, which according to her students' journals were the cars in fashion. Lakeland University students tended to be either rich and capable of paying private-college tuition or poor and on scholarship. The middle class had long since disappeared into state universities. She supposed she would have been on the poor end of the scale, since virtually all of her education was funded by scholarships.

She didn't envy the girls' cars or perfect haircuts. It was that they were driving away on their own, alone, that fascinated her.

Chapter 12

Sometimes facts were what allowed Lily to sleep at night, facts, not theories or promises or hypotheses or any of those rationalizations that got most people through the day. Particularly her husband.

By the time she'd reached this point in her musing, Lily had opened the front door of their 1920's two-flat building. They lived upstairs. The stairs seemed particularly steep this morning, her legs feeling as though she were wearing weights around the ankles, as they were after Jane's pronouncement. When she reached her front door, she fumbled the keys, dropped them, bent down to pick them up and fumbled them again. The second time she bent over, she slid down the wall and sat. The building was quiet. She held her hands out in front of her. They were steady. Inside she felt like a hidden guitarist was thrumming her nerves. She wasn't a drinker, but maybe she ought to start.

She pulled herself to her feet, got the key into the lock and herself inside the apartment's front hall. There was a framed mirror over a small breakfront, both crafted by Nate. Staring back at her was a woman who could have just come in from her morning jog. No wonder Jonas went into critical mode. She shrugged, spotting the shrug in the mirror out of the corner of her eye as she headed into the bedroom. The room took up the front of the apartment, overlooking the street. It was bright, sunny, and perfectly neat on Jonas' side; as disheveled as she felt on Lily's side. She pulled off her old tee shirt and threw it in the neighborhood of the laundry basket. Maybe Jonas should buy her a new shirt, since he cared so much about clothes. Whatever.

At that "whatever" in her thoughts, she heard herself laugh. "Whatever" was her students' favorite word to display complete lack of interest. When it came to clothes, "whatever" pretty much covered it for her. She stripped off her damp bra and underwear, took a quick shower. Then she found a clean pair of jeans, light blue blouse and sandals. The long hallway outside the bedroom led past the expansive living room, which they rarely used; guest room, which was never used since Jonas hated guests; another bedroom that served as her office; and the tiny second bathroom, which was technically hers.

There she stopped to redo the knot in her hair. She looked at herself in the mirror again, trying for Jonas' critical eye. A little color wouldn't hurt. She found the powder blush in a drawer. Perhaps some earrings? She returned to the bedroom, fished in a carved box on her dresser and came up with some small hammered silver hoops that Nate had given her for a birthday when she was in high school. When she returned to the bathroom, her reflection looked healthy, at least. No one enjoys being fired, but at least she looked as if she'd survived the event.

"It's show time." That's what she always thought before walking into a classroom to face her audience of students. Today she had a different audience in mind.

...

The plaque on the outside of the door read "Dr. Leonard Altawa, Sterns Chair and Professor of Biology," which sounded impressive. The office was the Prairie Shores equivalent of a double-wide mobile home, with years of journal back issues piled on the floor and every chair. There was a path from the door to his desk. "Len," Lily said, "I thought the department was giving you a student worker this summer to organize all this."

Len bent over his desk, white hair showing the track marks of that morning's wet combing. When he looked up, his ruddy face broke into a smile. He stood up and opened his arms. She rushed into them to receive a bear hug. Then he held her at arms length, looking her over with the care he usually devoted to his beloved fruit flies. "Lily, how are you? I searched for you after I heard about Hardy's insanity." He led her to the chair next to his desk, lifting the journals onto the floor and seating her with all the deference due a visiting dignitary. "You look great today."

Len and Lily had team taught for the past two years. They'd spent days planning the course, pulling together the reading materials, batting out the syllabus. The two couldn't have been more different, but they'd hit it off. Nate noticed and built a magazine case for Len. The professor had installed the case in his tiny house, in a place of honor: the kitchen, Len's other love.

Len sat in his office chair, fingers laced across his comfortable belly. "So, my dear. This is an interesting mess."

"Jonas is delighted I'm out of here."

"No surprise there." Before she could ask, he went on, "Jane's timing is suspect. She could have released you in time to go on the job market."

Lily leaned forward. "Are you implying malice on the part of my former department chair?"

His white head nodded thoughtfully. "Yes. But since Jane rarely shows her hand, I'm thinking your former department chair was making a point or a show of support. What I haven't determined is to whom."

"She's aiming up the ladder. So whoever she's trying to impress has to be at the dean level or above."

"Not sure about that. Jane's actual intent never becomes evident until much later, in my experience. Though of course I only see her at faculty meetings. Same in department meetings?" Lily shrugged. Obviously she should have paid closer attention to Jane.

He steepled the fingers across his middle; Lily had seen him do the same when pushing a student to reason through a problem. "Does it matter?"

"It matters. That's why I'm here." Her thoughts circled around their red center, the fact of being fired. "I need to know why. Not so I can come back here. After this morning, yes, that's history." Her face burned. "I called Jane a fool." Len pumped his fist in the air in approval. "But so whatever happened—well, if I can, I'd like to keep it from happening again, assuming I can land another tenure-track slot."

He sighed and shook his head. "You could sue, you know. That would be one way of finding out."

She waved away the idea. "I want to know what happened."

"Revenge is a dish best served cold?" he asked.

"Have I ever seemed the vengeful type?" Lily was interested in his answer, since revenge had never occurred to her.

"No, my dear. Not at all. But perhaps you should be. In the meantime, let me see what I can find out."

...

Lily spent the rest of the afternoon talking to fellow professors, lunchroom colleagues and English faculty. Most acted like skittish grade school kids, treating her as if she had cooties. She couldn't find the math chair. When she finally tracked down her friend Diana, the dean of students, all she could pull out of her was an implication that something was up. "But I'm only sniffing the air," the dean insisted. "If I find out anything, I'll call you. What are you doing this summer?"

"Research."

"You could take some time off."

"That's what Jonas said."

"Of course."

After collecting her mail and a few things from her Prairie Shores office, she found herself driving down the lakefront road knowing nothing more than she'd known that morning. On this drive, though, she noticed the cathedral ceiling of leaves overhead, the deep blue of the lake peeking through trees and houses. She tried to bring some of the old joy of the drive inside herself. But she felt unfinished, unraveled at the thought of searching for a new job when she hadn't the faintest idea what had gone wrong on the old one. It was as if she'd lost her one focus.

She got home before Jonas. In the little bedroom office, she dumped her mail on the desk, listlessly thumbing through it.

One return address caused her breath to catch. National Endowment for the Humanities. Touching the envelope with a delicate finger, as if it might explode, she tried to summon the courage to open it. Her hand pulled away of its own volition. She couldn't bear more disappointment. Not today. She started to put the envelope in a drawer, then stopped. Show a little backbone, she told herself.

She had to know. Picking up the envelope, she slit it open.

...

Jonas opened the door to the apartment and placed his briefcase next to the credenza. When he caught his reflection in the mirror, he smoothed his hair. He had liked it better long, the way it had been in high school and throughout college and grad school. But he'd never have scored an almost-six-figure salary at Lakeland looking like some guy who hung out in clubs at night.

The building was quiet. He didn't think about his wife until he walked into their bedroom. Her side of the room was a pit. She was getting slatternly in her habits. Well, now that she would be depending on him for support he could finally fix that. He removed his suit and hung it up in his closet, pushing other hangers away to make room. He'd talk Lily into giving him half her closet space, since she never used it.

After changing into pressed jeans and a polo shirt—no more dry cleaners, he promised himself, visualizing Lily ironing for him—he headed toward the kitchen, intending to see if there was anything remotely like dinner planned. When he passed the little room that Lily claimed as her office, he stopped. He'd thought he was alone, but there she was, staring at some letter in her hand. He waited a few moments, expecting her to notice him. This was an aspect of his wife that Jonas intended to change, that she could be so absorbed in something that she failed to notice his presence. He cleared his throat. Nothing. "Lily," he said in his normal voice. Still no response. It wasn't until he crossed into the room and stepped on a creaking floorboard that she looked up.

By the time he reached her side, she'd straightened the pile of mail on her desk. Whatever she'd been looking at had disappeared. "Jonas, you're home early."

"What were you looking at just now?"

"I don't know."

"You don't know?" He crossed his arms.

"Sorry, I just got lost in my thoughts. It's been an eventful day. There's a lot that I have to digest."

"What's for dinner?"

"There's some chicken in the freezer."

"Vegetables? Fruit?"

"I'll look." She got out of the chair and waited for him to precede her out of the office. He had the passing notion that she wanted to hide something from him but dismissed the idea. Lily wasn't devious.

On the way into the kitchen, he asked, "Got any plans for tonight?"

Without looking at him, she said, "Why? What did you have in mind?"

"Some cleaning."

"There's a thought."

Chapter 13

It was midnight and Lily was back at her desk. She'd cooked dinner for Jonas, cleaned the kitchen, then allowed him to direct her in straightening her side of the bedroom. What he saw as her mess was nothing that she couldn't have picked up in a few minutes, but he managed to draw out the experience to a half hour or more. She'd drawn the line at sharing her closet, telling him she had plans for that space. Now he was in bed, stretched out neatly under the summer blanket, snoring lightly.

She slipped the National Endowment for the Humanities letter from the other mail on her desk. Once again she opened it, once again she felt that flash of wonder. Dr. Lily Atwood had been awarded a grant for her continuing research on the writing relationship between Edith Wharton and Henry James. The amount of money was more than sufficient to cover traveling to Connecticut, New York, New Jersey and Massachusetts this summer for on-site work. Since Jane Hardy had finagled her firing, the percentage of the grant earmarked for administration would also go to Lily. In her mind, she saw those Lakeland sorority girls driving off by themselves. Was it that she felt ten years younger? She shook her head. She was going east. She'd have to consult with her travel agent friend tomorrow to see if it made more sense to fly and rent a car, or to drive.

She thought about how happy Jonas was earlier that evening, ordering her around the bedroom, pick up this, fold that, put that in the laundry. "See," he'd said, "if you'd do this a little at a time, the place would be clean all of the time."

"Or you could do it," she'd pointed out.

"What?" Really, he hadn't heard her.

"Or you could do it," she'd repeated.

"Why?"

"Because it makes you happy?"

"No." He'd put his hands on her shoulders, holding them down hard. "It makes me happy when you do it."

"Of course."

"You know that."

She'd shrugged.

What she knew was that she had better things to do with her time. The NEH letter was proof. She walked across the office, neatly sidestepping the creaking floorboard, and closed the door. Without a sound, she danced around the office, whirling, arms out, the letter waving from one hand.

She crept into bed after dawn, pretending to sleep when Jonas got up a half hour later. She dozed while he showered and dressed, getting out of bed as soon as she heard the front door close.

On the kitchen table she found a note he'd left, listing what she should do that day. Vacuuming, laundry and ironing his clothes featured prominently. Was he trying to turn her into his mother? Had his mother even done that? Both his parents were dead long before Lily and Jonas met and he never talked about them. She shook her head. Five years ago he'd married a professional woman, and being fired yesterday hadn't changed that. Her research was funded and she was in business. She was officially an independent scholar.

She savored the term, loving the sound and feel of "independent" and "scholar" when she said the words aloud.

Settling onto a chair on the sun porch, she phoned a grad school colleague who'd taken up the travel business. It was only 7:30, but Bridget was probably already working her phone. She taught college as an adjunct Spanish professor, hoping always to find that elusive full-time position. Sure enough, she answered the phone. "Travelight. If anyone can get you there, I can."

"Bridget, it's Lily Atwood. I need you to get me to New Haven."

"If I could get you to New Haven, I'd get me there. Did you know I applied for a tenure-track slot at Yale last hiring season?"

"Any response?" Lily asked.

"Nada. Form letter saying many qualified people had applied yadda yadda yadda."

"Is that Spanish?"

"Not that I know of. Maybe that's why I didn't get an interview. Now, what about Yale? You got an interview there?"

"No, no. I need to go to the Beinecke Rare Book and Manuscript Library to do some research, and from there to Lenox, Mass."

"Oh." Bridget sighed. "Wharton again."

"Wharton, continuing. Are you sitting down?"

"Why?"

"I got an NEH grant."

"Holy shit. That ought to get you tenure right there. They don't hand out those grants to just anyone."

Lily decided not to mention that she'd been driven off the tenure track. "I've got enough money for a summer of travel. You want to find out whether

I should drive east or fly then rent a car? And find me some reasonable but nice bed and breakfast type place to stay. I want to base around Yale, if I can."

"New Haven is either disgusting or expensive. But let me see what I can do. Connecticut's tiny by Midwest standards, so I could probably find you something in easy commuting distance. Why not rent an apartment for the summer? Might be cheaper."

"Do you get a commission for that?"

"Finder's fee. When do you want to leave?"

"In two or three days. I need to make arrangements with Yale to work there, and things are slow in the summer. See what you can find and call me back. I wouldn't mind hanging around Connecticut if I have to."

"Jonas coming?"

"Not for the summer. He's got a new job at Lakeland, in development. He'd better mind the store." When had she learned to lie so smoothly? First hiding the letter from Jonas, now this. "How soon can you get back to me?" She gave Bridget her cell phone number.

"I'll call you this afternoon with anything I've found."

"Wonderful." After they'd said good-bye, Lily thought about Bridget's question: "'Jonas coming?'" It was a logical question. During grad school he'd always hung out with her while she was buried in the library. Sometimes she felt as if he were keeping watch over her. She'd come to like it, found that her concentration improved when he was there. After they were married he hung over her all the time; she'd gotten much more done when he was elsewhere.

She was too excited about the summer's promise to allow him into her plans right now. She'd present him with a fait accompli. What she didn't want to think about was hiding the NEH letter from him. When she'd heard his step in her office yesterday afternoon, she was re-reading the dollar figure in the letter. What had popped into her mind was, no, this is research money. *My* research money. Burying the letter had been an automatic response.

She stood up, marched down the hall, and put a china pot of water in the microwave for tea. Breakfast was a pleasure, tea, peanut butter toast and a piece of dark chocolate, with the *Chicago Tribune* all to herself. Now that she had a plan, she could enjoy her free time. Leisure was wonderful only when it wasn't enforced.

Her phone made that text sound again. Checking, it was Cara again. What was going on? Cara never texted her and now, what, half a dozen times since yesterday? Lily's phone buzzed. It was Cara.

"There's something you need to know."

"Not now."

"It's about you, not me."

"Anything to do with being fired?"

"Oh, yeah."

"Do I want to know what you've been up to?"

"I'll tell you everything. But I have to show you something. This is really, really important. Can you meet me at my apartment?"

"Now?"

"Now."

"Well, all right. I'll be there in half an hour."

"Text me when you get here so I can let you in."

"Where's Nate?"

"His wife is in town. I met her a couple of days ago. She's way cool. Leaves town again tomorrow, I think they said. So he's, uh, otherwise occupied?"

"Love in the golden age. Probably not refinishing the kitchen cabinets. See you in a bit."

Chapter 14

The apartment looked all right. Neat but then that was Cara's habit. Izzy fit right in, since he turned out to be quite particular about the cleanliness of his litter box and his fur coat. He even brought her the rubber cat brush to remind her. At first she found it on her pillow but now that they'd worked out a routine he left it by the bedroom chair. He was getting to know Nate and vice versa. Nate allowed Izzy in the workshop as long as there was a human around. Cara sensed that Izzy understood he was on probation. She'd whisper to him, "Do your job" before opening the door separating apartment from workshop stairs. Never did he dash downstairs without sitting on the top step, ears pitched toward the sound of Nate's tools as if contemplating strategy. Then he'd step down the stairs, tail straight with that slight curve at the tip that declared "cat in charge."

This would be the first time Cara had invited anyone up to her apartment. She secretly thought of Lily as her mentor and her model. Lily had protected Cara. She'd taught Cara to attack problems intellectually, to follow through and ask the next question and the next. It was unacceptable to see her Lily, her mentor, broken as she was yesterday morning..

When Lily texted that she was out front, Cara went downstairs, Izzy right behind her. Cara disabled the alarm system, let Lily in and reset the system. Nate insisted that the alarm always be set when he wasn't there and actually it made Cara feel safer. Sooner or later she figured Angel would track her down here.

"Come on upstairs." Cara turned to see Lily kneeling in front of Izzy, who carefully sniffed her outstretched finger before rubbing his cheek against her hand. He let out one of his rumbling purrs. "Meet Izzy."

"Hello, beautiful," Lily told him. "Where did you get those gorgeous green eyes?" When she stood up, Izzy threw all twenty pounds of himself at her ankles. "Careful there or you'll knock me down. Come on and give me the tour."

The cat led them upstairs and into Cara's sitting room. An east-facing window was open to the breeze off the lake. Morning sun caught one wall that Cara had painted saffron. Two of Nate's earlier chairs, these with leather upholstered seats, stood on either side of a low table. Cara's laptop stood open on the table. Nate had advanced her the money for a used Mac Pro. Cara had already repaid him.

"Cara, you're taking wonderful care of this place. However did you talk my uncle into letting you paint that wall?"

"It was okay with him as long as I didn't make a mess. That was easy since he provided drop cloths and stuff." Cara sat down on the floor in front of the computer. She pointed at the nearest chair. "I have something to tell you."

Lily settled into the chair while Izzy stood on his back legs and reached up so his front paws prodded her thigh.

Cara interpreted for him. "He's too big to sit on laps. But if you'll scoot over he'd love to sit next to you." Lily followed directions, watching as Izzy stretched out next to her. "He likes you. He's a good judge of character."

"Quit stalling, Cara."

Cara took a deep breath, straightened her shoulders and neck, then began her story. She hadn't gotten very far when Lily interrupted. "You discussed what happened yesterday with a student who works for the department chair?"

Cara sighed. Professors never understood what was going on right in front of them when it came to students. It was like they thought students were interchangeable or maybe invisible. "Lily, it's me, Cara. I know Steph from helping her with math and biology. She's going to be an English major so when work-study offered her a place in the department head's office she jumped at it. But that doesn't mean she doesn't pay attention to what's going on right in front of her. Students know lots more about what's going on around campus than faculty give us credit for."

"It still makes me uncomfortable."

"But you have to let me tell you. You taught me to ask questions until things make sense. So I did. Why would Hardy want you to go? What's in it for her? People don't do things without reasons, even if the reasons aren't clear to them at first." Without waiting for a response, she told Lily about Jane Hardy's guy. About how he visited at least weekly at the beginning of the school year. When he disappeared for awhile Hardy became jumpy, easily aggravated by the smallest thing, snapping at the department secretary.

"Never a good idea. The secretary knows where all the bodies are buried," Lily put in.

"Steph said Hardy acted like she was on some drug that she couldn't get anymore. She was describing an addict jumpy for his next fix, you know?" But something changed about halfway through spring term, Cara went on. The guy was back. Jane became serene. Not happy, she didn't do happy, Steph said, but back in charge of herself.

"Yesterday, since Hardy seemed so contented, we figured he'd make an appearance." Cara placed the computer so that Lily could easily see the screen, then hit a few buttons. "I set my phone up on Steph's desk. As soon as we heard footsteps, I clicked on video."

In silence they watched Jonas Atwood sweep Jane Hardy into his arms and kiss her soundly on the mouth. He held her in his arms and stroked her hair while she said, "We did it."

He placed a finger over her lips and smiled down at her. "You did it. I had nothing to do with it."

Jane narrowed her eyes, protesting, "You removed part of the grant request form."

"Are you sure Lily didn't just misplace it? She does that, you know, forget things. Lots of women do," he said complacently.

Pushing against his chest, Jane stepped back and stared at him. Her face hardened, lips tightening, eyes narrowing. She wiped her hands on her skirt as if unconsciously trying to rid herself of his feel, while tipping her head to the side. When Jonas tried to kiss her, she strong-armed him away. "I see. It's like that, is it? You're an interesting specimen, Jonas Atwood. Is that why you managed to finish your Ph.D in psychology?" Then she swiftly crossed into her office, closing the door. The loud click of the lock rang out of the computer.

A pleased look crossed Jonas' face as he turned to go. "Done," he said.

"Run the video again, please," Lily asked. They watched her husband and her former boss a second time. "Would you send the video to my phone?"

"Sure." Cara's fingers clicked the keyboard, hitting the final key with a bang. "Sent."

"That's what he does, you know. Lure people in then turn them loose when he's drained what he needs from them." Lily closed her eyes and slumped down in the chair, almost dislodging Izzy, who resettled himself against her after butting his head under her hand. His purr sounded like an out-of-tune engine. One of Lily's hands stroked his forehead; her chin collapsed into the other hand, eyes still closed. "Except me. He's never turned me loose."

"Why did your husband set you up to fail?" Cara asked.

"Oh, baby, it's such an old story." Lily opened her eyes but looked out of the window, toward the light. "Edith Wharton was married off to a ne'er-do-well named Teddy Wharton. She was twenty-three and by nineteenth-century standards, long past her marriage sell-by date. So her widowed mother just arranged things. Marriage is an economic institution. It was then and it still is, well over a century later. The big difference now is that married women are in charge of their own money if they want to be."

That's what Steph was trying to tell me yesterday, Cara thought. That's what she meant by old-fashioned. But it wasn't old-fashioned. Cara's mind flashed a picture of Angel holding her down, attacking her, saying that he owned her. His tone then reminded Cara of how Jonas Atwood sounded talking to Jane Hardy. She reasoned through a few more steps. "That means your husband wanted you penniless. I mean, not bringing in any money of your own. Since that doesn't make any sense, like why would anyone want for the family to bring in less money, there has to be something he wants more. If he's like Angel, he wants to own you." She turned to Lily. "Does he?"

Now Lily opened her eyes. She wasn't exactly smiling but somehow Cara felt that her teacher was proud of her. "I'd say my husband wants to control me."

"But why wait until now?" Cara slid across the floor to the other chair and draped herself over it. "Haven't you been married for awhile? What changed?"

Lily pictured the last time Jonas had taken her to bed. He never waited until they were both in bed. Sex was an event. Carefully he would remove her clothing, piece by piece. Sometimes he'd take her into the tub and wash every bit of her. His foreplay was long and thorough. By the time he was ready to enter her she was on fire. This is the way it always was. Only in the last couple of years she'd stopped wanting sex between Jonas' events. The physical act that had been an addiction no longer was. She liked it well enough except... Except for what wasn't there. Maybe it was what other people called love. Maybe it was the connection between people that Wharton wrote about and acted on in her real middle-age. Until yesterday, Lily thought that her marriage was a contract and as such both sides would honor it.

"Lily, why was Jane Hardy acting like she was addicted to your husband?"

Slowly, Lily lips sketched an upside-down smile. "There's one thing that Jonas does very well. He never would say how he'd learned, wanted me to think it was the arena where he was the master artist."

"Are you talking about sex?" Cara asked. Lily nodded. "Seriously?"

"When we were in grad school, women would follow him around like they could smell it. Maybe they could. I couldn't. So Jonas followed me. Maybe, until now, I've been a challenge to him. Who knows?"

Lily hadn't moved from the chair or the cat but she looked indefinitely older, as though her skin sagged. She leaned her head back and rubbed her closed eyes with her free hand. Softly, so softly Cara had to lean toward her to hear, Lily said, "Wonder what it would be like to connect with a man emotionally and intellectually as well as physically?" Opening her eyes, she nodded as if to herself. "That's why Jonas did this. He sees me drifting away. He doesn't have the emotional wherewithal to hold me and somewhere deep down he knows that. He's smart. But limited. Something I didn't figure out until after we were married."

For her part, Cara was trying to digest the notion that Jane Hardy, who was probably about the same age as Cara's mother, was dancing to a guy's tune for sex. Without thinking, she said aloud, "That means your husband did this before. Play around. Hook up."

"The exact term is adultery," Lily said. "The thought had occurred to me lately but I preferred not to consider it. It was," now she sounded tired, "too much trouble. There were other things more important to me."

"Like what?" Cara asked.

"Like proving that Edith Wharton wrote one of Henry James' most popular stories."

"Why?"

"Why did she write it or why do I care?"

"Why do you care?"

"Because of the authors. Because if Wharton did what I have clues that she did, it will alter literary history if just a tiny bit. Because out of a family that cast her in the role of chattel she rose strong and finally took charge." Lily shrugged. "Or call it the thrill of the chase. This time it's me, Lily Miller Atwood, who is doing the chasing."

"Because you got the grant." Cara hopped up and reached for her backpack. "I forgot," she said, before seeing the stunned look on Lily's face. "How did I know?"

Lily nodded.

"Steph distributes faculty mail. She guessed what was in the envelope from NEH. Which I now know stands for National Endowment for the Humanities." Fishing into the back zip pocket of the backpack, Cara pulled out envelopes, including a large manila one. "Steph is giving your mail to me to give to you. After what we saw, we don't trust Hardy to send it on to you." She handed the mail to Lily, waving a last envelope at her. "This came in yesterday. We think you might be getting another grant."

The return address was indeed another agency to which Lily had applied. Quickly slitting open the envelope, she read the attached pages. "This grant is in support of the NEH grant." She frowned at Cara. "You and your friend will keep all this quiet, correct?"

"Of course." Cara was hurt that Lily would think otherwise. "We're all in this together, you know."

"I didn't know," Lily pointed out. "But I continue to learn." She patted Izzy before heaving him to the floor. "What do you feed this beast?"

"Cat food."

Lily stood up and reached for her bag. "Cara, I'm going to go open up an account at Nate's bank in my name only, into which I am going to deposit two quite substantial grant checks. Then I am going to go out and treat myself to a bang-up lunch at the most expensive place in this tiny town, paid for with cash from my purse. I would be honored if you would join me."

"Steph and I did good?"

"You followed the information where it led. You did brilliantly."

Cara jumped up to follow Lily. She wanted to make sure Lily got everything done before she crashed, because for sure that was going to happen and soon.

Chapter 15

Lily and Jonas were sitting on their sun porch, having a glass of wine before dinner. There was salmon marinating in the refrigerator, ready for the grill on the back porch. Green beans made with soy sauce and bits of almonds, a tossed salad with Lily's special oregano vinaigrette. There was even Cherry Garcia ice cream for dessert. Jonas was impressed. All right, so she hadn't said anything about the list he'd left her that morning, but she'd obviously spent the day thinking about him. Right then, with her hair pinned up, a flush in her cheeks from the heat in the kitchen, and a low-cut tee shirt over her cutoffs, she could have fit his ideal of the perfect woman. It was an ideal he'd had since high school, when he'd seduced his chemistry teacher, a woman twice his age and a knockout. Once, just once, she'd met him at her front door dressed in tank top and cutoffs. Maybe if the chemistry teacher had done that more often, he'd have taken more time with her.

"Jonas, I'm thinking of going on with my research this summer."

Of course, he thought. He slid down in his own chair, legs straight out, bare feet in deck shoes. He'd have to do something about that, like he had with the grant application he'd found in her desk. He liked to look through her desk. He must remember to break the lock on the drawer.

The face she turned to him then had eyes lit up. She sparkled. God, she could be sexy when she was like this. He leaned closer and put his hand under her shirt. Other than shifting a few inches away, she didn't respond.

"With what?"

Finally she turned to look at him. Chin to one side, eyebrows together, her face a question.

"Where will you get the money?" he said patiently.

"I thought you said you'd support me. You did say that, you know."

Her calm irritated him. "You've planned your summer without consulting me. What about my plans?"

"Did we have plans?" She raised her eyebrows. The flush in her cheeks had darkened.

"I was going to surprise you," he invented. "We could actually take a vacation to the Caribbean, like we've always talked about. We can afford it now."

"When did we talk about a vacation?"

"You know."

"Where in the Caribbean?"

"Barbados. You know that."

No such discussions had taken place. He knew that but also thought she would believe him. Why wouldn't she?

His wife got up and went into the house. He thought about following her but by the time he'd made up his mind she was back. In her hand was the checkbook in its worn blue cover. When she sat back down, he noticed she also held a calculator. In silence, she brought the checkbook balance up to date. "Let's see, we have three hundred forty-seven dollars and thirty-eight cents. My final Prairie paycheck will arrive sometime this week but the Visa bill has dibs on pretty much all of it, thanks to your new summer wardrobe. We owe rent, which will have to come out of your check."

He felt the anger build. It would be such a relief to let it rip that smile off her face. Not his way. Hold on, he told himself, just hold on. "You do what I tell you to do." He didn't realize that he'd said the words aloud.

"Where did you get that idea?" she asked.

"You've always done what I tell you."

She backed away, toward the porch railing where this had started. "How have I always done what you've wanted me to do?"

"You're such a pushover," he sneered. "You always have been. Paying so much more attention to Edith," he pronounced it EEE-duth, like a little whining child. He thrust his index finger at her. "I could arrange your whole life and you wouldn't even notice."

His wife leaned closer, eyes traveling over his face as if it were a jigsaw puzzle that she was slowly assembling. Then she got up and lit the grill before going into the house. He heard her in the kitchen. She returned with salmon and handed it to him. "So arrange this on the grill."

"You're cooking."

"Yes, I am," he heard her say as she disappeared into the house. He looked down at the salmon, thought about throwing it to the floor and threw it onto the grill instead. By the time he'd followed his wife into the apartment, he heard the front door closing. Racing to the living room window, he saw her drive off in their old Subaru. When he called her cell, he found his call blocked. He smelled something burning. When he reached the grill, the salmon was on fire.

No problem, he reassured himself. His silly wife had left their checkbook on the porch railing. She wasn't going anywhere for long.

Chapter 16

Lily tried to convince herself that she believed in heavier-than-air flight. Since she was ensconced in the window seat of the last row of an airplane, theorizing about science she didn't understand was one way of bringing down her fear level. Passengers crammed the aisle, shoving carry-on bags into overhead bins. Lily had thrown caution to the wind by checking her bags. There wasn't even a change of underwear in the tote sitting on her feet beneath the seat in front of her. What was in the bag was her research notes, representing one summer's work in Austin and another summer in Indianapolis. Every few minutes she reached into the bag to touch the manila files and flash drive, reassuring herself that they were safe and, therefore, that she was safe. She tried not to watch the action out on O'Hare's tarmac, as men and one lone woman in flame orange vests prepared the plane for takeoff. Had 9/11's near bankrupting of the airlines cut back the hours by maintenance crews? Would the rivets hold that engine looming over her right shoulder when they lifted clear of the runway? "Stop it, Lily," she chided herself.

The tall blonde young woman in the next seat glanced over. She smiled and nodded. "I'm afraid to fly, too."

"You?" Lily blurted out. The blonde could have been one of those supermodels, at least six feet tall with that perfectly-streaked hair.

The woman made a face. "Yeah, I know. I'm tall so I'm supposed to be in control." She took some denim-blue knitting out of the bag at her feet. Glancing at Lily, she laughed. "Yeah, I knit, too. Keeps me calm. Tends to throw people off in their instant judgments."

Lily looked abashed, but ventured, "When you're short and round, you're invisible."

"That sounds wonderful," the blonde said. "If I were you, I wouldn't do anything to change that." Then she focused on her stitches, ending the conversation.

Lily's thoughts crept back to her research. Jonas had accused her of placing her work at the center of her universe instead of him. Edith Wharton was invisible until she, Edith, took her life into her own hands. She was so invisible that the invitations to her wedding failed to mention her name. Lily knew the wording by heart: "Mrs. George Frederic Jones requests the honor of your presence at the marriage of her daughter to Mr. Edward R. Wharton, at Trinity chapel, on Wednesday April Twenty-ninth at twelve o'clock." Edith's mother Lucretia, as a widow, was allowed to be in charge of her own life. But Edith herself was not. The wedding merely transferred ownership of her from Lucretia to Teddy Wharton.

When Lily first read about the invitation, which also failed to mention the year of the wedding, 1885, she had shivered. Did Edith feel trapped into marriage or had it freed her from her mother? In her fiction, Wharton would equate marriage with prison for both parties. In any case, she herself remained invisible until her short stories started selling big. After that, no one in her upper-crust New York / Newport milieu knew how to treat her. She was an insider who told the world what she knew, for money. Unforgivable.

Lily leaned over to pat her research notes and laptop one more time before gripping the armrests for takeoff. The plane accelerated down the runway, rose into the air. Then it paused, as though trying to decide if it, too, believed in heavier-than-air flight. This was the moment that always petrified her. She was so relieved at the plane's continued ascent that a rush of well-being, of sheer glee, pushed her back into her seat.

Maybe, she thought, being invisible would be a help when she was at the Beinecke. According to the library's on-line information, she had some thirty-seven feet of boxed Wharton papers to inspect over the next month. It would be nice if no one paid her much attention. Because if she found something that would lead her to what she thought-hoped-dreamed might be out there, she wouldn't be invisible much longer, at least not in her world.

What if she didn't find it? She thought of her last meeting with Bethany, the cheerleader-turned-serious Prairie Shores student who'd asked to keep in touch with Lily over the summer. Lily had loved having Bethanys in her life. It wouldn't be such a bad thing focusing on teaching. If some college would let her do that. She sighed and envied her neighbor's absorption in knitting. Lily, too, could use such a distraction.

Instead, she pulled out her marked copy of Wharton's autobiography, *A Backward Glance*. She'd been reading it in the evenings last summer while digging through the Wharton collection in the Lilly Library at Indiana University. Her research led her to read between the the autobiography's lines. She'd gotten to wondering just how closely Wharton had worked with Henry James. Why did Edith care so much for Henry James? When he wrote about Wharton, his words radiated fright. In James' view, women, especially strong ones like Wharton, chewed up and swallowed men. After all, that's what his mother had done to his father. Women were dangerous to be around. Yet the two were fast friends, sharing an interest in gossip as well as the arts.

Edith and Teddy Wharton possessed a car and driver, a rarity at the turn of the last century. James had become addicted to what they termed "motoring." Wharton and her husband would swoop down on James and carry him off to areas within one or two days' drive of his home near the English Channel, Lamb House, in Rye. When he visited them at their Berkshires mansion, The Mount, in Lenox, Massachusetts, he delighted in such car trips. Same for when he visited them in France.

That they welcomed him into their homes didn't make him reticent about criticizing Edith's writing. The autobiography contained references to a few of his blistering commentaries. Yet Wharton loved and admired him. Why? When Lily pondered this, the thought kept coming to her: because he needed her. The only other time in her life when Edith truly felt needed, during World War I in France, she'd come through with trumps. France awarded her the Legion of Honor for working with refugees. She often spent her own money to help. A childless woman in a loveless marriage to a man who shared none of her intellectual interests. James was uninterested in women sexually, so the usual man-woman connection was out. Would it make sense that Wharton would try to mother James?

It was not such an absurd thought. After World War I, divorced but with a steady collection of friends and staff who became her real family, Wharton became quite maternal. But before the cataclysm of the war, Wharton was already doing for James. In 1908, she arranged and may have paid for James' formal portrait to be painted. The next year, James and Wharton colluded to funnel money through James' publishers to Wharton's lover and James' old friend William Morton Fullerton. Then in 1911 she was the brains and instigator of a plan to capture the Nobel Prize in literature for Henry James. Her efforts succeeded in getting his work considered by the Nobel committee, though they awarded the prize to another author who promptly disappeared into obscurity.

But then in 1913, James managed to abort a Wharton-led effort to raise money from friends for his seventieth birthday. He was so appalled that their friendship faltered temporarily. About the same time, without James' knowledge, she had persuaded one of her publishers, Charles Scribner's Sons, to offer James a huge advance for his next novel. She was so convinced that she'd done the right thing that she left a note "for my biographer" telling how she'd given Scribner's $8,000 to encourage James to go on writing, "as he was so despondent about his work. The result was successful and no one ever knew."

When Lily read here and there in the Wharton collection at Indiana, the idea tugged at her that Edith Wharton had done even more for her friend without his knowledge. Could it be?

Foolish parents sometimes do their children's homework for them. Over the years of her friendship with James, Wharton had learned to mimic him perfectly both in speech and on paper. It was a crazy idea that Lily kept to herself, but an idea that occupied her mind to such an extent that it carried her through the endless paperwork of applying for the NEH and other grants.

• • •

The rented Honda Civic smelled of roses. Lily pulled to the side of the rental car parking lot to fiddle with the dash buttons until she got the ventilation system going. The car must have baked in the summer heat for days, because the rose odor shoved her in the face when she first opened the door, sparking a headache. Nothing was worth a migraine. Maybe they cleaned the car with something flowery. She looked around to see if anyone was watching, then cautiously sniffed the dash. No. She tracked down the culprit—the floor mat in front of the passenger seat—and dumped it in the trunk. Her incipient headache cleared immediately.

Bridget, the travel agent/ adjunct professor, had booked her a small apartment in Guilford, about a half-hour away from New Haven on Long Island Sound. The route from the Hartford airport was simple enough, down Interstate 95 and something called the Boston Post Road, until she got into Guilford. All the streets radiated off a large square park in the center of town, and led right back to it. On her third circuit of the park, she pulled in behind a police car, turned off the Honda and approached. Chicago and Lakeland police were not prone to helpful behavior. This cop had a shaved head and sharp eyes but he smiled at her through his car window. He lowered the window and asked, "Lost?"

"Well, I got to Guilford, but I can't seem to figure out how to get to Green Street."

He laughed in a friendly way, then pointed to the park. "That's called the Green. This is Green Street. What number?" She told him, and he got out of the car so he could point again, this time to a coffee shop across the street. He towered over her. "Sounds like you're renting Maria's upstairs apartment. You here for the summer?"

She extended her right hand. "I'm Lily Atwood. I'll be working at the Beinecke Library this summer."

"Ed Sharply," he said, shaking hands. "There's a parking space behind the coffee shop. They make great muffins, by the way. The smell will probably wake you up mornings."

All of the sudden she was hungry. She looked at her watch. Three o'clock. "Where's a good place for dinner? And a grocery store?" Ed suggested a fish place, told her to get there early, and wrote down directions on a notepad he took from his uniform shirt pocket. By the time she pulled into her parking place behind the old red-brick building, she felt welcomed in a way she usually felt only with Nate.

She didn't feel invisible in Guilford. How odd.

The apartment had a small living room, slightly larger bedroom, and a huge kitchen with a window overlooking the Green. This was much nicer than she'd had any reason to expect, given the modest price. Bridget had said the owner was looking for a quiet tenant, no children, and no teenage group looking for a place to share for the summer. How had Bridget discovered this gem? Lily reminded herself to drop a thank-you email as soon as she got her computer plugged in. There was a large scrubbed-pine table in the kitchen that she immediately decided would be her desk. She could eat at one end of it. In the bedroom, she unpacked her few clothes. Then she returned to the kitchen, bright in the afternoon light. She put her laptop computer on the table, plugged it in, found the phone line and attached it. She was in business.

She took the pins out of her hair, shook it out over her shoulders, then opened every window. The air smelled of ocean. She was here. She was on her own. She was free. For three months, anyway. When she looked at herself in the bathroom mirror, her cheeks were pink, her eyes bright. The bags under her eyes had retreated. On a whim she pulled her hair into a ponytail. Then she found a vivid violet tee shirt to wear with her jeans and went to the seashore fish house the cop had recommended.

The restaurant was full of people who looked like they worked for a living, maybe on the water, many wearing denim work shirts featuring interesting stains. Faces were sunburned or tanned, lots of leathery-looking skin. Not the perfectly ironed shirts of rich tourists. Or Jonas. The restaurant's walls were covered with bright tee shirts for sale. The menu leaned toward the fried. Lily ordered crab cakes and a salad. "That all?" said the young waitress. "Saving room for dessert?"

"Should I?"

"Key lime pie's pretty good. We make it here. Real tart today, though. You like it sweet, come back tomorrow when my mom bakes."

Jonas wasn't here to frown at her for eating sweets. "Sounds wonderful." The waitress made a note and left.

A few hours later, she returned to her new apartment with two bags of groceries. As she arranged her purchases in the refrigerator and on the neatly-papered kitchen shelves, it occurred to her that she should text Nate that she was here. And Cara. Then she fell asleep in her new bed, which smelled of freshly-laundered sheets.

Chapter 17

Sure enough, around dawn the next morning the seductive aroma of baking woke her, just as the cop predicted. She knew immediately where she was, choosing to lie cocooned beneath the covers, planning her day, saying a short prayer of thanks to whoever was taking such good care of her. One of the day's many treats would be to find a good local bookstore. There were bound to be great ones in New Haven, but she wasn't living in Yale town. Before she approached New Haven and the Beinecke, she wanted to put her research questions in order. Now, finally, she would have a day to think about her crazy idea. No interruptions except of her own making.

Until Jonas came into her life, solitude buffered Lily, surrounding her with calm. She was by nature a reader and a writer, not particularly gregarious. Her mother didn't approve of Lily's addiction to solitude; in her opinion, Lily would be a better judge of people if she needed them more.

Lily had always been sure that her ever-critical mother was wrong, but missing the signals that Jane Hardy was ready to fire her had cost her that certainty. Her thoughts traveled to the kind police officer, Ed, and the waitress at the fish house. All right, Lily thought, I'll analyze my conversation with Ed. He made fun of her for what she didn't know, but more like a brother would tease a sister. He seemed to know everyone in town, certainly who owned her apartment. Should she have asked questions about Maria? No, that would have made her seem too curious. But Ed did make her feel as though she might be able to belong here. Was that his professional demeanor? She had no idea.

Morning light framed the blinds in a bright aura. She got out of bed, turning to smooth the covers. Jonas would approve. "But," she heard herself say, "I wouldn't make the bed if he were here." That stopped her. Why wouldn't she? Had she become that passive-aggressive in her marriage? The thought made her stomach clench. "Later," she said aloud. "One thing at a time. No hurry. Muffins first." She put on jeans, tee shirt and her ancient pair of Birkenstock sandals, found her wallet and clambered down the back stairs.

A screen door separated the cafe from a small covered porch. There was a distant clatter, as if someone were washing dishes a few rooms away. She tried the door, which opened onto a small hallway with scuffed wood floor and pale yellow walls. Then she followed her nose into the kitchen, where was stopped by a dark-haired woman, whose olive complexion was marked with laugh lines and what might deepen into a dimple down one side of her mouth. "I really prefer customers to use the front door." Her words had a rolling quality, as if English had not been her first language.

Lily instantly apologized. "Your baking—I couldn't resist it. What a wonderful fragrance to wake up to." She pointed toward the ceiling. "I'm the new tenant."

The dark-haired woman wiped a floury hand on her denim apron. Now there were two dimples, parentheses around a soft smile. "You must be Dr. Atwood. I am Maria. Of course you may use the back door. Let me introduce you to my muffins. The lemon-poppy seed have just come from the oven."

"You have my complete attention," Lily laughed. "Please call me Lily."

Maria escorted her to a table in the front. The walls were rough red brick, the floor a continuation of scuffed wood; two square wood columns supported the pressed-tin ceiling. A cool breeze streamed through the open front door. Lily felt like a duckling paddling behind mama duck until her landlady pointed to a chair at a table already occupied by Ed the cop and a couple in their forties. "No, no," Lily protested, "I don't want to interrupt."

"Sit here while I bring you a hot muffin," Maria said. "Tomorrow morning you stand in line."

"Do we get the same service today?" Ed asked.

"What do you think?" Maria responded, but she was looking at Lily.

"They get the same?" Lily answered. Then, more firmly, "My treat."

Maria nodded. "My treat this morning. But they'll hold you to your offer tomorrow." She strode off toward the kitchen, pushing chairs under tables and whisking empty paper cups into the waste container as she went.

"I've never seen her when her hands weren't busy," the woman next to Ed commented. "Though she never seems like she's in a hurry."

"I've never heard her offer free muffins before," Ed said, eyes on Lily. "She must like you."

Lily sat down at the table, though she felt uncomfortable. Unless Jonas ate breakfast, a rare occurrence, she usually absorbed a good portion of her daily solitude over tea and toast. Now three people looked at her expectantly, as if she were their morning entertainment. She started to sigh, stopped, and smiled, then worried that her discomfort would be obvious.

Ed came to her rescue. "I see you found your new apartment after all." He turned to the other two at the table. "This is Lily Atwood. I found her circling the Green yesterday afternoon, looking for Green Street."

The woman wore a tailored yellow shirt dress, with pearls on her ears and around her neck. She would have looked elegant on that June morning except that her curly red hair stood out in a slightly messy halo around her pink face.

She nodded at Lily. "I'm Donna Stone. This is my husband, Larry." Larry had a square face and jaw and, from what Lily could see, a square body. He had a rather mild expression on his face, as if he knew from experience that he might scare people otherwise.

"They're Feds," Ed said.

Lily blinked. "I beg your pardon?"

"We work for the FBI," Larry said, his deep voice sounding apologetic. "Donna's in management these days, while I fool around with all these neat high-tech toys."

"Get him to show you his car sometime," Ed suggested. Larry frowned at him, but Ed didn't look worried. "They work over in Hartford, but they live at the corner of the Green." He turned to Donna. "Can you see the apartment upstairs from your house?"

"Sure." She glanced at Lily. "Not that we'll be watching you. What do you do?"

Before Lily could answer, Maria appeared at her elbow. Lily and Ed cleared space in the center of the small table, which Maria filled with a plate of huge muffins. She put a paper cup of something hot in front of Lily. "I guessed tea. Earl Grey." When Lily started to thank her, Maria lifted her palm. "I was right?"

"Completely."

She nodded in satisfaction, and left.

"Let her take care of you," Ed advised. "It's how she gets to know people."

"Thank you," Lily answered, thinking perhaps she could learn something from this man.

"So, you were going to tell us what you do," Larry said, reaching for one of the muffins.

When Lily started to talk about her research project and Edith Wharton and Henry James and the Beinecke, she expected not to have to say very much. The usual reaction to her explanation was a quick change of subject. But the three listened, asked questions, even put in a comment about some movies they'd seen based on Wharton and James books. At one point, Larry said, "Don't be so surprised. FBI agents are required to have college educations, you know."

"My husband has a Ph.D., and he's not interested, " she said, then covered her mouth with her hand.

"Why not?" Donna asked, eyes on Lily while her fingers snitched the last bite of her husband's muffin.

"I don't really know. Perhaps because he's been hearing about Wharton since we met in graduate school?"

"What's his specialty?"

"Raising money," Lily said.

"You can get a Ph.D. in that?" Donna asked.

"No, his degree is in psychology. But he's a vice president of development at Lakeland University. He was too impatient to stay on the academic side of the college business."

"Is he crazy?" Larry asked. He looked serious, not teasing, and Lily didn't know how to take his question.

His wife said, "Honey, maybe you should offer a little background to that question."

"The Agency shrinks frequently seem a little nuts themselves," he said, "so I wondered whether your husband fit into that category."

Lily didn't know what to say. Jonas' thought processes were completely different from any other people she knew. Whether they were crazy or not was something that she hadn't considered. She thought about it for awhile. When she realized the others were watching her, she said, "I don't know. I have to think about it." The three faces turned toward her showed such varied expressions that she laughed—Ed looked interested, Larry looked worried and Donna, mystified. "I have to start paying more attention to people who are still alive," she added.

Donna mercifully changed the subject. They gave her directions to New Haven, including how to find the good parking lot in the middle of town, across the street from the Yale bookstore, "Now a Barnes and Noble," according to Larry. Donna suggested the RJ Julia bookstore just down the Boston Post Road in Madison. Ed wrote down directions for her, tearing another leaf out of his pocket notebook. Larry suggested he just put them in Lily's phone but was ignored.

None of them seemed to back away from her, as had her colleagues at Prairie Shores, even before she was fired. Memories flashed through Lily's mind of the times that administrative types had treated her as if she'd committed some egregious faux pas. Like the time the v.p. for development, Jonas' former boss, abruptly walked out of his office just as she looked in to say hello. Yet now none of the people sharing breakfast with her seemed to want anything from her. Could human relationships be this straightforward? When the Stones headed for their mysteriously-equipped car, they stopped, looked back, and Larry called, "Don't forget that you're buying the muffins tomorrow morning." She waved and nodded. Maybe she'd have a chance to find out.

Lily finished her tea, went upstairs to her apartment, and messed up the bed. No, that wasn't right. She liked it better neat in her apartment. She remade the bed. When she tried to imagine Jonas in this room, all she could picture was him moving things around to suit himself while telling her that it was what she'd wanted all along.

The clock in the front room chimed nine, stirring Lily into action. Taking her cell phone out of a jeans pocket, she switched it on.

She wanted to keep all problems at a distance on this lovely morning. She looked through the opened window at the Green, which positively sparkled. She could swear she smelled the ocean. When she and Jonas met, there was an ocean nearby, a real one, not the inland sea that is Lake Michigan. But that brought her right back to the question she hadn't ever answered about Jonas and suddenly realized she'd have to, if not right that minute then soon. The question of why Jonas chose her and chose to stay with her. Once she had that information, she could answer the next obvious question.

Chapter 18

Instead, she opened her email and found a long missive from Bethany with the subject line, "Outside."

"I've been sitting by the pool for the last few weeks, covered in 60 SPF sunblock and wearing a big hat and sunglasses."

Ah, thought Lily, literally outside.

> I probably look mysterious. But I know all the women around me. I used to lead half of them when I was cheerleading captain. Now they seem like strangers. Is that what happens when you go away to college? Or would this have happened if I'd stayed?
>
> Every morning, the pool is crowded with young mothers minding their toddlers. Dr. Atwood, most of them aren't much older than me. The mothers, that is. They went straight from high school into marriage and family, skipping college. They look happy, sort of contented, most of the time. But they do seem to screech at their kids too much.
>
> I have a lot of time to think. Cary, my boyfriend, works with his dad on their farm all day, weekends, too. They grow soy and corn and raise pigs for market. Sometimes the pigs smell, but most of the time they don't. They're a lot cleaner than people think. Though pig shit—phew. Cary's idea for our future is to take over his dad's farm, marry me, have kids, I'll run the house and help him run the business. Family farms that have survived are like big businesses. Since his dad owns the land free and clear, and Cary's the only child, what he wants is real. He's thinking of taking a few courses at the ag school, but otherwise doesn't see much use for college. His dad is pretty advanced, selling options on the pigs in the Chicago market, that sort of thing, so Cary's learning at home.

Here Lily sat back and shook her head. She couldn't see Bethany fitting into this twenty-first-century pastoral novel of an existence. But maybe she didn't know her all that well. She read on.

> I don't know. It all sounds pretty good. Last summer, it all sounded just perfect. I went to college because I got that scholarship. Maybe

if I'd just stayed and gotten married? Because I feel like I'm watching my town from a distance. I sit outside all day guarding moms and their kids and sometimes old people and always teenage girls, but teenage boys don't come much, they're too busy. The pool closes at six o'clock, way before the men get in from the fields. Sometimes the guy who owns the hardware store shows up for a half hour right before we close, but that's about it. Everyone has specific roles around here.

I'm trying to imagine myself as one of those mothers yelling at their kids, coming to the pool in the morning to wear out the little ones so they'll take a nap and I could get some chores done. Part of it sounds really appealing, comfortable, you know? Safe.

Then my heart starts to race, the way it does when I'm scared.

Here's the thing: It all sounds hard and bright and perfect.

I'm not.

Well, I don't know why I wanted to share all this with you. Maybe because I'm used to writing for you, so you seemed to be the person I ought to be writing for now. Anyway, I hear you've gotten a grant or something to do some research. I know you're really busy. But you know if you could email me, it would be awesome.

I know, I know, define awesome. Right now, I can't.

Bethany.

Outside on the Green, a young woman holding four leashes escorted two Labrador retrievers, a husky and a Weimaraner into the park, the husky firmly in the lead. A nice life, she thought, but not for her. Did Guilford have a fixed social order, like geologic strata whose relationships never changed? That's what Bethany's hometown sounded like. That's the geology that Wharton explored through much of what she wrote, the hard strata of New York, Newport and New England social upper echelons, where she was born and grew up and married.

But the subject line of Bethany's email intrigued Lily: "Outside." Outside because she spent her summer by the local swimming pool? Or outside the strata? Was Bethany indulging in figurative language? Where did she come up with "hard and bright and perfect"? Because that was a paraphrase from one of Wharton's most famous books, a book that, as far as Lily knew, Bethany hadn't read. She'd pick up a copy of *The Age of Innocence*—she'd left her own in the apartment, in the boxes of books she'd moved from her college office—and look up the reference. Or go online, though she still didn't trust the accuracy of books scanned onto the internet.

She found her canvas satchel, stowed notes and laptop, and went downstairs to the parking lot behind the cafe. The stairway smelled of chocolate.

It wasn't until she'd found her way to New Haven and the parking lot across from Barnes and Noble that she concluded she was running. She'd skipped the jaunt to the Madison bookstore. Sitting in the car, whose rose scent was now barely noticeable, she forced herself to examine why she didn't want to think about what Jonas had done.

One of the few things she'd fought with Jonas about was where to place the breakfront Nate had built for her as a wedding present. She'd insisted on pride of place in the front hallway of their apartment. Ever since, Jonas had been suggesting moving the breakfront to the front room, to her office, to the sun porch, but she'd ignored him. He'd continue trying to get his way, of course. That's what Jonas did, agree with her for the moment. No decision was ever final unless it was his decision. As long as he'd stayed out of her professional life, that had been fine with Lily. He hadn't trespassed, hadn't crossed from the personal into her teaching or research, she had told herself.

No, idiot, she yelled in her mind, he didn't trespass. Instead he worked from behind the scenes to exile her from her teaching life. Not to mention having had a good try at derailing her grant applications.

Since that night when she'd left him with the checkbook out on the porch, he called her constantly. With Cara's help she'd installed a phone app that immediately sent his calls to voicemail. Jonas had tried to reach Nate as well, but Cara had put the same app on his phone.

Cara's question was the central one: Why did her husband so want her to fail?

Jonas' list of chores for Lily rose in her mind, the list he'd left on the kitchen table the morning after she'd been fired by Prairie Shores. The list she'd also ignored. He didn't really want her to be the little wife, did he? He couldn't have changed that much in the course of their marriage, could he? Had he ever before presented her with such a list? She reviewed their years together, as doctoral candidates, as beginning professors, then as fundraiser and assistant professor. No list. Just the constant refrain: it's all right to fail.

Fuck that, she thought, and went to work.

• • •

Before he could switch off his new phone, Jonas noticed that there was a new text message. Well, he'd wait until the next rest stop. He loved being out on the road and didn't want another interruption. There was a really nice stop about fifty miles ahead that he'd found visiting one of his upper-upper-middle class donors. Prairie Shores donors, of course; LU donors wouldn't be caught dead with a summer place out in the cornfields.

When he finally checked his messages, there was one from the probate court in his home town. How had they found him? Not that he'd been hiding, but he thought that no one back home cared much one way or another where he'd gotten to over the past decade and a half. Why would the probate court be looking for him?

He deleted the message.

Then there was another message. It was a photo of a pale woman, white hair and white skin and pale clothes, dusting off a grave.

He looked closely. Could it be?

No way.

He deleted the photo.

Chapter 19

Lily rounded the corner onto New Haven's Wall Street, and there was Yale's Beinecke Rare Book and Manuscript Library. She'd been here before during a rainstorm which had blocked from sight what she could see now: the sheer weirdness of the library building in its wild contrast to the surrounding Gothic architecture, soaring spires, and limestone residence halls that looked more like miniature castles complete with moats. The rare book library was a modern white five-story box crouched over a plaza sunken one story down, to the basement level.

Lily stood on the street corner and gaped. She'd read somewhere that the architects had originally specified onyx for the outer sheath, only to discover that there wasn't enough onyx in the world to do the job. They settled for thin sheets of Vermont white marble. The morning sunshine played on the building, sometimes finding black or gray veining in the marble, sometimes bouncing off white marble to blind the observer. It was imposing but it was also a paradox: Yale's main library, Sterling, looked like a cathedral of books, with the cold formality of stained glass set in limestone. Modern thought housed in Gothic building, rare books housed in mid-twentieth-century modern architecture.

She crossed to the edge of the sunken plaza. One story down perched three Isamu Noguchi sculptures—a pyramid, a hollowed disc and a cube. The reading room on the lower level, where she'd be spending her summer, looked out onto the sculptures through a windowed wall.

Time to get to it, she thought, and walked inside the library, only to stand gaping again. Sunlight had warmed the marble on the inside to pale gold, but what held her attention was the inner glass tower of incunabula, six levels of ancient books, the first visible on the story below her, the other five above her. You'd never guess from looking at the outside what was on the inside. What you see versus what you don't see, Lily mused.

Unable to resist, she climbed the stairs to reacquaint herself with the Gutenberg Bible. Approaching the Bible's display case, she caught sight of a student reflected in its glass walls. Scuffed Birkenstocks, jeans, tee shirt, hair in a ponytail. My God, she thought, that's me. She stared and backed away, disconcerted that she looked as though she'd never grown up. She fled down two flights, coming up finally against the black granite counter opposite the reading room.

A petite woman, shorter than Lily, watched her calmly, her lips curved in what looked like a smile she was trying to press back. "First time here?"

"Second. The first time was when I was a graduate student."

The woman nodded. Her name tag identified her as Constance Cordrey, senior reference librarian. She fingered a large green pear-shaped jewel that hung from a fine gold chain around her neck. "Now?"

"I've got a grant to research Edith Wharton's relationship with Henry James."

"You are in quite the right place. Have you some identification?"

Lily pulled out the grant letters from NEH and the smaller foundation.

The librarian carefully examined both as if they might be new accessions for the library. Lily was rather expecting she'd comment on the generosity of the grants, but the librarian merely returned the letters before pointing to some computers. They looked oddly at home among the tapestries and paintings hanging over teak walls and between teak bookcases. "Start there. We have catalogued a good bit of the Wharton collection, but there are new acquisitions that we have yet to catalog."

"Are they available for study?" Lily asked.

"Oh, yes. We are just not quite sure what we have yet."

That sounded promising, Lily thought.

"How long will you be with us?" the librarian inquired.

"Most of the summer, I think."

"In that case, let me show you the lockers and the readers' lounge." She beckoned Lily with her index finger, leading her past the long counter to a doorway hidden at the end of the room. The lockers were built of more shining teak.

"I thought you'd show me school lockers."

"Not here. One of the donors had these installed." She turned at the entrance, took another few steps and opened a door set in the wall to her right. Inside was a large room lined with upholstered couches sitting on more oriental rugs. Here walls were hung with huge framed maps of Connecticut. Lily went up to look at one that showed the coast and Long Island Sound. It was an original, the ink fading. The librarian nodded at the look of awe on Lily's face. "The inside does not match the outside." She glanced at Lily's student garb. "Like most people, I sometimes think."

Lily looked at the librarian's jeweled pendant and her short curly light brown hair, answering, "Quite often, yes."

Cordrey's laugh was tiny and bright, like the woman. She handed Lily request forms. "I assume you have come prepared with a list of the boxes in which you are interested?"

Lily straightened. She was back in her territory, the place she'd always been most sure of herself. "Let's start with the uncatalogued boxes, please."

"Ah, one of those, are you?"

Lily smiled. She was indeed one of those, a literary detective, snooping for what had yet to be found. This was where she got to test out her crazy idea, to see if there existed primary source material—preferably correspondence in Edith Wharton's handwriting—to prove her right. To anyone outside of her particular addiction to print and handwriting and the real materials handled by Wharton and James themselves, her quest might seem hopeless. Plodding. Time-consuming. God knew Jonas thought so. In graduate school he'd perpetually tried to pull her away from her research. Maybe he had an ulterior motive even then. Later, she told herself, later. For awhile 'later' would become her mantra when it came to thinking about the Jonas problem.

Lily settled herself near the window in the library reading room at one of the large wood-topped metal tables. White-painted walls and pale beige carpeting added to the workmanlike atmosphere of the place, while the sunken sculpture garden on the other side of the plate-glass windows lent an otherworldliness. It was a place out of time. Lily's kind of place. She opened her laptop, took out a pencil (no pens allowed in this library) and tried not to think about what she hoped to find. One of the library's undergraduate pages wheeled in the first box of materials. She thanked the young man, removed the lid, took a deep breath and plunged in.

Chapter 20

Lily forgot the twenty-first century until Constance Cordrey tapped her on the shoulder, saying "We close in five minutes. The library page has been trying to get you to return this box." Lily had worked through lunch and realized she desperately needed to pee. She grimaced at the librarian. "Oh, dear, where's the bathroom?"

Cordrey pointed the way, saying only, "I shall wait with your things."

Lily didn't want Cordrey to look at her work but she didn't have time to protest. "Thank you," she called as she ran out the reading room door, past the long granite counter to the bathrooms. She made it just in time. Sitting in the stall, she had a moment of déjà vu. She'd gotten so involved that she'd almost wet her pants when she'd worked the previous summer at Indiana University's Lilly Library. She flushed the toilet, washed her hands and returned to the reading room.

The Wharton box had disappeared. Cordrey was reading her notes. Lily started to grab them away from her, but the tiny woman shook her head. "Not to worry. Your secret is safe with me. We librarians here are rather like priests, you know. What we know about our researchers' work is privileged information."

. . .

Constance could tell Lily didn't believe her. That much was clear from Lily's closed expression and the haste with which she gathered her belongings. Constance tried to help her, pushing the laptop across the table. Constance had a hunch about the connections for which Lily was searching in those uncatalogued boxes of Wharton material. At that moment, Lily was clutching her book bag to her chest, glaring. Constance had seen that behavior before, from other academics who needed success in their Beinecke searches. Needed success too much. But Constance could tell there was something else driving this visitor from Illinois. Casually, Constance said, "Do you have another appointment now?"

Lily looked surprised. "No."

"Care to go for a cup of coffee? There is a nice place nearby."

Lily blurted, "Why would I want to do that?"

"For a shot of caffeine before you drive home? Perhaps some food? To have an opportunity to discuss your work with someone who cannot tell another soul?"

Lily frowned. "Cannot? Or should not?"

"Cannot. It is not worth it to me to gossip. I would lose my job."

Constance had come to the Beinecke ten years before, after graduate school and a short tour at the New York Public Library. She had left an ex-husband in New York, coming to New Haven to find calm and quiet in her work, safety, and a little house for herself and her dog. On the surface she fit the stereotype of the spinster librarian, if one didn't know her history. It wasn't often that she found herself interested in the academics who came to use her library. More interesting were the questions she fielded from around the country. But she had a fondness for Edith Wharton, having been brought up in Wharton's milieu nearly a century and a half after the author's upbringing. Wharton had nailed those sons of bitches, she'd always thought. Not that she would actually voice those specific words. "I too am an Edith Wharton fan," she added.

Lily's eyes narrowed. "What about Henry James?"

"The man or his writing?"

Lily smiled, though her shoulders remained hunched and she still cradled her book bag protectively. "Good answer." She glanced at the reading room clock. Her shoulders relaxed. Ah, thought Constance, a decision. "Meet you upstairs at the exit?" Lily asked.

"Yes. About five minutes."

Precisely five minutes later, Constance collected Lily at the front door. Ten minutes after that they sat in the scented warmth of Claire's Corner Copia cafe. The menu of soups and salads and vegetarian entrees was handwritten on huge blackboards in colored chalk. Lily's stomach growled loudly, and she looked amused and embarrassed. "Maybe I'd better have something to eat."

"I would become lightheaded if I missed lunch," Constance said.

"Have you been watching me all day?" Her shoulders rose again.

"Hard to miss you, rooted in the same chair right in my sight line. Should I pretend that I did not see you?"

Then the woman said something that actually surprised Constance: "I'm not used to people paying attention to me."

"But that makes no sense," she responded. "You have a doctorate?"

Lily nodded.

"Then a whole group of professors must have paid attention to you at some point. You have a university appointment?"

"At one point, not now," Lily admitted.

"But someone must have interviewed you."

Lily grinned at the librarian. "Used to paying attention to details, are you?"

"It is my job. Any research has to be a logical progression. If you have a point of illogic, then eventually the entire project collapses."

Lily turned to read the chalked offerings. "How's the soup here?"

"Excellent. Especially the chowdery things." Constance stood. "We should order." She led the way to the counter piled with cakes and cookies.

Lily glanced with apparent longing at the chocolate mousse cake. She ordered a bowl of corn chowder and a glass of brewed ice tea. Constance decided to tempt her. "Care to split a piece of that cake?"

"If I did that, I'd have to take up exercise."

"Care to borrow a dog?" Constance suggested.

"Say what?"

"Dog-walking is my exercise of choice."

"I don't think my landlord would approve of my having a dog, since her restaurant is downstairs."

"You might be surprised," Constance said. She led the way back to their table, carrying a piece of cake and a glass of iced tea for herself. She allowed Lily to eat about half of her soup before saying, "Now, do you think you will find the connection you are looking for between Wharton and James?"

Once again Lily surprised her, merely looking up at her to say, "Do you?"

"Oh, yes. It is there."

"How do you know?" Lily said, her tone businesslike now.

"I couldn't have known Wharton and James, but I know people like them. A woman doing a good deed for an unappreciative man? Keeping her role secret?"

Lily put down her spoon, her expression again suspicious. "What are you, a speed reader? I wasn't in the bathroom that long."

Constance said, "You did not have to be."

• • •

The next morning, driving to New Haven, Lily was more prepared for a full day of research than she'd been the previous day. Next to her on the passenger seat was a paper bag containing a huge turkey and havarti cheese sandwich, an orange and a bottle of water. If the Beinecke could come up with antique oriental rugs in the readers' lounge and teak lockers, she bet there'd be a refrigerator somewhere. If not, she'd ask Constance to use the staff fridge. She felt she could do that, after last night's conversation. How was it, she wondered, that people here seemed to want to help her, when back in Illinois everyone just wanted to run her life or avoid her? Or maybe it was that here she was willing to let people help her? She thought about that as she circled off the highway and into New Haven, but couldn't answer her own query. What she didn't think about was Jonas. Again.

This time she walked into the Beinecke as if she'd worked there forever. The guard at the door nodded at her identification. The sun-gold marble interior warmed her but couldn't distract her. This morning she took the steps down to the research floor with the distinct feeling that she was home.

Constance greeted her with a smile, gesturing with her hand toward the reading room. "Same box?" she asked from her spot behind the counter.

"Yes, please."

"The student page will bring it to you in a moment."

"Thanks." She showed her brown bag lunch to Constance, who told her where to find the refrigerator. Back to the Reading Room, the Noguchi sculptures' familiarity drew her to the window wall, where Lily arranged her laptop. She plugged in to check her email. Cara had sent a photo of Izzy watching Nate sanding a table. Bethany had written again.

The email began:

> I brought my laptop to the pool today. My mom says I'm nuts, that it'll get wet and ruined, not to mention that I'm supposed to be watching the pool. Well, I can't just read all day. I mean, I can, but I need to write, too. Somehow I think you can understand that. Remember when you used to tell us about Edith Wharton and how she'd write every morning from her bedroom, tossing the finished pages onto the floor, knowing that her secretary would pick them up for typing. I don't think I'll fling my laptop onto the concrete at the bottom of my ladder. There's a little covered shelf behind my chair that ought to keep it safe enough. I could have brought pen and paper, if I had any.

At this Lily shook her head. Students never seemed to own pen and paper during the school year; it wasn't reassuring to find out that a bright one like Bethany couldn't put her hand on such basics at home, either.

> Maybe I'll stop at the store on the way home. There's the usual crowd of mothers and little kids in the pool right now. But there was a little excitement last night. This really hot guy showed up about an hour before the pool closed. He's older, not a teenager, DEFINITELY

not from HERE. He bought a day ticket at the gate, came in, took off his clothes. When he dropped his pants, every mother's eye was on him. What was he up to? But he had a pair of swim trunks on under his jeans. He dived into the part of the pool that's kept for lap swimming—you know, divided into lanes. He swam and swam this really nice crawl and then breast stroke until we called closing time. Every female here watched him the whole time, but he didn't seem to notice. No, he had to notice. I mean, I can always tell when someone's watching me. But he didn't look back.

The funny thing is that when you looked closely at him, there didn't seem to be any reason for him to be HOT. He was nice looking enough, regular features, fat-free body and everything. But he didn't have great muscles or the perfect pecs or anything beefcake like.

Oh, wow, why am I telling YOU this?

And that was the end of the message.

Why indeed? Lily thought. Bethany had sent the email about the mystery guy when she could easily have deleted it. Lily read through the three paragraphs again. Playing her own teacherly hunch, she wrote back,

Bethany, you're trying to describe something that you can't actually see. That kind of description is difficult, but you're almost there. Keep telling me the story. Don't be afraid to fill in what you can't see with what you feel. Much of what interests us about others is our impressions of them, which may come from how they look or from the contrast between how they look and how we react to them. In the movies, the heroines are always falling in love with the guy who's the nerd or punk instead of the clean-cut blonde guy, and the whole point of the movie is why he's the right or wrong guy, from the heroine's point of view.

So if your hot guy returns to the pool, see if you can figure out what his story is FROM A DISTANCE. Stay away from strangers.

Lily wanted it on the record that Bethany shouldn't approach this guy. She changed FROM A DISTANCE to boldface. She sent the message, wondering how fast Bethany would get it, whether the girl still had her own computer on at the pool.

Before stopping herself, she emailed Cara to ask if she knew Bethany. The two young women seemed introspective, not all that common in their age groups. Then she emailed Bethany to ask if it would be all right to forward her emails to Cara, that she thought the two younger women might enjoy getting to know one another.

Women helping women. It was a new concept for Lily. She had helped Cara, Cara had helped her. Help was not a strong enough word. But there it was, that connection. Not dependency, not control. Something else, a positive something else.

Then the library page said, "Dr. Atwood?" She looked up to see a student holding her Wharton box. She laughed at herself: "her" box already. She pushed the computer to the side as the boy slid the box onto the table in front of her. Breakfast, she thought wryly. And lunch. Dinner. Dessert. The whole feast.

Chapter 21

July

"Frustrated?" Constance asked a few weeks later.

At this point Lily had occupied her seat in the reading room for so many hours and days—if the Beinecke was open, she was there working—that she and the librarian had taken to sharing mid-morning breaks. In the readers' lounge on rainy days; outside overlooking the sculpture garden on dry days. Lily had come to fit in at the Beinecke. Over the past few weeks, Constance had introduced her to other librarians, to security men and women who watched over the priceless books, to student pages. Lily was happy there, unhappy with her the progress of her work. She'd had her fill of Wharton, something that she never would have thought possible.

Constance had brought a huge thermos of iced coffee laced with cinnamon. Cradling her cup of coffee, careful that the lid was tight so as not to spill onto her new tee shirt—she hadn't packed everything the evening she'd left Jonas and the grilling salmon—Lily looked down ten feet at the sculpture garden. It reminded her of the photographs she'd seen in books about Japanese gardens, so smooth and, to western eyes, empty. It should be calming. Instead, the three stone sculptures irritated her. According to Constance, the pyramid shape stood for earth, the sphere for the sun, and the cube for chance. That last one particularly annoyed her, since she was relying too much on chance these days. She glanced over at Constance, who was watching her with her usual bright interest.

"Frustrated?" Constance repeated.

"Sure," Lily said, dangling her feet over the side of the wall surrounding the sunken garden. Seated cross-legged, Constance fit perfectly on the narrow top of the wall. Her eyes held Lily. The green pear-shaped jewel pendant that Constance always wore was so striking because the emerald was the exact color of her eyes. Lily said, "I'm trying to think of the right word. Overwhelmed? Yes, but I expected to be, with thirty-some feet of boxes to go through. Impatient, sure, I expected that, too. But what bothers me is that I feel overfull, like I've eaten too much, and not necessarily of a good thing."

"Too much Wharton?"

"Jonas was always hopeful I would finally tire of her."

"Was?" Constance said in a neutral tone. "You never talk about him. Did you realize that? And how odd it is that you fail to mention your husband?"

Once Cara had shown her that it was Jonas who had instigated her dismissal, she'd been insulated by a feeling of detachment.

Constance's words exploded her detachment.

Anger and fear that she had kept at bay washed over her. It seemed to her the Noguchi cube—Chance—turned dark red, blood red. She stretched her arm back and threw her paper coffee cup as hard as she could at the sculpture. The lid flew off as the cup struck the stone. Black coffee dripped down the face of Chance. Lily froze, appalled at what she'd done, afraid to look at Constance.

"Well, two points for nailing Chance, my dear," Constance said, upper-class New York vowels sounding rounder and consonants more bell-like than usual.

"Oh my God, will the coffee come off?" Lily gasped.

"Those sculptures have survived more than fifty years of student abuse. They are tough. So are you."

Lily hunched her shoulders. "Oh no I'm not. I'm really good at denial is all. I can't do this. I can't bring this research off. It means too much."

"Like what? It is a lovely project." The librarian offered another cup of iced coffee to Lily, who shook her head, afraid of herself.

"It means tenure. Somewhere."

Constance set down the coffee with care, then slammed her little fist into Lily's shoulder, knocking her backward onto the grass.

"What the hell was that for?" Lily rubbed her shoulder. "That hurt."

"Wake up, will you?" Constance stood over her. "Tenure? You are not fighting this hard for tenure. I watch you slog through box after box of Wharton papers, hour after hour, forgetting to eat half the time. Tenure? Some ditzy articles about Wharton's use of parenthetical phrases will get you tenure. What are you really fighting for? Or against?"

Pulling herself up onto her elbows, wincing at the pain in her shoulder, Lily finally brought herself to her feet. She glared down at Constance. "Who the hell are you to assault me?"

"Maybe the first real friend you have ever had." Constance glared back at her, those green eyes dark with some emotion that Lily couldn't fathom. "Certainly the first one to completely empathize with your situation."

"What's going on with you today?" Lily demanded.

"With me? Did I decorate Chance with coffee?" Constance sat back down on the edge of the wall and spoke in the direction of the sculptures. "Though I have been waiting for you to do something like that. I have never met anyone with as much banked anger as you have."

"I'm not—" Lily began, the words stopping when Constance pointed to the coffee that now covered most of one side of the stone cube. "I saw red," Lily admitted. "Blood red. I always thought that was the stuff of junk novels." She sat down next to Constance. "How'd you know?"

"A psychiatrist would call it projection. I have endured that level of anger. I left all that behind in New York."

"Freedom," Lily said. "The success of this project means freedom. I can do what I love and support myself."

"Got it in one."

"Freedom," she repeated. She remembered how in June she envied the Lakeland U sorority girls driving off alone in their cars, and told Constance the story.

"Freedom," Constance announced, "requires strategy."

"I got the grant. I'm here." Lily thought a moment before adding, "Maybe I confused escape with freedom." She nodded, then looked at her friend. "Got any suggestions?"

"You have been working through the boxes as they are listed in the different databases."

Lily said in a low voice, "What I'm looking for could be anywhere. The last place I look is where I'll find it. If I find it."

"Hmmm." Constance sipped coffee, then leaned her head back, closing her eyes to the morning sun. "How far have you gotten in the uncatalogued database?"

"Dipped into it a couple of weeks ago. Why?" Lily turned to face Constance. "What are you thinking?"

Those green eyes were open and light again while her fingers played with the pendant. "If what you seek was catalogued, someone would have found it by now. But the new stuff? Most of it no one has taken the time to look through." She grinned at Lily. "You could catalog it for us."

"No, thanks." She watched coffee drip off Chance. "So Constance, what do you think I'm looking for?"

"A short story by Wharton that was published under James' name. That may or may not exist. But," she said, holding up an index finger to halt Lily, who'd opened her mouth to speak, "what we may well have is reference to it."

"How do you know?" Lily demanded.

Constance waved the question away. "Talk about that later. The library has recently accessioned collections of letters Wharton wrote to her publishers from her home in Lenox, Massachusetts, and from abroad. So far we have organized the letters by date, more or less. Have you determined when Wharton would have pulled off her sleight-of-hand?"

Lily snorted. Sleight-of-hand. "More like her good deed. No wonder she had to leave New York and Newport. I've never been able to imagine those people actually wanting to take care of each other except for selfish reasons."

"They still do not," Constance said. "Something else I left behind in New York." She waved her hand again. "Stay on topic. You assume that Wharton cared about James. When she first knew him, he would have been the celebrity. But at some point she surpassed him. When? Year?"

"Because if she wrote a story to boost his reputation, it must have been when the public was losing interest in him," Lily said. "I've been looking for any references to that. I've skipped the correspondence for the period when James was still the Stephen King of his time."

"The what?" Constance said, eyebrows raised.

"He generated verbiage as fast as King, but he lost sight of what people like to read, unlike King. A good story. Strong plot, stronger characters. These days we'd say he didn't know how to write an airport book." She stopped. "Sorry, didn't mean to lecture. Look, will you ask one of the pages to bring me the boxes from her publisher, the new ones?"

"Recently accessioned," Constance intoned. "No, I will not unless you specify a time period."

"Oh, that's easy. After 1908, before 1911. Probably closer to 1908, before she got involved with Fullerton and spent most of her emotional energy on her delayed sex life and dealing with her husband's madness, then the divorce. Well, either 1908 or 1911, at the end of all that. It's probably something, some correspondence maybe, to do with Scribner's, because she was threatening to leave them to go with new publishers. Scribner's would do anything to keep her—that's how she managed to get them to offer James a huge advance that she funded. Scribner's played along, making James believe it was business as usual. My guess has been that whatever I find will have to do with Scribner's."

Constance gazed in the direction of the now brown and white Noguchi sculpture. "Chance looks a lot better now."

Chapter 22

Chance took its time, and so did Lily. Constance's suggestion about the uncatalogued boxes reduced her search from thirty-seven boxes to ten. By the time she'd reached the eighth box at the beginning of August, she hadn't quite given up hope. But she was certainly running out of time: NEH expected a progress report by the end of September. So far she'd come up with nothing more than an annotated inventory of the uncatalogued collection, useless to Lily though it pleased Constance and the other librarians. She'd run across letters here and there from Wharton to her publisher that mentioned James, but nothing that could be remotely considered a hint that what Wharton had in mind involved actually writing under James' name.

Lily wouldn't give up. Her research style was persistence long past the time others would have gone home. Still, she was having a hard time making herself believe that persistence alone would lead to a significant discovery, one she could hold in her hand and say, "See, I found something," at least to herself and to Constance. The latter tried to cheer her up, to tell her she was on the right path. It wasn't until Lily muttered something about seriously considering whether she should bother going on to box number eight that Constance clamped her hand around Lily's wrist and dragged her outside.

The day was hot, the sky white. Constance pulled her across Wall Street, cut between Berkeley College and Harkness Hall to Cross Campus Park before she'd release Lily's wrist. Then she pushed roughly against Lily's shoulders, barking "Sit down, damn you." Her behavior was so out of character that Lily froze. Constance pushed again, harder, gave up and sat down in a patch of shade.

"I have a story," the librarian announced.

Lily immediately sat down beside her. The grass was cool. Summer school was out, undergraduates gone; a few graduate students dotted the commons, out of earshot. "I'm up for a story, especially if it doesn't involve Wharton or James."

"If it does?" Constance's eyes glittered, appeared hard, something that Lily hadn't seen before. Her friend's hand gripped the faceted emerald pendant so tightly that it must be cutting her palm.

"Are you all right?" Lily asked, leaning towards her. "What's going on?"

Constance shrugged, then looked carefully around. "Do you know those stories that begin something like 'once in a place far, far away'?"

"You mean like *Star Wars*?" She sounded like Cara. "You're telling me science fiction or fantasy?"

"Of course not. But I must tell you a family story. Not my family, my ex-husband's. Just do not ask for any more details than I give you. Deal?"

"No," Lily said.

"Then no story," Constance said. She put her hands flat on the grass and started to push herself up.

Lily waited for her to get halfway to a standing position before grabbing one of her ankles. If she pulled, Constance would topple over. "Constance," she said.

"What are you doing?"

"Do you trust me?"

"Not right at the moment."

Lily grinned. "Do you really think I'd pull your foot out from under you?"

There was a silence. The two stared at each other. Neither moved.

Finally Constance said, "All or nothing, is that it?"

Lily nodded. "You're in or you're out. Choose. You know everything there is to know about my project and what it means to me."

Constance began to lower herself back to the grass, and Lily let go. "You are locating your tough streak," Constance remarked.

"I think I have to."

"The contract works both ways. You must tell me about your marriage."

Lily took a deep breath, stretched her head back and looked at the sky. Talking about the Jonas problem was something that she never considered. It was her secret. Her, what? Embarrassment? But why should she be embarrassed? Always her thoughts worked themselves into endless loops that didn't produce any answers. She contemplated Constance. Such a logical mind in a delicate curly-haired package. Would it be worth the risk? Hands covering her eyes, she nodded, feeling as if she'd just jumped off the high dive into the shallow end. "And you must tell me about your marriage," Lily said.

Constance nodded. That was it, the contract of trust.

The librarian plucked a few blades of grass and began to braid them. Without looking up, she said, "I heard a rumor, possibly a family myth, when I was married. My husband's family was related to Teddy Wharton."

Lily looked at her, mouth open.

Constance didn't notice. "My—I do not know what you would term it—social level, the families I knew growing up, for generations the same families married each other. New blood became acceptable about forty years ago if accompanied by money. Though the money part is beside the point."

Constance picked more grass, then tossed it away. She crossed her legs Indian fashion, then straightened them out in front of her, leaning back on her hands. Her toes pointed toward her knees, stretching and pulling the Achilles tendon, then straightened and flexed.

Lily remained quiet, allowing her to come to her own decision.

Finally she looked at Lily. "One of the reasons I moved from New York is that my husband turned on me. In the few years we were married, he changed into a different man. He used his fists. He stole money from me, shifting my salary checks from our joint account to another opened in his own name. He could not reach into my various family trust accounts, though he tried. His family is wealthy in its own right. His stealing from me was about something other than money."

Lily said, "When Teddy Wharton got older and bipolar disease overcame him, he took to spending Edith's money on secret projects of his own, including other women. The final insult was taking fifty thousand dollars from her, partly to buy his mistress an apartment. A century ago, that was a fortune."

Her gaze still on her toes, Constance said, "It was the same madness that descended on my husband. I did not know it at the time. I just knew that he scared me. I left. Got an order of protection, eventually a divorce. He lives at McLean's now, the same mental institution that Teddy Wharton's father was in."

"Oh, Constance. I never would have guessed." Lily leaned forward. "Wait. Are these the details you didn't want to tell me?"

"Partly. But as you say, context is everything. Now you have context. In my husband's family, one of the ongoing myths was that Teddy Wharton, before he went totally crazy after Edith divorced him, helped Henry James write for the public."

"Teddy Wharton? The gentleman athlete? The husband as parasite? No way," Lily blurted.

"Exactly. Remember, I was working in the reference section of the New York Public Library before and during my marriage. I looked into the rumor by looking into Teddy Wharton. No way, indeed. The man made it through Harvard on charm alone. It simply makes no sense that an intellectual aesthete like Henry James would listen to any literary ideas from a Teddy Wharton."

"Besides," added Lily, "until his mind went, Teddy was his wife's biggest fan. He may not have understood everything she wrote, but he was intensely proud of her for her work and her mind. In awe. He would never write for Henry James, even if that was in his skill set."

"Which makes the story even less plausible."

In Lily's family, stories tended to be based on someone's version of the truth. But from what little Jonas said about his family, stories were just that—fiction. Families believe what they want to believe. "Family myth frequently is a twisted kind of truth," she said.

Constance nodded. "My thought. So I considered the possibility that Edith was advising Henry James."

"Read her autobiography," Lily laughed. "He could dish out criticism but he couldn't take it."

"Which leads me to think the only way my former husband's family myth could be true—"

"—is if Edith Wharton secretly wrote for him," Lily finished excitedly. "Exactly my working hypothesis." Her excitement died. "But where, damn it? Where? I've been through seven boxes of the uncatalogued Wharton stuff and another seven of the catalogued. Where?" she shouted, pounding the grass with her fist.

"I am unable to tell you where. But I know it is there and that somehow Teddy Wharton is involved." Constance stood up. She held a hand out to Lily. "Come on. You have work to do."

...

A week later, Lily pulled a faded note out of the front of the ninth box. It was on the letterhead of Edith Wharton's publisher, dated April, 1909. "Dear Mrs. Wharton," it began. "Are you certain that this is what you want to do? The story would probably work as you suggest. But I feel that there is perhaps information I am missing. Please advise before we take the next step." The top of the letter was marked "copy for Wharton file." The note didn't mention where the original was to be sent.

Where was Edith Wharton in April, 1909? France?

Maybe this means nothing, Lily told herself. Maybe you're interpreting it the way you want.

Lily looked at the next letter. And the next. She dashed out of the reading room to the library counter and put in a request for the eighth box, the one that she thought she'd checked so thoroughly, and returned to her table. Deep breaths, she told herself. Don't mess this up.

While waiting, she pulled all the letters, memos and notes out of the ninth box one by one, arranging them on her table in chronological order. None of the pieces dated before April, 1910 contained any reference to Edith Wharton's request, whatever had prompted the publisher's "are you sure this is what you want to do?" response. She read them all through again, considering the possibility that Wharton had written in euphemisms so thick that her note would appear to be in code, even to Lily, who spoke and read Wharton's language fluently.

After what seemed like hours, the library page delivered box eight. Before opening it, Lily put away all the material she'd removed from box nine, this time in chronological order. This, after all, was uncatalogued material; the order was not yet important to anyone but herself. Then she organized the contents of box eight on the table in chronological order.

She spotted a note in Wharton's hand, undated but pinned to another letter from her publisher. The publisher had written, "Interesting story, not your usual style. In what venue would you like it published? You've completed your contract with Scribner's Magazine, but we are always interested in your work, as you know."

Wharton's note read simply, "What do you think of this? Does it sound too much like James?" Her stationery was headed, "The Mount, Lenox, Massachusetts," the mansion that Edith and Teddy had built and that Edith had decorated to much acclaim.

Suddenly, a chronology of her own was writing its way across Lily's mind. Could it be that Wharton had composed the story originally as an exercise? Or a tribute to James, anticipating or perhaps during one of his visits to The Mount?

The Reading Room clock struck. Lily had less than three weeks to find out what she could before her grant report time ran out. She had to look over the rest of the eighth box again, plus the tenth box. It was four o'clock.

She looked across the room toward the black granite library counter. She could see Constance, finishing up something for the end of the work day. Lily had a plan that involved Constance, if she was game.

Lily hoped she could talk her into it. Bribe her. Bring the dog. Bribe the dog. Whatever it took.

Chapter 23

It was an indulgence, but Lily figured she was due a reward after all those dry weeks at the Beinecke. She'd been minding her pennies, eating breakfast in her apartment, taking brown bag lunches, heating canned soup for dinner. This morning she wanted people and pastry and a really good cup of coffee that didn't come from a thermos. The scent of cinnamon had awakened her at dawn. She spent the next couple of hours lying in bed, thinking about what she'd found, dreaming about what she might find. Then she got up, showered, put on a clean black tee shirt with white shorts, and clattered down the wooden stairs to the cafe.

Maria greeted her. "Sticky buns this morning."

"I'll have two," Lily said.

"No you don't," Maria said automatically before asking, "Why?"

"I'm hungry. I've got a long day of driving ahead of me. I'm happy."

The proprietor looked her over. She wiped her hands on her jeans, patted Lily's cheeks, and pointed to the table in the front window. "Your friends are looking for you."

"Friends?"

"Go on. I'll bring you breakfast."

"Coffee?"

"Go." Maria turned her toward the front and gave her a little shove.

Lily found Ed, the town cop, with Larry and Donna Stone, her FBI agent neighbors. She'd seen them occasionally over the last couple of months, not sharing coffee and muffins with them since the end of June, when she began to live like a poor graduate student. When she reached their table, Ed and Larry stood. Ed pulled out the chair next to him.

"We were hoping you'd show up this morning," Donna said as the men resumed their seats. "We were just talking about how to find you if you didn't."

Donna's face looked pinker than usual, but it might have been sunburn. Still, Lily sensed a tension around the table. Ed looked worried, but smiled quickly when her glance moved to his face.

"Maria said you were looking for me."

Larry looked soberly at her. "We need to ask a, um, a personal question."

Lily couldn't imagine what he'd regard as personal. She'd been living the life of a nun, an academic buried in a convent devoted to research. "Sure, I guess," she said.

"Have you got a boyfriend?" It was Donna who put the question.

Lily was astonished. "Boyfriend?" She held up her left hand with its plain gold band. "I'm married." The faces around her looked if anything more worried. "What's going on?" Lily demanded in her classroom voice.

"Do you remember that Larry works with all these wonderful high-tech toys that he brings home to test drive?" Ed said.

"Like what?" This time Lily's voice was suspicious. What had this group been up to? She found that she'd pushed back a few inches from the table. She pulled forward and leaned in toward the cop and the two Feds. "Tell me what's going on." To her surprise, the three snapped to attention.

"The last two nights, I've been trying out a new pair of night-vision binoculars," Larry said. "I tested them out on the front porch, then decided to see how useful they were to see the outside through window glass. So I went upstairs at our house and checked out the Green. I saw dog walkers—did you know there's one guy who has three miniature Schnauzers?—and teenagers and a couple of people who were just loitering. But then I noticed one figure who had parked himself behind that big tree." He pointed to a vast old oak about thirty feet into the Green directly across the street. "At first I couldn't tell if the person was male or female."

"Since your husband never came to visit," his wife said, "we thought maybe you were separated or something, maybe you'd found another man." She looked directly at Lily.

"Good heavens, no," Lily said. "The only man I've had any serious conversation with besides Larry and Ed is Henry James, and he's been dead for a century. That's what I do, you know. Commune with dead authors."

"Weird way to make a living," Ed said. "But doesn't sound dangerous."

"It could be, if I found something significant," Lily said absently. Which she may just have done, she reminded herself, but only as of yesterday. That was a mere hint of something valuable. No one would have watched her the night before last, not for any reason that she could think of.

Then what Larry had said hit her. "Dangerous? What do you mean?" Her tablemates' expressions made her feel as though a doctor had handed her an ominous diagnosis. "What? What's going on?"

Larry said, "What I determined immediately was that the guy—turned out to be male—was watching your apartment windows. He was there again last night. When I told Donna, she insisted we tell you. Ed agreed. I didn't want to worry you, but Donna just said, 'woman living alone,' and that decided it." His face reddened and Donna took over.

Lily heard their words as if from the other end of a dark tunnel.

"What did the man look like?" Donna asked Larry.

"All I can offer right now is the classic eyewitness description: medium height, medium build. He wore dark clothes but no hat; his hair appeared dark." He shook his head. "Sorry."

No, Lily thought, no one would waste time watching her. These two FBI agents evidently didn't have enough to do. She didn't like being someone's practice object, professional or not. "Are you sure this person was watching my windows? He could have been watching the cafe."

"Why do that?" Ed put in. "If he wanted to talk to someone here, it's a public place. He could just walk in."

"Unless," Larry said, "he wanted to see someone without her seeing him."

"Exactly," said Lily.

"There's no one here at night except for you," Donna said. "Maria closes mid-afternoon."

That someone might be stalking her seemed more unreal than threatening. "I'd go out tonight to see who it is—" Lily started, but Ed interrupted.

"No you won't. You'll stay away."

His sharp tone made her realize that the others at her table were scared for her. The end of the tunnel rushed at her, making her dizzy. Bile burned her throat. She couldn't move.

Instead of three worried neighbors, she saw a class full of twelve-year-olds. Suddenly she was back in seventh grade, the teacher jeering at her in front of the other students, cornering her. Then, too, she'd felt dizzy and immobile. Why was this man after her day after day? What had she done? Or not done? The other kids leaned away from her, she remembered, as if she were tainted. Twenty-some years ago and still so vivid an event in her mind. Over the years she'd wondered why it continued to haunt her.

Now she knew. Then she didn't have the maturity needed to understand what was going on, to take the offensive herself. Easy for the teacher to threaten a young girl, to corner her. But she wasn't young now.

She wished Maria would bring the coffee because her throat was suddenly dry. She reached over to Donna's glass of water and lifted it for a sip.

Whatever was happening, it was her fight. "If someone's stalking me, I'll face him."

"No you won't," Ed barked.

"Don't give me orders," Lily snapped. Ed leaned away from her.

"Of course not," Donna said. "But let us help you do it. Take advantage of our experience."

"Is that what you would do in my situation?" Lily demanded.

"I'd never go in without back-up," the agent said.

"Actually, I may be able to get you a photo," Larry broke in. "We've got another new toy for me to test drive, a night-vision camera. I'll bring it home with me this evening."

"I won't be here," Lily told them. "I'm going to the Berkshires for a few days. A librarian from the Beinecke is coming with me."

"You've found something," Donna said.

"Maybe," Lily said, voice cautious. "I don't want to tempt fate." She thought a moment. "I want to give all of you my cell phone number so you can tell me what you find out." Ed pulled his phone out of his uniform shirt pocket and handed it to Lily, who added her information to his contacts. Ed forwarded it to the other two, and then put his own and the Stones' numbers in Lily's phone. "If you get a picture, text me," Lily said. "Next time," she added, looking at all three of her companions, "don't debate whether you should bother me or not. Tell me what I need to know."

Donna raised her eyebrows. "Yes, professor," she said.

Lily laughed. "Sorry." She looked at the oak tree standing guard across the street.

Maria spoke behind her. "Breakfast. One sticky bun," she leaned over to place the dish before Lily, "and two eggs scrambled. You need protein." She handed the others cinnamon rolls. "Coffee next."

"What is this urge people have to take care of me around here?" Lily said.

"Only around here?" Ed asked.

"Yes. Do I seem particularly needy or something?" Lily quickly pulled off a bit of roll and put in her mouth. It was wonderful, sugar melting with butter and cinnamon.

"New England towns," Ed said. "We tend to take care of our own."

"With my very own stalker."

"Go away and leave him to us," Larry said.

"No." Lily straightened her back and glared at the others. "Get me what information you can. Please. Then I'll decide what to do."

"We'll decide," Donna said. "We know better."

"Not about my life, you don't."

"Agreed," Donna said. "But about stalkers we do know more. I meant we all decide, all four of us. All right?"

"Absolutely," Lily attacked her eggs. She was suddenly quite hungry.

· · ·

She went upstairs to pack an overnight bag and check her email.

Sitting at the kitchen table, she opened her laptop and signed on. There was an email from Bethany.

Bethany who had written to her six weeks before, talking about that strange man at the pool. Bethany whom Lily had forgotten. Cara and Bethany had connected, as Lily had suggested. Lily knew she'd been absorbed in her research at the Beinecke, but that immersed? Had she blocked herself from the world outside the library? She opened the email and scanned it for bad news, then sat back to read it carefully.

Today, right now, she'd respond to Bethany. Enough of this hiding or whatever she'd been doing. Right at that moment, Lily disliked herself. Not guilt, dislike. Or as Nate would say, enough already.

> Dear Dr. Atwood,
>
> It's been a strange summer. At the same time that I'm enjoying the routine of work and home and seeing my boyfriend, I'm not enjoying it. I keep thinking about school and my dorm room. I'm going to have a single room, the first time in my life I have time completely to myself if I just close a door, except for maybe the bathroom at home, and not even then. I'm running out of things to talk about with Cary. He's pushing to get married, insisting I could transfer from Prairie Shores.
>
> How could he not get that I don't want to leave there? I've tried telling him but it's like he doesn't hear me or understand my words or something. I'm too young to get married. I've got things to do first, even though I don't know what those things are right now.
>
> Marrying him and moving back here permanently and being a farmer's wife, I don't know, but sometimes I can't breathe at the thought. It's like the times when my brother and sister and I would play fort at home on a rainy day and we'd get the blankets all draped around the couches and tables and sit inside and after awhile we'd have to put our heads outside because there didn't seem to be enough air. You know that feeling?

Absolutely, thought Lily. All the time.

> So I'm going back to school a week early. I got a resident assistant position at the new dorm, which is why I'm getting a single. That means room and board are paid for, which means my scholarship money will go farther. I know I'll be bugged night and day by the

kids on my hallway, but I'm looking forward to that. Their problems aren't my problems, so they're easier to solve. Does that make sense?

What are you doing? Cara told me about your grant and all, and what that nasty Hardy pulled on you. I'm really glad you connected me and Cara. We've been emailing and texting back and forth all summer. We're going to get together when I get back to Prairie Shores. I can't wait to meet Izzy.

Oh, and do you remember I told you about that hot stranger who bought a day ticket to the pool? He's been back a couple of times. After the first visit, he tried to start a conversation with me. But all the women around the pool were staring at us, so I put him off. Once he even asked if I wanted to get a cup of coffee after work. Coffee? It was like over 90 degrees here that day—that's what made me think he might be some crazy. Then the last time he was here, Cary was with me. Cary may not be the perfect boyfriend, but he's big, played football in high school. He just sort of stared down at the guy, loomed over him, you know? The guy was smart enough to leave. I haven't seen him since.

But you said to describe him, so I took notes. His face was kind of square, his hair a chestnut brown, all flyaway after swimming in the chlorinated pool and drying in the sun. He looked younger far away than he did close up. Close up I could see the beginning of lines between his eyebrows and around his mouth, like maybe he's a smoker. No laugh lines around his eyes. His eyes were a sort of non-color brown/green—hazel, maybe. He looked like the kind of guy who probably looks better in a suit, because it would give him wider shoulders, and because clothes would hang on him just right. Or maybe I'm imagining how clothes would hang on a woman but on a man? Anyway, he looked male-model-ish far away but not close up.

Once he came up to me wearing just a Speedo, you know, a really small swimsuit, and I could see his stomach was flat. There was quite a bulge in the Speedo. Maybe I shouldn't have written that, but you did say to describe what I saw. I definitely saw that. He looked at me sort of sleepy-eyed, as if he expected me to melt at the sight of him. But you know, he's too old for me. Or I'm too young or something, because there wasn't chemistry. But like I said, after the time Cary was here, the guy didn't show up again. To tell you the truth, he gave me the creeps.

Are you coming back here? Can I come see you, even though you're not going to be at Prairie Shores?
Bethany

Lily hit "reply."

Dear Bethany:
Your description of the pool stranger gave me the creeps, too. You're doing quite well picking up detail. Either you've always been perceptive or by writing about it you're becoming so. Either way, it's a saving grace. Nurture your attention to details.
Yes, I'll be back. I'm researching Edith Wharton and Henry James. Today I'm driving up to the mansion Wharton built in the Berkshires—that's western Massachusetts, two hours from where I am in Connecticut. Time is getting short. I find I have so much more left to do. Sometimes a research project works out like that.
Of course you can visit. In the meantime, keep the emails coming. I'm enjoying your writing.

Lily shut the computer. She didn't tell Bethany her real preoccupations, the guy behind the tree and the clue in Lenox. She slipped the laptop into her book bag, where it nestled against inches of research notes, grabbed her duffel bag and left by the back stairs. She got to the first landing, put the bags on the floor, and returned to the apartment door. She tried to turn the knob. Locked. Only after that did she gather her bags and leave the building and its comforting cafe sounds of talk and rattling dishes coming from the ground floor.

· · ·

Jonas' phone announced another anonymous text. This was getting annoying. He should just delete the damn things before looking at them. Or block the number.
In spite of himself, he looked. Another photograph, this one of a black-gritted track. He turned the phone to view the photo in landscape mode. Then widened the photo. It was a running track. It really resembled the track he'd run on in high school. He widened the photo again, bringing the phone close to his eyes. Was that a ghost on the edge of the track?
What the hell?
He couldn't delete the photo fast enough.

Chapter 24

Constance and a middle-sized dog that looked like a wheat-colored Airedale emerged from the front door of her orange brick house in New Haven. Constance came up to Lily's window. "How about we take my car? Then you don't have to explain dog hair to the rental car agency. This is Bob." Bob wagged his tail while looking at Constance. When he looked at Lily, the tail stopped. She could have sworn she heard a soft growl.

"Well, all right," Lily said, "but I was looking forward to driving. You know, most of Illinois doesn't tend toward hills."

"Pull into the garage." Constance pointed to where the brick driveway curved around the back of the house. "You can drive my car."

Lily drove the rental car into the garage, which was neat and clean, not even an oil stain on the cement floor. Constance and the dog followed her. Lily got out of the car, opened the trunk for her belongings, and all three of them went back down the drive. The librarian led the way to a small dark blue SUV parked across the narrow street. She opened the back door for the dog, who leapt onto the seat. Lily added her bags to the ones already stowed in the hatch and slid into the driver's seat. "Hey," she said, "this is a Subaru."

"So?"

"That's what we have."

"Useful in the winter, four-wheel drive and such. Now, I must introduce you to Bob. He needs to know that you come under his protection. Otherwise, he might decide he needs to defend me against you."

The dog looked harmless, with all that curly blonde hair, but when Lily turned in her seat, bringing her closer to Constance, she heard that growl again. "Is he growling at me?"

"Do not let Bob's appearance fool you. Wheaten terriers were bred originally to protect. Most that you meet are not trained properly. Bob is. Ready?"

Lily nodded, though she didn't know ready for what.

"Do what I say, nothing else," Constance instructed. She ordered Bob to sit. He'd been lying down on a dog blanket, but he rose into a sitting position. Then she put a palm on either side of his face so he could see only her. "Bob, this is a friend. Protect a friend. Understand?"

Bob looked up at her. One hand still on Bob's head, Constance took Lily's hand and brought it to the dog's nose. He sniffed. "Friend. Protect." The dog seemed to think about this. Constance repeated the command, adding, "Now show me." Bob looked at Lily's hand, which she held steady even though she was convinced he was about to bite. He sniffed, leaned into Constance's hand, then tentatively licked Lily.

"Now scratch his head with your free hand. Move slowly."

Lily touched Bob's head gingerly. Though it looked wiry, his fur was soft. She scratched his head. He shifted weight, now leaning against her hand and sighing.

"All right," Constance said. "Good boy. Remember: friend." She handed Lily the keys. Lily had moved on to scratching Bob's other ear. Reluctantly, she turned to face the steering wheel.

"Want me to navigate?" Constance asked.

Lily said, "No kidding. That I found my way from Guilford to the Beinecke is a miracle, GPS, Siri or not. I'm used to streets on a predictable grid, not this meandering stuff you specialize in around here."

"Indian paths," Constance said. "They came first, became roads." She told Lily how to get to the highway.

Lily drove, but her mind wasn't on it. After she'd almost missed two turnoffs and got honked at several times when she drifted into another lane, Constance directed her into the parking lot of a Dunkin' Donuts. "Let's stop for a bathroom break and coffee." Lily obligingly got out of the car. Constance held her hand out for the keys.

A few minutes later, they brought coffee and doughnuts back to the car. Constance clipped on Bob's leash and took him for his own bathroom break. When she returned, she slid behind the wheel, motioning Lily to the passenger seat.

Where Lily really wanted to be was in the backseat with Bob. "Can he have a piece of doughnut?"

"He could, but he prefers this." Constance pulled a plastic sandwich bag out of the console between the front seats. Bob immediately sat at attention, eyes on the bag. "Freeze-dried liver treats," Constance said. She broke off a tiny bit, handed it to Lily. "Give it to him while you tell him your name."

Lily held out the treat. "I'm Lily. Lily." Bob looked at Constance, who nodded. The treat disappeared in a wet lick. "Can we do that again?" Lily asked.

"Sure." Constance held out the bag.

Lily broke off another bit and held it. This time, the dog looked at her for permission. She nodded, the liver bit was gone, and Bob leaned over to lick her face. "What a great guy."

Constance started the car, saying, "Only after a lot of training." Her voice softened. "But yes, he is a great guy." She turned into the line of traffic heading back to the highway before adding, "You are the only person I have told him he should protect."

"I'm honored." After a pause, she added, "I might need it."

"You seemed, oh, distracted," Constance said, eyes on the road.

"You mean I almost crashed the car."

"Seemed like a clue." But Constance's tone was serious. "What happened?"

"The FBI thinks someone is stalking me," Lily blurted, then was ashamed. Technically that was the truth but it sounded so overblown. "Those neighbors I told you about that work for the FBI think they saw a guy watching my apartment last night and the night before." Lily shook her head. "Sounds like the plot of a bad gothic novel. The beginning of the horror, you know? The evil villain sneaks up on the innocent maiden under cover of darkness. The sort of crap Edith and Henry would have made fun of over after-dinner port at the Mount." Her words sounded to her like one of the flip literary discussions new grad students indulge in, that she'd indulged in a decade before.

They hadn't reached the highway. Without comment, Constance left the frontage road again, this time into a McDonald's lot. By the time she'd parked and turned the engine off, her silence grated on Lily. Then she turned in the driver's seat.

Constance's eyes flashed at Lily. "What the hell is going on?" She was furious. "Why did you not tell me immediately? Why are we out on public streets when someone might be after us?"

Her attack stung Lily out of her complacency. "I hadn't thought of that. Oh, God, I'm sorry. This is all so, I don't know, sudden. They just told me at breakfast. I thought that leaving town was a good idea."

"Who the hell told you that? The Feds?" Her friend spit out the words. Bob looked at his owner, alarmed. "Like they know anything."

Lily looked closer at Constance. She sat erect in the seat, mouth clamped, fingers white and bloodless against the black steering wheel. "This has happened to you," Lily said. She remembered Constance pulling her out onto the Yale lawn, how hard it had been for her to tell Lily about her ex-husband's insanity, his ultimate institutionalization. "Your husband. He stalked you. My lord, I'm so sorry, I completely forgot." The experience must have been terrifying, given Constance's reaction. Suddenly Bob jumped between the front seats. "Feds?"

"Feds, cops, all the same. None of them know what it is like. Here is what they and you do not understand: This is serious. This is dangerous. You can run but you will never be able to hide, never feel safe."

"I don't want to run," Lily said. Constance's attack had shaken her so that she began to cry, which in turn upset her more. She'd thought she was fine, taking charge of her life for the first time. Bob whimpered and crept into the seat with her. She buried her face in his fur. He let her cry for a moment before licking the tears off her face. That made her grip him tighter, which didn't seem to bother him. He just leaned into her.

Constance ignored her tears. "Going to the Berkshires is running," she said. "Look, these are your options. Face the danger. Or run. Your life, your choice."

Lily looked out her window, away from Constance and the dog, toward an overflowing dumpster. Yesterday the Berkshires was work, not escape. It was still work, though maybe if she found something it might—what? Her dreaming effectively dried her tears. She could hear her mother's jeering voice saying to her father, "She's off in fictionland again."

Lily looked at her friend and the dog, really looked. Concentrated. The dog's head was cocked, but Constance still gazed straight ahead, profile rigid. Think about the next step, not the last one, Lily instructed herself. If she went to Wharton's house with all this on her mind, would she be giving her research project the best chance? No, she told herself, you're still running away from what you need to face. This was all beyond her. What was a literary researcher doing worrying about being stalked?

"Maybe," Lily said, "Larry didn't really see what he thought he did."

"Maybe," Constance said, clipping syllables, "if it had been someone else. I dislike the cops, they were never there when I needed them, but they are realists. You said the person was using some sort of night goggles?"

Lily nodded. "What do you mean, 'if it had been someone else'?"

The green eyes turned to her. "I knew, after the first couple of times we talked, that you are just like I used to be. That the world could come rushing up like a storm heading in from the ocean, while I stood on the beach with my back to the water, admiring the view inland."

"My parents accuse me of being oblivious."

"At our age, it can be willful obliviousness. You never mention your husband unless asked specifically, he never seems to contact you, you have slotted him into some other part of your mind. Sometimes you talk about students. You tell lovely stories about your uncle. But mostly, the people most alive to you are Wharton and James. People dead for almost a century." She paused, leaned back in the driver's seat. "That was me. Buried in old books. In my nonprofessional life, I was a windsock for other people's emotions, low on emotion myself. Until I had the shit scared out of me and realized I had been fooling myself." Constance turned toward Lily, "Look, anybody who cannot bring himself to ring a doorbell is up to something. Someone who stands behind a tree in a park, watching, is creepy, probably dangerous."

Dangerous. There was that word again. Creepy—Bethany had used that word in her email.

"All right, that's it," Lily said. Left arm still around the dog, with her right hand she pulled her cell phone out of her jeans pocket. "We're going back to your house."

Constance's shoulders relaxed, and when she glanced at Lily, her eyebrows were raised in question.

"I've got to go back and figure out how to trap this guy."

"Not by yourself, damn you."

Bob growled.

"You want to help?" Lily asked.

"No," Constance said. She shifted the car into drive, and pulled back into the line of traffic headed for the interstate.

Lily dialed Donna's work number. While the FBI office phone rang, Lily checked the time on the Subaru's clock: just before 11:00. They'd be back around lunch time. Maybe she could get together with Donna unofficially, on her lunch hour. Was this unofficial? Did the FBI deal with stalkers? Should she call Ed? When Donna answered, Lily said, "Donna? Lily Atwood. What are you doing for lunch?"

"I thought you were going to Massachusetts."

"New Haven. New plan." She turned to Constance. "Your house okay?"

Constance didn't respond for a moment, evidently making up her mind. "Cops in my house?" She shivered, then looked as if she consciously squared her shoulders. "Yes. My house. Tell them to bring sandwiches."

Her decisiveness caught Lily by surprise. She heard Donna's voice say, "Lily? Are you there? Lily!"

"Donna, can you and Larry meet us?" She gave Constance's address. "Bring something to eat. We won't have time to stop. And Donna?"

"Any other orders, Dr. Atwood?"

"Just one. Ask Ed if he can join us."

There was a brief silence. Then Donna said, "I see. Yes. See you about 12:30." The phone went silent.

"What the hell have I gotten myself into," Constance said to Bob.

• • •

This time the text message on Jonas' phone came from the judge of the probate court. Didn't judges have clerks to do that sort of thing? Or maybe it was the clerk. Caller i.d. read "Probate Court Judge," though not which court or county or state. Weird. The message read, "Come see me."

Come see who?

Jonas deleted this message, too.

Chapter 25

Dark gray clouds had rolled over New Haven by the time they regained Constance's house. Her neighborhood of red brick townhouses, so old that the brick had smoothed and faded to the color of tomato bisque, seemed to blend with the trees. Lily noticed that the only reason Constance's house had a garage was because it was on the corner; the garage looked newer than her house. "Did you add the garage?" Lily asked as they went through the covered back porch into the house.

"Yes." They were in the kitchen, which had a slate floor, light wood cabinets and what looked like marble countertops. She gestured toward the table, which matched the cabinets. Instead of chairs there were cushioned church pews on either side. Constance settled herself on the pew facing the kitchen, evidently her usual place. Bob stretched out on the floor by her feet, while Lily sat across from her.

"This house was my bolt hole when I left New York. I refused to leave my car out on the street. I was afraid of what might turn up in it or on it or done to it." Constance's hands clasped in front of her on the table. The fingers tightened. She looked down and said, "I was afraid all of the time. Always. Until my husband's family incarcerated him at McLeans. Even then, until I got Bob here and trained him to watch over me." One hand reached down toward the dog, who automatically stretched so the hand landed on his head. The other hand remained clenched on the table.

Lily had reached over to place her hands on top of Constance's when the doorbell rang. Constance said, "Here we go again," and started to rise. Lily held onto her. "I didn't mean to drag you into anything. Are you sure you want to be involved in this?"

The librarian shook her head at the same time she said, "Yes," then laughed a short, mirthless laugh. "When I saw you at the Beinecke that first time, I felt a kinship. After we talked, I had a bad feeling about what was going on around you. I could have backed off then. Maybe I should have. But I did not. Could not. So here we are." She stood and led the way out of the kitchen.

They passed through a small dining room, dim because of tiny leaded windows, dark furniture and wainscoting. Next to it, a large square living room looked bright, with worn oriental rugs on a polished parquet floor, equally worn soft couches and wing chairs, and books lining every wall. Here the leaded windows were larger, the glass slightly wavy, giving Lily the sensation that she was underwater. The front door stood at the end of a narrow hallway paved with random shapes and colors of marble, pink and gray and pale blue and white. A tapestry covered one wall—no, when Lily looked closer, she realized that it was knitted of what seemed an infinite number of fine yarns in similar but more vivid hues of the marble floor. "Is that knitted?

"Yes," the owner said.

"It's a work of art."

"Thank you."

The bell rang again. Constance looked out through the peephole, then yanked Lily over. "Do you recognize these people?" Only when Lily nodded did she open the heavy wood door. She stood back. Donna and Larry came in, bearing brown grocery sacks that smelled of vinegar and fresh bread. "Good lord," said Constance, "did you go to Mario's?"

"Oh, yeah. Soon as Lily here said where you lived, we figured it was a great chance to get Italian deli for lunch," Larry said.

Lily introduced the FBI agents. Constance closed the door behind them and flipped the lock. Lily glanced at her, thinking it overdoing it to double-lock when you've got two agents in the house, and, judging from the bulge in the back of Larry's seersucker jacket, at least one of them armed. It must have been habit. Constance took another look at the grocery bags and went back toward the kitchen, saying, "Well, we might as well be comfortable."

"Why did the address say Italian food to you?" Lily asked Donna when they reached the kitchen.

"This has been an Italian neighborhood for over a hundred years," Constance answered for her. She was pulling down white ceramic plates from the cabinet near the sink. "My family invested in this neighborhood fifty years before that." When she turned to put the plates on the counter, a small diffident smile was on her elfin face. "My family buys property. We never sell."

Donna nodded, as if Constance had confirmed something she already knew. Had the agents checked out one Constance Cordrey, owner of this house, before coming here? Lily wondered. She saw Larry's expression. They had.

"But you own this house," Donna said. She was pulling containers out of a bag. She opened one, which contained olive salad. Another had what looked like a marinated artichoke salad, or maybe an antipasto. Lily's stomach growled.

"It was transferred to me when I took the job in New Haven." Constance opened a cutlery drawer. "After a century of tenants, the house was worn out. It took over a year to get it in shape."

"Your home is lovely," Donna said. She was looking around admiringly.

Constance stood back, crossing her arms. When Donna began taking huge Italian sub sandwiches out of the second bag, Constance seemed to come to a decision. She nodded. "Would you care for a brief tour?"

For the first time since Lily had met her, Donna looked excited. "Yes, please. I would love that." She gestured her husband over to the sandwiches. "Would you slice these?"

Constance put a cutting board on the marble counter and found a serrated knife, handed it to Larry, and the two women disappeared.

"What was that all about?" Lily asked.

"Donna loves old houses," Larry said. "Why do you think we live on the Green in Guilford when we could live in a new apartment walking distance from where we work?"

"Why?" Lily asked.

"It's where we can afford."

"Got it. Housing prices around here are like where I live, Chicago's North Shore. The only reason Jonas and I can afford to live there is because my parents bought our two-flat when the area was urban renewal."

Larry shrugged. "What's going on here, Lily? Why the sudden change of mind?"

"Shouldn't I wait to tell Donna?"

"She'll be getting the story from your friend." He looked around the kitchen again. "Your rich friend."

"House rich, anyway."

"No, rich." He was slicing the last of four subs. "We checked."

"Why?"

He shrugged. "Never hurts to be careful."

"Why?" she repeated.

"Because you've only known her for a few months."

"Same as I've known you."

"You can trust us."

"Can I?"

Larry put aside the knife. "You've chosen to?"

"Me, yes. I'm not so sure about Constance."

"Her husband was a piece of work."

"You found all this out in the last hour?"

"The restraining order was easy to find." Larry finished putting sandwich sections on plates, then took them over to the table. "I'm surprised she's willing to get involved with cops after her last experience."

"You may have to talk her into it," Lily said. "And for sure you're going to have to talk me into it." She went through the cabinets until she found some bowls for the salads. "Constance is worried about the stalker. I'm worried that she's worried." She looked up at Larry. "Does that make sense?"

"Yeah, you're numb. See it all the time." He reached over and poked her forearm. "Feel that? This is real. Numb is okay. Dumb isn't." Before he could say anything else, Bob was at his feet, growling. "Jeez, who's this?"

"Bob. Our guard dog. He's saying look but don't touch."

The two women returned to the kitchen at that moment. Donna said, "Words to live by."

Constance introduced Bob, but didn't go through the friend instruction, as she had with Lily.

The doorbell rang again. "That will be Ed," Donna said. Constance went to get the Guilford cop. "Everything all right?" Donna asked.

"Hard to say," her husband said. "How about with you?"

"Same." She shook her head. "That's one tense woman." She narrowed her eyes at Lily, who felt herself blushing. "Why is your friend tense while you're not?"

"Would you prefer it if I fell apart?" Lily said in her best professional tone.

"Well, how do you handle danger?"

"Truth? I have no idea. The last time I felt like I was in real danger, I was twelve, and I didn't understand what was going on. I was fired from my tenure-track job a few weeks before I came here, and I didn't see it coming." She didn't feel the need to explain that her husband had engineered her firing.

"Numb and dumb," Larry repeated.

"Stop that," his wife admonished.

Constance returned with Ed. Her face was pale. Lily saw her hands were once again clasped tightly. Ed was talking away about something, not paying attention to Constance's reaction. It was his uniform. He had on the full cop belt, the gun and nightstick and all. He reached up to flip off the radio on his shoulder.

Lily put her arm around Constance's shoulders, led her to the pew behind the table and sat next to her. She gestured the other three to sit down across from them. Donna started to say something, but Lily shook her head. "My turn to talk." Briefly, she told the others about Constance's ex-husband, how the cops weren't there when she needed them, how she associated cops with her husband.

"Behavioral conditioning," put in Larry.

"Quiet," Lily said. The others looked surprised. "I know it seems like Constance has been doing all the worrying for me up until now. So I want to do two things. One." She cleared a space in the middle of the table, pushing aside sandwiches and salads. She pulled Constance's gripped hands from the woman's lap and gently put them on the table. Then she grabbed Donna's hand, and Larry's. "These are good people. They've been watching over me when I didn't realize I needed it." She shook her head at the other three, warning them not to react to what she was about to say. "Protect Constance." Bob sat up. "These are Larry and Donna."

Ed added his hand to the other two. "And Ed."

"Friends. Protect Constance."

At that, Constance burst out laughing. Tears ran down her face. Then Lily realized her own face was wet.

"All right," she said. "Do we have that cleared up?"

"I think the dog might be a bit confused," Ed said, looking down at Bob.

"He'll figure it out," Lily's sense of being underwater was gone. The room seemed brighter, which was illogical—rain streamed down the tiny windows. "Now, we need to plan. Because I'm not going to wait to be stalked."

...

Five text messages later, Jonas had just about had enough. Each message said, "Come see me." He didn't have to go anywhere, except work, and really, he could do that from anywhere he had a phone. When he was actually at his desk, the executive vice president of development hovered around, hinting that he should be out shaking the trees for cash.

But curiosity was getting the best of him.

His return message to the judge: "Why?"

Chapter 26

"I'm going to do the stalking."

"But," Ed started to interrupt. Lily stopped him.

"Here's my question: What's the best way?"

Donna held up her hand. "You're not trained for this. Three of us at this table are."

Three sets of cop eyes narrowed at Lily. Constance leaned out of the pew, patting Bob's head. By distancing herself from the discussion, Lily thought her friend was letting her know that she, Lily, was on the right track. "Would you agree that I'm the one who is in danger?"

"Maybe," Ed conceded. "Maybe this is all nothing."

"Damn it, Ed, you know better than that." Donna sat forward to glare at Ed. "What are you trying to do?"

"Inject a note of calm."

"I'd say she's too calm already." Larry pointed at Lily.

"Enough." Lily sat back, arms crossed. "My question: What's the best way?" Before the others could start arguing again, she added, "I see myself walking through the park, coming up behind this man."

"He might be carrying," Larry said. "Surprising him could make him shoot."

Lily used her imagination, the same imagination that had cushioned her from the world. "We know about this guy because of the night-vision glasses you were using."

Larry whacked his palm on his head above his ear, as if trying to knock water out. "Did you hear me? I said he might be armed."

"Where were you when you used the glasses?" Lily persisted.

"Why the hell aren't you scared? Don't you get it? Someone might be trying to hurt you."

"Where were you?"

"Just answer Lily," Donna said.

"In our spare bedroom. It's upstairs, looks over the Green from the side street."

"How far away do you think you were from the stalker?"

"Maybe a hundred feet?" Larry looked at his wife, who said, "That's sounds right."

"What could you see of the man? Did he look like he was carrying a weapon?" To herself, Lily sounded like a character in a Raymond Chandler novel. Stop that, she told herself. No more fictionland, not now.

Larry was thinking about her question. "How could I tell?"

Constance stopped scratching Bob's ears, turned to glare at Larry, then cast a significant glance at Lily.

"Forgive him, for he has committed the sin of being human," Lily said.

"Then what do we need them for?" demanded Constance.

"Protect?" Donna suggested gently.

"How?" Constance said.

"This is what I think." Lily continued her imagined scenario. "Tonight we go to your house. You've asked us to dinner. Bob, too."

"Yes?" said Donna.

"We sit around on the front porch for awhile, talking. Pretty soon I need to go in to use the bathroom."

"Which is upstairs, next to the spare bedroom," Donna added. "You happen to notice the night vision glasses, and Larry shows you how to use them. The two of you check out the Green."

Lily smiled at her. Donna had imagination, too. This was someone with whom she might actually be able to connect. "If our stalker is there," Lily said, "I take Bob for a walk." She put her arm around Constance's narrow shoulders. "Would that be all right?"

The shoulders tightened. "Let me think about it."

"Then what?" Ed said. "In your fairy tale?"

"Scenario," Lily corrected. "Bob takes me to the stalker, I see if he looks familiar. In the meantime, the three of you have placed yourself behind your own trees."

"I have a suggestion." Donna was staring out the window at the rain. She turned back to the table and looked at the group. "I think I should sneak around to Lily's apartment, go inside and turn the lights on. Be the woman the stalker is looking for."

"Distract him." Larry nodded. "Good. You'll dress for the occasion."

"Of course. Just in case."

"Will the boss know about this?" The FBI agents had dropped into husband-wife talk, seeming to forget the others.

Donna said, "Yes. We'll tell him what we're up to. Just in case."

"What if he wants to help?" Larry asked.

"When has that ever happened? We're just covering ourselves."

"Bureaucratically?" Lily asked. She understood the concept though had never applied it.

"Exactly," Donna said. "What do you want for dinner?"

"How about leftover Italian?" Lily looked at the mass of food spread over the table and counter.

• • •

Constance decided to join them that evening, partly, she told Lily, because she was worried about her, and partly because she didn't want to miss the action. That second reason was hard for her to admit.

After lunch, when the cops had returned to their day jobs, Lily and Constance lingered over iced tea. When Constance offered tea, Lily had expected her to brew it before icing it. Instead, she made instant Nestea. This was Lily's favorite summertime drink. When she confided that to Constance, the two giggled. "They'll throw us out of academe if they find out," Constance joked.

"I'm already halfway out the door," Lily said.

She'd changed the subject back to the evening. Neither woman appreciated surprises, so they made plans of their own. They practiced in the park two blocks away, Bob leading the way on his bright red leash. It only took an hour or so. But as Constance had said, Bob was very bright.

• • •

That night the five of them ate Italian on the FBI agents' front porch. Donna offered iced tea—brewed, to the amusement of Lily and Constance. "Way above our station," Lily told their hostess when she asked what was funny. "We're strictly instant tea."

"Do they allow that at Yale? I'm surprised," Donna laughed.

The five of them were on alert, feeling as though they were playing the part of a summer porch party for an unseen audience. They told jokes intended to cause loud laughter, told embarrassing stories about themselves. If anyone had been listening, he would have learned a lot about Larry's tendency towards nerdism, Donna's habit of falling asleep in the sun, Constance's mother's horrifying cooking ("Thank goodness we had a cook the other six days a week"), Lily's students' malapropisms (one wrote about the "whine cellar" in an essay; she and Nate joked about installing such a place where you could whine without annoying anyone else). Ed told stories about some of the too-rich Guilford women who called on him to carry their packages and pick up their children from school. "The concept of 'cop' seems beyond them. Don't they ever watch television?" he said.

After dark, Lily went upstairs, followed by Larry. He used the night-vision glasses, but didn't see anyone.

No stalker.

The next night, dinner was take-out fried chicken.

No stalker.

"I'll give it one more night," Lily said.

"If he's no-show again," Constance put in, "you're moving in with me. I won't have you in danger."

"But I'd just be bringing the danger to your house."

"Which features an alarm system and a trained guard dog."

"Good point," Ed said. "I for one would feel better if you were there."

The third night, Lily and Donna made a huge Caesar salad. And a giant pitcher of iced Nestea. Constance had brought Donna the biggest jar she could find at the grocery. The weather had stopped cooperating, becoming damp and misty, so they'd moved inside. By this time, the group was comfortable enough with one another not to have to provide constant entertainment. When Ed turned on the television to check the evening news, everybody joined him. He did the same thing for the eleven o'clock news, at which point Larry and Lily went upstairs to see how the binoculars worked on misty nights.

Behind the second tree from her street, there was a man dressed in dark clothes. Was it a man, or was she assuming? She watched him step around the tree to avoid the people walking dogs. His movements were careful. After a while he moved to another tree. He unzipped his pants. Lily watched for a few seconds, then handed the glasses to Larry. "Is he doing what I think he's doing?"

Larry peered at the man. "Yep. Taking a leak. Ed could arrest him for that, if you want."

"Not right now," she said. He handed her the glasses, taking up an odd-looking camera in its place. He snapped several pictures while she watched the man zip his pants and resume his spot behind the second tree. "I'll go tell Donna."

Larry nodded, his attention on the man.

Donna put on a long black wig, black shorts and a loose yellow top over a bulletproof vest. From across the street, she'd look like Lily, or close enough. Lily had parked her rental a couple of blocks away. Now Donna walked to it through the back alley, drove it brazenly down the street in front of the stalker, and parked it in Lily's spot. In a few minutes the lights went on in Lily's apartment. Though she stayed well back, Donna-as-Lily could be glimpsed through the kitchen windows. While Donna was providing this distraction, Ed had moved onto the Green, a few trees away from the stalker.

With the others in their places, Constance clipped on Bob's leash and handed it to Lily. "Be careful," she said. To Bob, she added, "Protect. Protect Lily. Follow her commands."

Lily took Bob for his evening constitutional. They cut through two alleys before Bob walked Lily back toward the Green. There, they strolled, checking out all of the trees. They waited for the other dogs and owners to leave the Green. Lily spotted the man with three miniature Schnauzers. One seemed to be in the lead. They turned out of the park across from Donna's house, and disappeared down another side street. Lily stood quietly. Bob sat and listened. Finally she tapped his head. He stood, looking at her expectantly. She nodded.

Bob led the way to the man behind the tree. The man's attention was apparently riveted on the performance in the upstairs apartment. Donna danced around the kitchen, never coming close enough to the windows for the watcher behind the tree to see her clearly.

Lily and Bob came up behind him. Bob lifted his leg. He urinated on the man's shoe.

"What the fuck are you doing?" The man spun toward the dog, who had already stepped away. Bob stood between the man and Lily.

"Jonas, what are you doing here?"

"Lily, who is this damn dog? Goddamn it, you surprised me. Does he always take a leak on people?"

Bob growled.

Then Jonas turned back to look at the still-dancing Donna, then at Lily. "What did you do, set me up?"

"Yep, we set you up, pal." Ed emerged from dark, laughing. He grabbed Jonas' hands and forced him up against the tree. He patted him down, doing, as far as Lily could tell, a more than thorough job. "No weapon," Ed told Lily. "Just this." He handed her a cell phone.

It was a new phone, not the one Jonas owned when she'd left two months before.

When she turned it on, the screen picture chilled her.

It was Bethany. At her lifeguard post.

"Can you arrest him?" Lily asked Ed.

"Sure. For urinating in public."

"That's the dog," Jonas said sharply.

"Yep. Sure is," Ed agreed.

Chapter 27

Lily dashed across the street and upstairs to her apartment. When she banged in, Donna was already waiting for her, crouched behind the door. Lily bounced the door off of the agent's shoulder, and yelled, "Donna, where are you?" before slamming it. Donna grabbed her, put her hand over Lily's mouth, hissed, "What's going on?"

Lily pointed at Donna's hand and shrugged. Donna let go, saying, "Keep it down."

"Why? This is the only apartment in the building. The cafe's closed. We got the stalker. Ed arrested him."

"Tell me all," Donna said.

"Wait until I send an email. My computer is in the kitchen."

"I almost tripped its cord and sent it flying." Donna grinned. "While I was dancing. Did my performance succeed?"

"Who knew my husband could mistake a tall blonde for me." Lily left Donna in the living room with her mouth open and disappeared into the kitchen.

The laptop was unplugged, centered on the table. She plugged it in, hopping from one foot to another while it powered up. Then she ran off an email. "Bethany—tell me where you are RIGHT THIS MINUTE. Call me. Collect if necessary. Dr. Atwood. THIS IS URGENT." She added her cell phone number and hit send. The Mac made its rocket-blast-off noise announcing the message was sent. Lily left the mail program on, just in case Bethany replied that way out of habit.

In the meantime, she called 411 and asked for the phone number of any family with Bethany's last name, Dwight, in her little town. There were three. One of the men's names listed sounded familiar—had Bethany mentioned her father's name? She tried that one first. No answer.

It was almost eleven p.m. in Illinois, the time when Midwesterners understand that a ringing phone means something awful has happened. Lily hoped that something awful hadn't. That picture on Jonas' phone of her student. She tried the second number, asked the boy who answered if Bethany was home. "Well, yeah, of course, her weekday curfew is like ten o'clock."

"Please put her on the phone. Now."

"Uh, sure. Who is this?"

"Dr. Atwood."

The phone thumped down. She could hear shoes pounding against wooden steps, and the boy's voice yelling, "Hey, Beth, it's for you."

"Jeb, hush! You'll wake Daddy."

Lily heard light footsteps, then Bethany's voice. "Hello? Who is this?"

"Bethany, this is Dr. Atwood. Something has happened and I just needed to make sure you were all right."

"I'm fine. Wow, are you calling from Connecticut? Just to ask if I'm okay?"

Lily sat down suddenly on a hard kitchen chair. "Bethany, do you remember that stranger who appeared at your pool? The one you described to me?"

"Well, sure, Dr. Atwood. What about him? Are you sure you're okay?"

"Did he have a cleft chin?"

"Yes, didn't I say so?"

"Any hair on his chest?"

"Dr. A!"

"Please answer me."

"Not much, no."

"Dark mole on the outside of his lip, sort of like Cindy Crawford?"

"Now that you mention it." Bethany's words were drawn out.

"Did he ever come back to the pool? Did you ever see him anywhere in your town?"

"He came back once more, but my boyfriend was there that time, too. Cary thought he was weird and took a picture with his phone. I thought I saw him coming out of the coffee shop one day when I was driving to the pool, but I can't be sure. You know, I just saw him or whoever out of the corner of my eye."

"When was this?" Lily's head began to ache, a migraine flowering at the base of her skull. She dropped her head to her chest, relaxing her neck and jaw muscles the way the doctor had instructed. It didn't help. Donna was waving at her to get her attention. Lily ignored her.

"Let me think. Maybe a week ago? No, it was last Friday. Less than a week ago. Dr. Atwood, what's going on?"

"I'll explain all when I see you. And Bethany—you were right. That guy was doing something creepy. Now go back to bed. Stay safe." Lily hit the off button before Bethany could ask for the answers she deserved.

"What the hell has happened?" Donna demanded.

Lily held up her hand for Donna to wait. The agent followed her into the living room, watched while Lily found her migraine pills in her bag, and followed her back again to the kitchen. Donna grabbed a glass, filled it with water and thrust it at Lily. Lily swallowed the pill, then said to Donna, "I need to talk something out. It's going to sound crazy. I need the response of an objective, perceptive woman."

"Where's the stalker? Did you say he's your husband?"

"Yes. He's at the police station with Ed. I'm guessing Constance stayed at your house."

Donna tried to lead them into the living room, but Lily said, "No. I must have stashed something sweet to eat around here somewhere. Sugar helps my migraines." She started to look in the refrigerator, but Donna gestured her toward the table.

"You talk, I'll search. What am I looking for?"

"Anything but ice cream. Cold stuff makes it worse." Lily sat down at the table. The headache had reached the point where bright light and noise were beginning to hurt; she shut the laptop. If she hadn't taken the medicine in time, she was in for it. The last time she'd had a migraine was in May. June? Not since coming to Connecticut. Or perhaps, given tonight's events, it would be more accurate to say since leaving Prairie Shores, Lakeland and Jonas.

Donna gave up on the refrigerator and was checking out the cabinets. Lily said, "Remember, I'm short. Anything would be within my reach."

"Unless Maria left you a surprise."

"She's never done that."

"Did you check the freezer?"

Lily started to shake her head but the pain flared from the migraine that held the back of her neck in a vice-like hold.

"The stalker was your husband," Donna said. She'd found a box of Pepperidge Farm cookies over the sink, and brought them to the table. "Tea? That used to help my sister when she got headaches."

"Please. Hot." White pain migrated from her neck to her scalp. Her hair hurt. Her front teeth were on fire. Slowly, inevitably, the pain settled behind her left eye.

Donna found a mug, filled it with water, put it in the microwave and continued searching cabinets. She found tea bags. "But haven't you been talking to him all along? What am I missing here?"

Lily ate a cookie in two bites. Cara's video of Jonas and her former boss, working together—screwing each other to screw her. She thought about the last time she'd seen Jonas, the night before she left for the airport. She thought about his list of "suggestions," his "husbandly" demands. She thought about everything she had refused to think about.

Migraines brought about such a sense of unreality for her. She ate another cookie.

"Hey," Donna said. "Talk. There's a reward in it."

"Why, was Jonas on the most wanted list?" She was pleased with herself for making a joke. Donna didn't react. Migraines tended to hit when the stress was off. Interesting, she thought. Did her body think it was time to relax? Because Jonas was temporarily under someone else's control?

Donna was looking at her. "Looks like Maria's been here. I found a cinnamon roll in your freezer."

"Well, hell, thaw it out fast." Lily ate another cookie. "When I have a migraine, everything seems bigger and louder and brighter. Like I'm surrounded by magnifying glass." Donna put a mug of tea in front of her. "I need to tell you a story. Nonfiction. Actually, I really need to tell myself the story, see if it makes sense." She sipped tea, regretted it when it burned her tongue, got up and added cold water from the tap. "That's what I'm good at, analyzing narrative." Not marriage, that was for sure, a thought she didn't voice.

Donna put Maria's roll into the microwave to thaw. Now she joined Lily at the table with her own cup, but immediately got up again when there was a knock at the door. A voice called, "It's me. Constance. Donna, are you here?"

Lily sat back and closed her eyes for a moment. She could hear the two women's voices, but didn't bother to listen for words. When a cold wet nose found her hand, she braided her fingers into Bob's fur. "Thank you, my friend," she whispered. The dog's tail banged against her shin. Then she felt cool hands on her forehead.

"Headache?" Constance asked.

"It may be receding. Maybe I took the medicine in time."

"Migraine?"

Lily heard a chair scrape. She opened her eyes carefully. The light seemed bright but almost tolerable, so she sat up. Donna was putting the cinnamon roll on a plate. "Knife in the drawer next to the refrigerator," Lily said. "Iced tea in the pitcher for Constance."

Voice pitched low in deference to Lily's headache, Constance told them that when she couldn't stand the suspense any longer, she'd crept out the back door, into the alley and onto the Green. There she'd caught the evening's denouement, her dog following silent commands to pee on a stranger. When Lily had run off, Constance had caught up with Larry and Ed on their way to Ed's patrol car with the stalker. They'd handed over Bob. "Who looked too pleased with himself," she said. "Now, what's going on? Who was that guy?"

"Lily's husband."

Constance gasped. Lily squinted at her. "History repeating itself?"

"Is your husband crazy, too?"

"Lily was going to tell a story." Donna divided the cinnamon roll into three, pushing the plate into the middle of the table. No one reached for a piece.

Constance regarded Lily. "Did you have any idea he was the stalker?"

"None. I know he tried twice to destroy me professionally. He succeeded getting me fired by fucking my department chair. He also tried to ruin my grant applications by taking out key sections. Of course I reviewed each application before sending it in so I reprinted the missing sections. He's one success for two tries at causing me to fail.

"But this stalking thing really scares me. So I need to talk." She looked at the FBI agent, who'd stepped away from the window to take off her yellow top and the bulletproof vest underneath. She returned to the table dressed in her own tee shirt and jeans. Then Lily looked at Constance. The vertical line between Constance's brows had deepened and her curly hair stood out, almost electric. "Do you know, I've never had women friends. How odd." Lily sat forward, broke off a piece of sweet roll and dunked it in her tea.

"Let me get this straight," Constance said, her voice hard. "Your husband tried to kill your career but that's not what scares you."

"That was disgusting. That was something that I'll never forgive. That's grounds for divorce," Lily said. "But Jonas never frightened me. He's one of those people who feels entitled, who wants the best clothes and the fanciest car for himself. I've never understood how I fit into that entitlement. But it all struck me as either childish or anachronistic, you know, man wanting his wife to wait on him. Never crazy. Not until now."

Silence. Finally, Constance said, "You kept all of this to yourself. While working every hour of every day."

"I have the oddest feeling right now," Lily said. She ate more cinnamon roll. "As if the light is brighter."

"Migraine," Donna said.

"Could be, though it feels different. More a light-at-the-end-of-the-tunnel type of feeling."

"As if something makes sense that didn't before?" Constance asked.

"As if something's important that I never noticed before."

"Now you're making me nervous," Donna said. "Come on."

"The last time I talked to my husband was the night after I got my grants in June."

Sipping tea and eating sweet roll and cookies, she told her friends how she'd opened a bank account in her own name for the grant funds.

"My uncle always said Jonas wanted to marry me more than I wanted to marry him."

"Was he right?" Donna wanted to know.

"I never thought about it until this summer. Never. Considered how I felt, that is. Lately, when it comes to Jonas, I have discovered the relief of out of sight, out of mind."

"But this doesn't explain why he'd stalk you."

"Oh, it's worse than stalking me," Lily said. Then the bright light shattered. She burst into tears. "I've been so stupid. Blind, willfully blind and blind-sided."

She felt Bob lean against her legs while his owner said, "Come on, you are almost there." Donna handed her a paper towel to dry her eyes.

Lily told them about Bethany. She let them read Bethany's emails about the creepy stranger. She showed them the picture on Jonas' new phone.

"He's stalking you and people he thinks you care about," Donna said.

"Oh my God," Lily cried, and groped for her cell phone.

Constance glared at Donna. "Subtlety not your forte?"

The agent made a shooing motion with her hand. "No time right now."

They listened while Lily listened. The phone rang and rang. She gave up and dialed another number. That, too, rang and rang. Finally, she tried the first number again. Nate answered. "It's after midnight."

Lily's laugh was tinged with hysteria. "Are you all right?"

"What the hell is going on, Lily?"

"Suffice it to say you were right about Jonas."

"Meaning what?"

"Definitely the wrong guy."

"You getting rid of him?"

"Can you change the locks on our apartment, first thing in the morning?"

His laugh was so loud that Lily had to hold the phone away from her ear. "I would be delighted. In fact, I'll do it now."

"And check on Cara. Now. Please."

"Will do, though she was going upstairs to her place above my studio when last I saw her. I set the alarm myself. When are you coming home?"

"Soon."

"'Night, Lil."

She hit the off button.

"Is that it?" Donna said. "End of story?"

It wasn't, but Lily wasn't ready to continue. "Why?"

"Because what I do is look for holes in stories. It's my job description. I've got questions. First, why were you let go from that college?"

"They didn't think I played well with others." Lily took another cookie from the box, a chocolate one. This was getting serious. "I told you. Jonas had an affair with the department chair."

"Cut the crap. She knew you were applying for the big grant. She had to sign something, I'll bet."

Lily nodded.

"There had to be some reason why she was in such a hurry to get rid of you. Sex, adultery, all that stuff is common on college campuses. Don't you teach something that most people don't? Research or something?"

"Methods of literary research. It's a required course for English majors and grad students. To anticipate your next question, they didn't have anyone else to teach it, not even the person they hired to take my place."

"When did they start looking for this person?"

"Before Christmas. Wait, before Thanksgiving."

"Where was your husband? Then?"

"He'd just taken the job as v.p. for development at Lakeland University the previous July." Lily leaned forward to look in Donna's face. "What are you thinking? That I was let go because of something Jonas promised Jane?" But the questions her former department chair had asked at the beginning of the fall term began to float back to her. Questions from the head of development, Jonas' old boss. How the president of the college began to shun her. How all these things took place after Jonas left. How Jonas had seemed to leave in such a hurry, telling her he had a new job and within a couple of weeks moving into his new office. "Or something else that Jonas did at Prairie Shores?" She found she was telling Donna and Constance everything she could remember.

"You've got some research to do, and I don't mean about Wharton out in the Berkshires," Donna said. "You've got to find out about your husband." She rubbed her eyes. "Do you have any idea how often in my work I run into women who married a man they never got to know? Too many of them were in the hospital or the morgue when I first saw them. For the FBI to get involved in a domestic abuse case, it has to cross state lines and include, oh, kidnapping or financial fraud."

Now Lily felt petrified, as if she could never move again. She had the sense that she was next to an abyss, that she was about to fall in.

A hand caught her shoulder. "I have months of vacation due me," Constance said. "So, where are we going first?"

"Kansas." Lily hadn't known she was going to say it, but knew she was right when she heard her own words. "After I talk to Jonas. Now."

Donna took the phone this time, dialed her husband and went into the living room.

Chapter 28

Jonas had spent years courting her and married to her. What was he capable of? What had he already done? Well, it might take her a while to unravel his web. She'd take her time. Pain jabbed behind her eye. No, she wouldn't. She gave herself a deadline: September. Pain faded. Jonas was always jeering at her to "figure it out, research it, isn't that what you're good at? Doctor Literary Research?"

One of the students in her advanced literary research course had been a journalism major who'd remarked that the course was like taking Ultra-Advanced Reporting. He'd called it "Search and Destroy 501."

Yep.

She always taught her students to reason out their first step carefully, to consider the problem at hand rather than rush in. What didn't she know about Jonas? She knew almost nothing about his background, where he grew up. He'd never taken her to his home town because his family was dead. That she and Jonas married in Lakeland never struck her as strange. After all, traditionally the wedding is in the bride's hometown, paid for by the bride's family. In graduate school Jonas never had any more money than she did, though that had changed in the last few years. Now Jonas spent his money and hers. All he'd ever wanted, he said, when he was campaigning for marriage, was her. That had never made sense to her, which she'd put down to her lack of experience. Not so her uncle. There was something Nate read in Jonas that he couldn't or wouldn't explain to Lily.

She remembered how, after Jonas had asked her out twice in grad school and she'd refused, he'd said, "Just give me a chance. You'll see." Lily ate another cookie. She looked at her friends. That's what I'll do, just what Jonas always asked for: I'll give him a chance. But not the way he'd intended. For the first time, it was her own intentions that mattered. Because for the first time, Lily was discovering how she actually felt about Jonas.

The migraine must really be fading. She was at that point of absolute clarity that visited her after a headache. Reality sharpened, her perceptions came with instant explanations that more often than not turned out to be true. The clarity also tended to dissolve the veneer of good manners. She said to Constance, "How rich are you?"

"I beg your pardon?" Constance looked as if she'd been struck. Her green eyes searched Lily's face. "No one has ever gotten to know me well enough to ask that question. Except the people who already knew the answer." She smiled. "Why? What do we need money for?"

"Airline tickets. We're flying to Kansas City tonight. Bob needs his own seat."

"Be cheaper to fly to Paris," Constance said. "Tickets as such will probably be unnecessary, though. Then what?"

Lily was about to ask her what the hell she meant by tickets being unnecessary when Donna came into the kitchen and returned the phone to Lily. Lily stood up. Her head felt light, and she grabbed the table. "So, who's driving to the Guilford police department? Where is the Guilford police department?"

"Your car's parked in back," Donna said. "I'll drive. The station's out by the highway."

• • •

Donna drove Lily to what looked like a doctor's office in a strip mall. "My headache's under control," Lily said. Then she noticed the sign for the Guilford Police Department. She hadn't expected the police station in such a quaint town to look like something that could be a doughnut shop tomorrow with a mere sign change. "Good grief, this is it?" A basketball court was visible from the road. Even though it was after midnight, a game was in progress. "Who plays basketball in the middle of the night?"

"Everyone. No place safer than the police station. I'll bet those guys aren't even cops." Donna drove into the front parking lot.

Lily could swear she smelled doughnuts baking but maybe that was the tag end of the migraine. "Do you smell doughnuts?"

"Not funny." Than Donna sniffed the air. "Hey, I do." She glanced down at Lily. "Learning from Bob, are you? You know, a dog's sense of smell is better than its sight?"

"Migraine sharpens the senses, including smell." She followed Donna into the police station. Polished white floors, four matched chairs pushed up along one wall, next to a cheap silk plant. Fluorescent light bounced off the floor and the window running along the entire right side. Behind the window sat a policeman pecking away at a computer keyboard.

He looked up just in time to see Donna flash her credentials. "Here to see Jonas Atwood." The cop stood up and pointed to a door. When Donna and Lily got to it, the door buzzed and swung open.

Ed appeared, looking tired but otherwise as spick and span as usual. "Your husband's quite a guy," he said, leading Lily and Donna down a narrow hall.

"Insists it wasn't him we saw urinating against that tree. That therefore we have no reason to detain him. He seems to absolutely believe what he's saying."

Though the front lobby had been air-conditioned to goose-bump temperature, here it was warm and airless. Lily pushed back her shoulders and breathed deeply, then exhaled equally deeply. Ed must have noticed, because he put an arm across her shoulders. "You okay?"

"Yep. Better than okay." They arrived at another unmarked door in the pale yellow wall. Ed reached to open it. She put her hand on his arm. "I'd like to talk to Jonas alone, if I may."

"Is that a good idea?" Donna appeared on Lily's other side. The two of them are protecting me, Lily thought. After another deep breath, she said, "It's the only idea. You both can listen in. But I need to do this without help."

Donna looked at Lily, then at Ed. After a moment, they nodded to each other. Ed said, "Door's open. We'll wait in the other room."

Lily hugged him, then pulled Donna into the hug. "I need you both. But—"

"Some things a woman has to do by herself. I actually do understand," Donna said, and pushed Ed down the hall. Over her shoulder she added, "We'll be right down here, first door on the left."

"Eating fresh doughnuts. Guy in back's been baking," Ed put in. The two disappeared down the hall.

Chapter 29

Lily ran her hands through her hair and thought about combing it and applying some lipstick. Then she realized that's how Jonas had trained her, to meet him looking her best. She shook off that need. Her headache was gone and she was in the clarity zone. She trusted herself.

She opened the door and entered a windowless room with a rectangular table that took up most of the floor space. There was a large mirror on one wall. Jonas sat with the back of his chair propped against the wall, feet on the table, acting as if he owned the place. The air was stifling. Lily left the door open.

"Close the door, Lily." Jonas didn't move from his position, though he crossed his arms. Unlike Ed, he looked messy. His hair needed combing, and his dark pants and tee shirt were wrinkled. This told Lily more about his state of mind than his greeting had.

She ignored his request.

"The door, Lily. We have a lot to talk about. Including what the hell you think you're doing, disappearing like that, then having me locked up."

She moved around the table to the wall next to the one against which his chair was propped. She looked down at him. Slowly she made herself comfortable, leaning against the wall.

Forced to look up at her, Jonas frowned. "Close the damn door!"

She thought about the video of him working Jane Hardy. His list of demands. She thought about seeing him pee in the dark. In seven years, more than five of them living with him in small spaces, she'd never seen him do that. Heard him, sure, but not seen. Then she thought of Bob peeing on Jonas' shoes. That's when she began to giggle. The giggle turned into a laugh.

She was laughing and looking him over when he crashed the front of his chair down. Springing up, he aimed a slap at her. In her heightened state of perception, her body had known he was going to do that. She stepped toward him, throwing him off balance. He slammed his palms down on the table to catch himself.

"Sit down, Jonas." Though soft, her words seemed to ring off the walls.

Jonas tried to stare her down. She waited. All this childish stuff—why hadn't she noticed before?

Jonas pointed to the chair across from him. "You first."

She waited.

Finally, he pulled his own chair up to the table and sat down in a manner meant to convey dignity.

A dignified eight-year-old, Lily thought.

"Lily, your behavior is completely inappropriate," Jonas said. "You know better."

"Jonas." Her voice remained soft. His head turned toward her—unwillingly, it seemed. "From here on out my behavior will always be inappropriate." He opened his mouth but before he could say anything, she repeated, "Always." She smiled with her mouth. "You can rely on that."

Trying to take control of their meeting, Jonas said, "Why didn't you call me from Connecticut? Were you blocking my calls?"

Lily dug his new cell phone out of her pocket and opened it. The picture of Bethany on her lifeguard post flashed on. Lily placed the opened phone on the table, out of Jonas' reach. "She's a beautiful young woman. What you don't know is that she's lovely inside as well. But then that isn't something that you usually know."

In the voice she knew so well, his snake-charmer voice, Jonas said, "What makes you think I don't know her very well?"

It was like she was looking at a cheap tabloid picture of someone whom she vaguely recalled. "Then I assume you know her boyfriend, too. Nice boy. Played football. You were never big enough for football, were you?"

Jonas flushed. Next to Lily, he'd always seemed tall. He dressed to make himself look taller.

She should have been shaking at this encounter. In the past, when Jonas tried to take charge she'd let him. It was easier that way. Now she was simply interested, analyzing the proceedings as part of a research project. She knew their history together but realized that was insufficient. She needed prior information.

"I missed you, Lily." His face assumed a kindly expression.

"Here are the rules, Jonas."

His expression broke apart. He sneered, "Rules? You're making rules?"

"When you return to Lakeland, you'll have to find another place to live."

"No way." But now he blustered. He'd always refused to consider buying their apartment from Lily's parents, preferring to spend money on other things.

"By the time you get back, your clothes will be waiting for you at your office."

"You wouldn't."

"When I return, we'll see what we can work out."

At that, he smiled. He thought he had her, she knew. That she couldn't ultimately resist him. After all, he'd always succeeded in the past. She counted on this certainty about her. The idea that she was fooling him for a change appealed to her.

She stepped to the doorway and called, "Ed." While she waited for him, she watched Jonas. He couldn't sit still, fingers drumming on the table, crossing and recrossing his legs. When Ed appeared, she said, "You can release him now. Please have him escorted to the airport."

"No ticket," Jonas said. "I'm staying here like I intended."

"As I understand it, sir, you haven't checked into any hotel," Ed said.

"I'm staying with my wife."

Lily said to Ed, "Chicago. From there he's on his own."

"I want a lawyer," Jonas announced.

Ed said, "Why? You're not under arrest. We're just taking you to the airport."

"Then I can go anywhere I want."

"Jonas." Lily returned to her spot on the wall, looking down at him. "Headline in the *Guilford News*: 'Big Ten U. development officer discovered stalking coed, charged with urinating in public.' I'll make sure the newspaper clipping lands on your boss' desk. And that copies go to Jane at Prairie Shores." She smiled. "Just for starters, you know."

They looked at each other. Lily thought she should be proud that she didn't flinch, but really, it wasn't any effort. Moments passed. She handed the phone to Ed, who fiddled with it. When he held it up to her, Bethany's photo was gone. He handed the phone to Jonas, who pocketed it.

Ed cleared his throat. "Would you care to go to the airport, sir?"

Jonas stood up and pushed away from the table. He looked Lily over, then shook his head. He pushed by her, stepping on her toe. When he joined Ed in the doorway, he said, "You'll have to follow me to the airport. I have a rental car to return."

"No problem, sir. Someone here will return it." Somehow Ed had Jonas out the door and down the hall.

This time Constance appeared in the door. "Bob is in the car, I packed a bag for you and told Maria you would be gone for a few days. A jet is waiting to drop us in Kansas City. Ready?"

"Absolutely. Just not Hartford Airport." Lily's eyes flashed in the direction of the departing Jonas.

"Oh, no," Constance said. "Money gets you Westchester Airport."

"Wait," Lily said, turning to confront Constance. "Did you say there's a jet waiting for us?"

"We are hitching a ride on a plane heading to one of the Dakotas for some oil thing." Constance flapped her hand. "Come on."

"You didn't have to buy tickets?"

Constance made a face. "Get real."

When they got to the airport, Constance parked her car in a lot marked "owners only," and flipped a card onto the dash proving it. A mid-size jet waited for them. A young man helped them stow their bags then gestured toward a large cabin. "Make yourselves comfortable. I'm waiting for clearance to MCI now."

Lily started to thank him, but he just waved and sat in what looked to be the pilot's seat. "Who is that?"

"Chance," replied Constance, who was showing Bob to a seat that appeared to have been designed for pet passengers.

"You're kidding, right?"

"About what?" Constance didn't look up from putting a seatbelt around Bob.

"Chance?"

"His name is Caldecott Chancellor IV. Nicknamed Chance since birth."

"Our pilot is named Chance. I love it. I think."

"Sit down and quit babbling."

"Let me guess. He's your cousin."

"Hush."

Chapter 30

Kansas City International Airport turned out to be a series of half-moon shaped terminals boasting a former elegance. Lily could imagine that the wood parquet floors had probably been beautiful when the buildings were new in the previous century. Chance had touched down just before dawn, leaving them to enter the airport building when fresh light flooded through the tarmac-facing windows, lending a pink flush to floors and curved interior walls. She felt as if she had emerged from a long trip through a dark tunnel.

They took a shuttle bus to one of the car rental buildings on the airport perimeter and got a car big enough to allow Bob to stretch out in the back seat. They also got a map. Lily studied this while Constance drove, following the on-board computer directions out to Interstate 29. Then Lily navigated them onto Interstate 70, which the map identified as the Kansas Turnpike. After a while, when all traces of city and rolling hills had vanished behind them, ahead only flat wheat fields, Constance said, "I feel like I've left civilization behind."

"You're equating civilization with buildings. How do you know that farmhouse over there doesn't contain quite nice people?"

"They could also be watching us through the sight of a high-powered rifle," Constance replied. "Or manufacturing meth."

"Just like the city?"

"Touché. How far is it to Parthenon, anyway?"

Lily returned to her map and estimated another hour's drive, at least. "Do you want me to drive?"

"Not a chance. No double entendre intended. Get some sleep."

Lily lowered her seat back, which prompted Bob to come forward and squeeze next to her. She reached her arm around his comfortable warmth as he leaned his head on her shoulder, and they slept. When Constance said, "Lily, wake up, Parthenon," she opened her eyes and felt as refreshed as if she'd slept eight hours.

Parthenon, Kansas, appeared less dreary than Jonas had always portrayed it. The road wore new asphalt and was edged by mature trees. They followed signs to the center of town, where there was an unexpected sight: a green, smaller than Guilford's, but blooming with late-summer flowers. Lily pointed at a purple garden, full of salvia and lobelia and lavender and purple sage, outlined in dusty miller. "Someone around here has time to garden."

"I wonder if they would be interested in coming to my house? This level of gardening usually is restricted to museums. Wait until you see the gardens around Wharton's house. Though come to think of it, they are not as lush as these." Constance parked in a space next to the green. When they got out and the August heat hit them, she added, "How do they keep the flowers from wilting?"

"Maybe we'll find out. Jonas first."

"Right." Constance opened the back door of the car and Bob hopped out. He pulled the leash toward the flowers. "No. Right here, young man." She pointed him toward a tree near the car. When he hiked a leg, Constance grinned at Lily. "Speaking of Jonas."

Lily ignored her. "We need a place to stay and a map of town." She pointed toward a small building off the green. "Let's try that. It looks like it might be a police station, though I don't see a basketball court."

But Constance and Bob were already heading toward a church built of rough-cut limestone across the street from the park. Lily followed, trusting her friend's instincts. The church doors were open, and after their eyes adjusted to the dimness inside, they could see four women dusting and arranging flowers on the altar. "Is there a service today?" Constance called. Her voice carried over polished wooden pews and echoed back from the slate floor. Inside it was a pretty little church, cool, with light coming through one enormous stained glass window.

A woman with the whitest hair Lily had ever seen answered, "Evensong." She came over to them and bent down to pet Bob, who, at a warning look and leash tug from his owner, allowed it without growling. "What a lovely dog."

"Thank you. He's a little tired. We just drove here from Kansas City."

"Are you visiting family?"

"We're looking for my husband's family," Lily said. Constance nodded. On the plane, they'd agreed that they'd be straightforward in their quest. If people liked Jonas, they'd be happy to talk about him. If they didn't, they might be happy to gossip about him. If he had family, Lily didn't want to sneak up on them. "His name is Jonas Atwood."

The woman's brown eyes widened, and her eyebrows shot up. "Jonas Atwood? You're his widow?"

More Jonas lies, Lily thought, saying only, "Jonas is alive. I saw him last night." She pointed to a pew. "Would you mind talking to me for a few minutes?"

"But wouldn't you like to meet his mother?"

At that, Lily collapsed into a pew. "His mother? But his mother is dead."

"Well, we seem to have a mystery." The white-haired woman held out her hand. "My name is Betty Anderson." She pointed toward the other women. "Ladies Auxiliary, altar guild."

Lily introduced Constance and Bob. "We're here from Connecticut."

"Just to find out about Jonas?" Betty appeared confused. "He could have told you. If, as you say, he's alive." Then she shook her head. "No, I expect he wouldn't. His father ..." Her mouth pursed, she looked across the little church to the women working and chatting. She seemed to come to a decision, saying, "Wait here."

Betty went down the aisle and up the step to the altar, separated a slender red-haired woman from the group, and walked her to the back of the church and Lily.

While she did this, Constance and Lily glanced at each other. "I don't get it," Lily said. "How could we find people who know Jonas the first place we go?" She shook her head.

"Small town," Constance explained. "It is hard to keep secrets in a place like this if Kansas towns are anything like the ones I know in Maine and South Carolina. Everybody knows someone who knows someone else, and everyone is interested in everyone else's business. The old ones regret the demise of telephone party lines, but they managed to recreate the same web of information exchange. If that makes sense. Though how your husband managed to make them think he was dead—that would take some managing."

Lily didn't have time to answer, because Betty was introducing the redhead as Jonas' former high school principal. Up close, it was obvious the hair was dyed. Her face wasn't wrinkled though it showed age under eyes and chin, sagging skin around her neck showing above her skimpy blue tank top. The woman projected the sort of gravity that Lily associated with her own high school principal. "I'm Dorothy Cranmer." Lily shook her outstretched hand. "I understand you're Jonas Atwood's—" she hesitated. "Wife?"

Lily nodded. "Lily Atwood. This is Constance Cordrey." The redhead nodded a greeting. "Could we go somewhere and talk?"

Betty put in, "Where are you staying?"

Constance said. "Have you any suggestions?"

"Well, Jane has turned her house into a bed and breakfast. You just might be her first guests, if you'd care to chance it."

"Sure," Lily said. "Then could we talk?"

The high school principal looked Lily over carefully. She hesitated, thought a moment, and asked, "May I see some identification?" Her voice was low and gravelly, as if she was a smoker, though Lily couldn't detect the odor of cigarettes.

"Of course," Lily said. She sat down again to dig into her shoulder bag for her wallet. When she found it, she handed her driver's license to Dorothy, then flipped through the back pocket of the wallet. Finally she found what she was looking for, a small photograph of Jonas with Lily and her parents. It had been folded for so long a crease appeared between her face and Jonas'. She handed the picture to Dorothy. The principal took it and walked into the afternoon light thrown through the open church doorway. She held the photo at arm's length before taking a pair of half glasses from her shorts' pocket and perching them on her nose. She looked at the photo, shook her head as if angry, and returned it. "When was this taken?"

"About six years ago," Lily said. "Before we were married."

"That son of a bitch."

"Dorothy!"

"Come on, Betty. You know how much his mother has suffered thinking her prize production died all those years ago."

Lily looked from red head to white head and back again. "We're talking about the same person, then? The same Jonas Atwood?"

"One and the same," Dorothy growled.

Lily said to Constance, "I knew there was a story here. Hell, I think I've always known there was a story here. I could kick myself for not coming here sooner. Like about, oh, six years ago."

Dorothy said, "Oh, there's a story, all right."

Chapter 31

Parthenon, Kansas should have been a dusty little town, sun-faded and empty except for a few businesses clinging to Main Street. That's what Lily and Constance had expected, a town left over from the days of family farms, one that had barely survived corporate agriculture and Wal-Mart.

Instead, the place reminded Lily of expensive Connecticut towns like Guilford and Madison. Mothers pushed strollers past small shops and restaurants. Flowers filled huge terra cotta pots at regular intervals along clean sidewalks. The old gas street lights still stood sentry. There was a bank, an investment firm, and Lily could see two real estate offices. Since Parthenon wasn't within commuting distance of any city, she didn't get it. What was supporting all this? "Is there a big employer nearby?" she asked Betty.

"Nope." She looked around. "Hard to believe, isn't it? Place almost died."

"How did—?" Lily began, but Betty laughed.

"How did this happen?" She gestured to the street scene. "Sheer stubbornness, me and a bunch of others, all of us over sixty years old now. Old enough to remember the town when it was alive the first time, young enough to understand that times change." She steered them down a side street, past a cafe with outdoor tables shaded by a blue and purple striped awning. Young people, old people, people Betty's age filled most of the seats, tall perspiring glasses of what looked like milkshakes in front of them. "Homemade ice cream. You'll want to try it. No, what we did was invite technology to town. Started with a little local phone company which, with the town's help, put in what it needed to offer high-speed internet access. Now it's one of the biggest cell phone companies."

She stopped and pointed back at the ice cream shop. "All those families? They're business owners. There were empty acres nearby that now have warehouses that ship all over the country." She touched Lily on the arm to get her moving. "Well, maybe one of our biggest employers is UPS. Or Federal Express. But that's not where the tax money is coming from. Oh, and one of our group is a pilot. He suggested we put in a small airport, available to Parthenon taxpayers, including businesses. A lot of these families have their own Cessnas and such to go to K.C. or Wichita or New York or wherever, for business and what shopping they can't find here or online. Or in their own warehouses. The airport is expanding now, too, because a lot of our folks want to upgrade to private jets."

While she was talking, they'd reached the front garden of a Queen Anne-style house. Set far back from the street, the house was built on a foundation of more large limestone blocks, these painted white. The upper stories were pale blue clapboard edged in white gingerbread moldings. Screened porches wrapped around the ground floor. In the garden, boxwood hedges trimmed to no more than a foot high set off circles and ovals full of roses here, herbs there, more late-summer flowers nearer to the front porches. "Jane got into gardening in a big way when her husband died, maybe ten years ago. Lot of our altar flowers come from her. Wait 'til you see the back. She found some old book that showed how to design a maze and damned if she didn't manage to grow one. Nice place to sit in the evening, especially the part of the garden where she's planted moon flowers—you know, the ones that only bloom after dark."

The front porch was dim and noticeably cooler. "Why don't you leave your dog out here for now." Constance directed Bob to lie down; he found a cool spot in the shadiest corner. Betty opened the screen door to the house and gestured them in. "Jane must be around or the door wouldn't be open."

The entrance hall was floored in some dark polished wood. The walls were painted a pale color that might have been light gray or blue. A simple wood table in the same dark wood held a wide blue and white bowl with pink and apricot and white roses rising from the middle, as if they were growing out of the porcelain. "Antique Chinese porcelain and perfect Japanese flower arranging," Constance murmured. "In the geographic center of the country." She was smiling. Lily hadn't expected gingham curtains and linoleum, but style such as this startled her, too. Jonas, you ass, she thought, keeping all of this from me.

Unless Jonas didn't know about any of this. "Betty, how long ago did Jonas leave Parthenon?"

The older woman pushed both hands into her white hair. "Let me think. He and my son graduated from the high school the same year. We never saw Jonas after that." Her eyes searched the ceiling. "Yes, that's right. That was fifteen years ago."

A voice called from the back of the house. "Betty, come out to the kitchen."

They followed the voice down the hallway, past a large living room on the left and what looked like a paneled library on the right. A familiar scent of baking pastry grabbed Lily, pulling her forward as it did in Guilford on mornings over Maria's cafe.

The kitchen must have been a late addition to the back of the house. The kitchen pushed into the garden like a peninsula, with windows surrounding the end of the room. Metal shelving filled with professional-looking pots and pans covered one long wall. At the center island stood a tall, angular woman covered in a denim apron. Her graying blonde hair was tied back off her neck in a knot. She greeted them but didn't stop rolling out pastry dough on a marble countertop.

"Jane, you want a couple of guests?" Betty headed towards the windows and a cooling rack full of pies.

"Sure. Don't pick at the crust, Betts. You know I always send a pie home with you." Jane wiped her hands on the apron and smiled at Lily and Constance. "I'm Jane Budd."

Lily introduced Constance, who asked whether it was all right that Bob was out on the porch. "Oh, hell, bring him in out of the heat." After Constance left the kitchen, Jane asked where they were from and how long they wanted to stay. As soon as Jonas' name was mentioned, she grew quiet. Betty, who had come up to the kitchen island, just said, "Yep. He's alive. These two here are on a fact-finding mission."

"Interesting," Jane said. However, her friendliness had noticeably diminished. "Well, I charge a hundred dollars a night, and that includes breakfast and dinner. You're on your own for lunch."

"Jane," Betty exclaimed at the same time that Constance returned with Bob.

"That sounds fine," Constance said. "This is Bob. I assume there will be an extra charge for him."

Jane's expression softened at the sight of the big blonde dog. He peered up at her through his feathered fur, cocked his head and waved his tail once. Jane put a finger to her lips, thought a moment, opened the big stainless steel refrigerator and burrowed through it for a moment. She brought out some cooked beef roast. "All right if I give him a taste?" she asked Constance.

"Wait." Constance knelt down next to her dog to speak in his ear. He looked at Jane and glanced back at his owner. "Thank you. But make sure he works for it."

Jane cut two small chunks off the roast. "Lie down, Bob." The dog complied. She put the meat between his front paws. He ate it so quickly he might have inhaled it. "Now," Jane said, "can you sit and give me paw?" Bob did so. He ate the second piece out of her hand. "What a good boy." She looked at Constance. "Will he sleep in your room?"

"If that's all right."

"Of course. I'll give you the bedroom that has a door to the back yard." Then she looked at Lily and frowned. "Have you seen Jonas' mother yet?"

Betty answered, "Not yet. That's our next stop. Well, almost. We're going to the Velvet Freeze for ice cream first."

"Leave Bob here. She's afraid of dogs. Don't phone. Just go over there."

They were back on the front sidewalk before Lily could ask Betty, "Why not phone?"

"She might disappear. That's what Lil does when strangers are around, and sometimes when friends are."

Lily stopped. "Lil? Jonas said his mother's name was Helen."

Betty rolled back on her heels, arms crossed. "Woman, didn't you check anything about this man before you married him? That's what the internet's for."

Constance began laughing so hard she had to lean against Jane's garden fence.

Lily wanted to slap her. She asked Betty what "Lil" was short for.

"Lillian. Her husband called her Lily."

Constance's laugh cut off. "Jonas chose to pursue someone with his mother's name?"

Lily blinked hard, fighting back tears. She swallowed. When she managed to get herself under control, she said, "I should have listened to my uncle. He said to treat what Jonas said as claims to be double-checked. I just, well, I didn't." When Nate had told her that, she'd felt an enormous weight, as if what he wanted was too much work. She'd finished her dissertation and defended it; she'd published then landed a rare tenure-track position .She had wanted her life to be settled. She didn't want to hear what he was saying. Now here she was, six years later, doing what Nate had so gently suggested. "You must think I'm an idiot."

"Husbands lie," Constance said.

"Some do," Betty agreed. "Mine doesn't, but then I was never very trusting until he taught me otherwise. Now, before we go to see Lil, I think we need some ice cream."

Lily nodded.

They had covered the two blocks to the ice cream place and were sitting over sodas when Constance asked, "What about Jonas' father? Is he still alive?"

Betty looked as though she'd been hit. Odd, thought Lily, who said, "Dead, according to Jonas," and went back to her root beer float.

Betty put down her spoon, then rubbed what must have been cold hands on her thighs. "You know, I think we need to stop at the library before we go to Lillian's. There's something I want to show you."

"What?" asked Lily.

"Something you need to see. Look, I'm not trying to be mysterious. I just want you to see this in context."

Lily paid for their ice cream, saying to Constance, "This I can afford," before they walked two blocks over to the library. The outside was WPA-built of clean-cut stone, utilitarian, massive and impressive. Inside it was brightly-lit and humming with patrons.

Betty led them over to a bank of computer terminals. Sitting down at one, she Googled "Joel Atwood." There were three listings. The first, from the *Kansas City Star*, blasted Lily with its headline: "Bank Director Stabbed to Death; No Suspects; Found on High School Track."

Betty tapped the screen. "Jonas' father was a director of the Parthenon Bank. Kept quiet about it. This was after the bank had to foreclose on all those farms when the farmers borrowed too much against their land."

Constance looked mystified. But Lily understood, having grown up in the Midwest and heard the stories, some from writing by her students from rural Illinois, Iowa, Wisconsin, and Indiana, students whose families still lived with the consequences of borrowing beyond their means. "You know, Willie Nelson and the Farm Aid concert," she said to Constance. "That was, when, about 1985? Who advised the farmers to borrow?" She addressed this second question to Betty.

Betty nodded. "The ag extension agent. That would have been Joel Atwood."

Lily looked carefully at the date on the newspaper article. "But he was shot in 2000. That was over ten years after all those foreclosures. Were the farmers still in the area?"

"Gone, most of them. The ones that stayed, well, it was a big surprise to them that Joel was involved with the bank. After they learned about that, they were happy he was dead. Only one at his funeral was Lil."

Lily looked away from the computers. "Where was Jonas?"

"You know, that's what we all wondered," Betty answered.

Chapter 32

Their next stop was the cemetery attached to the church where Lily and Constance had found Betty. "It's on the way," the older woman said. Still, she seemed to have something on her mind. Given the last few bombshells she'd dropped into Lily's life, Lily wasn't sure she was all that eager to find out what was bothering Betty. To Constance, she murmured, "I thought I was ready for this."

Constance touched Lily's arm. "When I thought I had found out the worst about my husband, there was more. Always more." Now she bumped her shoulder against Lily's. "You are never ready for it. But you have to know in order to go on with your own life. Knowing is much less expensive than not knowing."

In their short friendship, Constance had given Lily a glimpse of her own pain once or twice, and only when it was necessary for Lily to understand what Lily's next step should be. She put an arm around Constance's shoulder, squeezed and let go. "My own life after Jonas. I haven't thought that far."

"You will when the time comes."

Lily pointed at her friend. "New Haven?"

"For me, the Beinecke is L.A.A.: Life After Alden."

Betty led them through the church, whose altar was now decorated with purple and white flowers, and out through a side door. The afternoon sun blinded them momentarily while heat clamped down over them like a metal dome. They followed her past another well-tended garden, through a gate hidden in a tall hedge, and suddenly they were at the edge of the cemetery. Grass was trimmed between gravestones. It was quiet. They could hear their feet crunch on the crushed-stone path.

Well away from the outer perimeter of the other graves stood a square stone that read "Joel Jonas Atwood, 1957-2000. Beloved husband." Betty stood back from the stone, glaring at it, arms crossed. "Lillian put up the stone." She pointed to a worn spot on the grass next to the marker. "She spends a fair amount of time right there."

Lily backed away, turned and spotted a bench under a tree about fifty feet off. Constance joined her, then Betty, who sank down on the edge. "Here's what the newspaper articles and Lillian won't tell you. You need to know it to understand about Lil when you meet her. Joel had to marry Lillian when she got pregnant with Jonas. Abortion though legal was never a possibility. Maybe having a child, particularly a son, appealed to Joel. However the marriage came about, he cheated on her from the first, and made sure she knew it.

"It was like he'd cast a spell over her. He moved out of their house before Jonas was in preschool. Joel would drop in when he felt like it, beat her when he felt like it, play with his son when he felt like it, support them when he felt like it. They never divorced, and every woman within a hundred miles knew the rules of playing with Joel: no commitment. Maybe his personality froze when they married. Me, I think he got exactly what he wanted. Always did."

Lily felt as though Betty had sprayed her with dirty water. Not because Jonas' father was, well, what he was. But Betty said Joel had cast a spell over Lillian. Lily suddenly understood her mother-in-law. For her, the spell had broken when she saw Jonas on the Guilford Green. But until then, Jonas got exactly what he wanted from her. "Tell me. Did Joel like spending money? On himself?"

Betty nodded slowly. "Seems to me there was a new car every year. He built himself quite a house outside of town. Had a sunken bathtub and a loft over the bedroom. One bedroom, no room for guests, including his own son. His suits and such fit him perfectly, as if he'd had them made to order." She turned to Lily. "That what you mean?"

Lily frowned, nodded.

"Jonas do that?"

"Yes."

"Spend money on you?"

"No."

"New car every year?"

"No."

"Fancy house?"

"We live in an apartment owned by my parents. Low rent in an otherwise expensive neighborhood."

"I see," Betty said. "No commitment, more cash."

True, Lily thought, though where it all went every month was something that required looking into.

"From what I've heard, after he died, turned out Joel had more than a million dollars stashed away in banks as far as K.C. He didn't bother with a will, which meant Lil got it."

"Did Jonas benefit?" Constance asked.

Betty squinted towards Joel Atwood's grave, then shook her head. "Now that's a good question. I don't think so. See, Lil just fell apart after Joel's murder. So a bunch of us who went to high school with her suggested to the local bank that maybe a trust would be a good idea, one that paid her bills, gave her some walking-around cash. It may have paid for Jonas' college education, but there wasn't anything else in the trust for him. Specifically, that is. After Lil goes, he'll inherit, I expect. I can't imagine that she'd think of making a will, either. She lives in the past."

"Especially since she thinks her son is dead," Constance said. "Was he declared legally dead?"

Betty raised both hands. "Don't know. Does it matter?"

Constance said, "Possibly. Some states will set aside a missing heir's part of an estate, just in case." She shrugged. "Librarians pick up random information and some of it sticks."

Lily stood up and walked toward the church. Then she began running as fast as her sandaled feet would let her. She slid out of the Birkenstocks, flying out of the churchyard barefoot.

She couldn't stand it. She had to think. How had she not had a hint of any of this?

She stopped, finding herself on the burning asphalt by their rental car. Her feet felt on fire. She ran onto the grass.

How had Jonas gotten her to follow him? What in her had he touched, enabling him to take control?

Before she went any further in this quest, she'd better figure that out.

• • •

When Constance caught up with her, Lily was standing in the center of the garden, itself at the center of the town green, hands on her hips, glaring at a fountain featuring cherubs spitting water.

"Those babies do something to you?" Constance said, panting. "No more sprints like that, or at least not until it is cooler than ninety degrees out." She handed the sandals to Lily.

"I can't do this right now," Lily said.

"Try."

"No, I mean, right this very minute." Lily turned to her. "I need to think." In the distance she saw Betty trudging toward them. She waved, slipped into her sandals, then walked to meet the older woman. They spoke for a moment.

For her part, Constance hung back. She could see from a distance that Betty looked relieved. The older woman reached over to shake hands with Lily before walking away. Constance hesitated before crossing the park to Lily.

Lily tried to smile. "Betty's going to come over to Jane's for breakfast."

Lily pivoted slowly, looking at Parthenon. "There are some questions I need to consider before meeting Jonas' mother. I told Betty we'd plan things in the morning." She tugged Constance's hand. "Come on, let's go get Bob."

"He is fine where he is."

"My current comfort zone requires Bob and you." Lily wiped a forearm over her perspiring face. "Somewhere out of the heat."

"What are we thinking about?" Constance asked while they walked toward their lodging.

Lily chewed the inside of her cheek. "Trust."

"Vast topic."

"How it's possible for Jonas to fool me into something so profound as trust."

Well, thought Constance, that narrowed it down somewhat.

...

When they returned to Jane's house, Lily cooled her stinging feet on the cement floor of the shaded front porch. She found a wicker chair upholstered in rough cotton and propped her feet on a matching ottoman. It was Constance who sought out Jane in the kitchen at the back of the house. Bob met her in the hallway, tail wagging, cold nose bumping her hand. She knelt down to hug him. He licked her face, then backed up and sat down, head on the side in his "What's going on?" expression. She said, "We will play it by ear." When she stood, he moved into heel position and the two of them went into the kitchen.

In the hour or so since she'd been here, two more pies had been finished and now decorated the table. Flour coated Jane's denim apron, forehead and one cheek. She was again rolling out dough, but it couldn't have been for pies this time. The dough was so thin that Constance could see through it to the black marble pastry stone. When Jane looked up at her and smiled, Constance hazarded a guess. "Strudel?"

"Sort of. My own concoction. Thin pie crust around strawberries, a little sugar. Kind of strawberry pie roll-ups." Turning, she opened the oven door, gesturing Constance over to look.

A glorious odor of baking pastry and hot oven overwhelmed Constance, transporting her back to the kitchen of her childhood, which was overseen by a cook who constantly tried to feed the tiny young girl she had been. Jane's voice asking if she wanted to try a bit brought her back to reality. "No, no. I just came in to say we would like to go out to dinner and to ask for a restaurant suggestion."

"Hmm." Jane's floury hand went to her cheek, adding more flour to what was already there. "Good thing you all want to go out. I don't have anything prepared. Let's see." She looked at Constance, who could feel her gaze checking out narrow shoulders, tiny waist and slim legs. Oddly, it didn't make her feel uncomfortable. Jane came to some sort of decision. "Do you all like fried chicken?"

"Love it unless it is fried in lard. Would that be southern fried chicken? Is Kansas southern?"

"Kansas is southern in a lot of ways," Jane said. "Lard's expensive, though, and too many people don't want to eat it these days. There's a place off Main Street that does it with canola oil. I've been trying to get the recipe from the chef but she won't play. I offered to trade some of my recipes, said I wouldn't serve it to guests, but nope. Anyway, order that and the Southern green beans. You eat bacon?"

"Sure."

Jane walked over to the phone hanging on the wall by the kitchen door. She wiped her hands on a clean towel then called the restaurant and made a reservation for her guests for an hour later without consulting Constance. After she'd hung up, she returned to rolling dough out even thinner, saying, "Go a little early. Have a glass of wine in the bar. It looks out over a kind of Japanese garden. You can see it from inside. Bob can stay here. Or he can go with you, stay out on the restaurant porch." She gave Constance directions to the restaurant, then seemed to forget about her. Constance watched for a moment while Jane peeled the fine dough off the marble with such a delicate touch that it didn't tear. Constance hoped there would be strawberry roll-ups for breakfast.

She and Bob walked down the cool dark hallway and out to the porch. They found Lily holding one foot in both hands, contorting so she could blow air on the bottom of it. She looked up at the sound of their steps and said, "I may have burned my feet."

"Wait here. I think I have something with aloe in my bag." Constance cut down the hall to her room at the back of the house. Her toiletry kit turned up a small bottle of lotion. The back of the bottle listed the second ingredient as aloe. That would do the trick until they could find a drugstore. She took the lotion to Lily, who massaged it into her feet.

"That's better," she said. "Not very smart, running shoeless in this heat."

"You were not thinking." Constance mentioned the six o'clock dinner reservation. Lily glanced at Bob and Constance said, "He can come, too." Lily looked relieved, more relieved than she had when she'd applied aloe to her burned feet. Constance stretched out on a wicker sofa, arm behind her neck, eyes closed. She figured Lily would talk when she was ready. They sat like that for half an hour, in silence except for the click of Bob's toenails on the porch floor as he crossed back and forth between them, sharing his attentions. Finally Constance decided Lily could use some prompting. "What made you go out with Jonas the first time?"

"There was no first time. He was just sort of there. He'd worked his way through most of the single females in the English grad program." She mused for awhile. Constance was beginning to think she needed another prompting when she added, "You know, I may have been the only one left. I never paid much attention to him or to any guy. I just, well, you know, never did."

"Did not know how? Not interested?"

"Yes to the first, no to the second."

Constance turned on her side on the sofa, eyeing Lily. A handsome woman with that blue-black hair and dark eyes in a pale complexion, her tiny waist setting off bust and hips of about equal size. She was highly intelligent. Lily's idea about Edith Wharton publishing her own short story as one of Henry James' was groundbreaking. If Lily was that capable of analyzing the motives of her research subjects then she could damn well figure out her own motives. "Come on, Lily. Why did you let him hang around? What did you see in him?" Constance understood from her own life how it was possible to fool yourself into marrying the wrong man—feminism had failed to prevent the pressure for a woman to be married, as if you were some sort of failure otherwise, as her mother had insisted. "Lily, what did Edith Wharton see in Henry James?"

"A brilliant stylist. A writer who understood narrative structure so thoroughly. A tough critic of her own work. The two of them connected at the most important level of her life, her art," Lily answered instantly. "They shared a fascination with what people do and why. Did you know the pair named her automobiles after each of George Sand's lovers?"

Constance considered how she could get Lily to back away from her own situation far enough for her to see it in perspective. Then Lily surprised her. "Henry James was everything Teddy Wharton wasn't. Edith married Teddy because it was time to get married, because her first love had died, and the love of her intellectual life wasn't getting around to romance."

"I thought James was gay."

"Possibly. Probably, though of course we'll never know for sure. But he's not who I mean. And I don't mean Morton Fullerton, either—he was later, and that was about sex. Someone she may have had in common with James, by the way. I mean Walter Berry. Walter Van Rensselaer Berry, was the first man to appreciate her brilliant mind, and therefore to take her seriously. Remember how women weren't supposed to be book smart, especially before the end of the nineteenth century.

"I didn't marry a Teddy Wharton. I didn't need to get married." Lily stood up, looked at her shorts and dirty feet. I want to put on some clean clothes for dinner. I'll be right back." She gave all these statements equal emphasis.

Constance stayed where she was, though Bob followed Lily upstairs. Lily was back within ten minutes, wearing black cropped pants and a loose light green shirt, both showing packing creases. Her feet were back in the old sandals. "Ready?" she said. "I'm hungry." She looked down at Bob. "Suppose they'll have anything for him to eat?"

"We will ask. If not, we will find a grocery store after dinner." She looked at Lily's feet. "Maybe do that anyway, find something to put on your burns."

Lily said, "I think the aloe did the trick. You know, Jonas was in the psychology department. The girls there didn't seem all that interested in him."

They went out the porch door. The evening was still hot, though the sun not quite so glaring.

"Jonas was studying psychopathic behavior. Not schizophrenics or bipolar or anything like that. Rather, the sort of psychopaths who might turn into criminals. He was interested in the ones who felt emotions, who had all their emotional faculties but still did awful things. He wanted to know why they did." They walked another block. Lily held Bob's leash, allowing the dog to check out every other tree. "He was interested in what made these people tick. I was interested in what made Edith Wharton tick. In a way, we shared an interest."

"Except that Wharton was no psychopath."

"Oh no, not at all. But her mother was, or close to it. Sociopath, anyway. Teddy Wharton turned out to be manic-depressive. Edith was surrounded by dysfunctional human beings, including one brother who tried to steal her inheritance. Women weren't supposed to know how to handle money, either. They were supposed to be protected by their ignorance."

Constance let that comment fester for another block or two.

"But you know something that I've always wondered is why Jonas didn't go on with his research after he got his Ph.D. When I asked, he always said that he'd gotten bored with the topic. I've never gotten bored with Edith Wharton, and he always made fun of me for that. He said the psychopaths got him the doctorate and that got him a leg up in development and administration. But one time he let slip that he didn't want to talk to the crazies anymore. That's how he referred to his interview subjects: the crazies. He refused to elaborate on why. Though every now and then he would comment that some of the people who give money to Prairie Shores or LU could have been in his dissertation. Then he'd laugh as if something was funny. I didn't think it was funny. But then he insists I don't have a sense of humor."

She stopped to let Bob mark a tree. Watching the dog, she said, "I'm not making him sound very likable." They walked the last block to the restaurant. "But interesting. Sexy. Jonas has this electricity about him when he wants to. I'd never been close enough to any other man to feel sexy and wanted and, well, gloriously female."

The restaurant was a yellow-brick house fronted by a glassed-in porch. The murmur of voices and muted laughter from inside could be heard on the sidewalk. "Busy place," Constance said.

A hostess dressed in pressed jeans and starched white shirt met them as they came through the porch. She looked at the dog and asked, "Jane's guests?" When they nodded, she pointed to a quiet corner of the porch. "He'll be fine there. I'll keep an eye on him. If necessary, he can go into the garden when it cools off some." Bob found himself leashed to a heavy table, sighed and curled up under it.

They were led through the bar to a corner table covered with a flowered cloth, by the back window. The promised Japanese garden was visible, lit by hidden yellow lights, a tiny stone bridge off to one side. The hostess handed them menus. "If you want fried chicken, you should put in your order right away. It takes awhile and sometimes we run out." They both ordered chicken and slow-cooked green beans. A waitress came by, took their drink order, returned with huge glasses of iced tea, then left them.

"So you married him for the sex." That Constance understood too well.

Lily looked at her iced tea, a rueful expression on her face. "I was drunk on the sex. I'm amazed I finished my dissertation in time." She looked up at Constance. "This is not something you can explain to a caring uncle."

Constance picked up on her thought, making the connection to something she'd said to Betty. "Certainly not to an uncle," she said. "Uncles, healthy ones, prefer not to think of their nieces having sex. What about your father?"

"Uninterested. To say my parents are ambivalent about being parents is a massive understatement."

Constance understood that completely. "So Jonas got you to marry him while you were high on sex?"

"Yes. After the honeymoon was over, he turned off the electricity. Well, he turns it on when he feels like it. But the electrical current definitely became intermittent." She shook her head. "Sounds trite, doesn't it?"

"Trite? Maybe. Manipulative? Definitely. Now, my friend, we have a line of questioning to follow."

Lily frowned. "What's that?"

"To whom did Jonas do this before you?"

Lily's frown turned to anger. "What makes you think he did? Maybe he just got tired of me."

Constance shook her head. "Uh-uh. Do not go there. Right after your honeymoon? Designed to make you feel inferior, unwanted. I sense a script. There had to be a rehearsal."

"But why? Why me? Why not a rich woman, like you?"

"Maybe there is something your husband wants more than money."

"After all," Lily said softly, "if he wanted money, he just had to kill his mother. Instead, she thinks he's dead."

"But," Constance pointed out, "so does the whole town. Hard for a dead man to be suspected of murder."

"No," Lily said. "Doesn't work. They've thought he's been dead for years."

Then she went pale, so pale that Constance waved frantically for the waitress. The hostess materialized at the table. "Brandy, please. A large one. Quickly." The hostess glanced at Lily, nodded understanding and returned in less than a minute with a brandy glass. Constance thrust it at Lily. "Drink. Now."

Lily obeyed, choked on the first sip, then drank more slowly. Her color returned after a few minutes. She put the glass down firmly. "You realize I may get a migraine from this."

"Oh, good lord, I had completely forgotten." Constance felt immediate guilt. "Is there something you can take? Do you have it with you?"

"Don't worry. I've taken to carrying the medicine after that episode."

Chapter 33

It seemed to Lily that her recent migraine happened ages ago. So much had happened in the meantime. Seeing Jonas at the jail. Coming to his hometown. Discovering his trail of lies. She took another swallow of the brandy, fending off Constance's cautioning hand. "Who," Lily said, "is the man I married?"

"Whoever he is," Constance said as the fried chicken was served, "you first met him after your honeymoon. Are you prepared to find out who he really is?"

"Why didn't I start trying to find out about Jonas a few years ago?"

Constance served herself chicken before handing the platter to Lily. "You have to learn to forgive yourself for making mistakes. Forgiving yourself for falling for Jonas may allow you to think clearly."

"But here's the thing: I didn't fall for Jonas. As soon as the lust cooled, he was just this man I roomed with. My husband? I don't think I ever loved him. I ought to know the difference between lust and love. It's in just about every one of the classic novels."

"Reading about it does not compare to living it. Think how Wharton's novels changed after she had real sex for the first time. What was she, over forty? Was it not after her affair that she could write *The Age of Innocence*?"

Lily nodded. She thought about that while she ate. At first she had little appetite. But the more she got her mind around the idea that perhaps it was forgivable to have chosen to marry the wrong person, the more food appealed to her. Before long she'd eaten everything on her plate. She found herself nodding when the waitress offered to tell them about desserts. "Something with chocolate, please. Just surprise me."

Constance added, "Bring an extra fork."

The waitress grinned and headed toward the kitchen.

"How's your head?" Constance asked.

"Fine. No migraine warnings on the horizon."

"One woman I know from the library says she had terrible migraines for years. They mysteriously ended after her divorce." Constance chuckled. "She always adds that she had the pain removed in court."

"Divorce," Lily said. "I suppose that could happen."

"Take your time," Constance advised.

"Oh, I intend to."

The waitress brought dark chocolate pie and two forks. Lily ordered a second piece.

...

The next morning at the breakfast table, Lily actually felt good, optimistic, as she often did at the beginning of one of her sieges of research. She rubbed Bob's head with her foot and felt his tongue lick her toes. Maybe she'd get a dog. Not now, but, well, later. After. She and Constance were just finishing up Jane's strawberry roll-ups when Betty joined them. They were sitting on the back porch, which was deep enough to shade them from the morning's heat. Constance had fed Bob dog food, much to his disappointment, and he was stretched out under her chair. Jane brought a fresh pot of coffee and sat down at the table with them. She topped up her guests' cups before pouring black coffee for Betty and herself.

Constance smiled at Betty. "Anything new?"

Betty smiled back, looking puzzled. "New?"

"Do we have a plan for today?"

Betty sipped coffee, put the cup back down. "Are you ready to meet Lillian?"

Both Constance and Lily nodded.

"Well, I stopped by her house on the way here. She's not home. That means she's at the cemetery. That's bad and good."

"In that order?" Lily asked.

"Bad because it means she's living in the past today, not to mention that it's blazing hot out there. Good because she tends to be more talkative when she's near Joel's stone. It's like she doesn't feel trapped when she's out there, like she does in her house."

"God, that house," Jane said. "It's more a memorial to Joel than his gravestone is."

"It's clean," Betty protested.

"Oh, sure. Joel beat her if the house wasn't clean, even after he'd moved out. That's one of the things I'm talking about. It's like she never had a life of her own after he latched onto her. He's gone and she's like…" Jane's voice trailed off. "Well, you'll see for yourself."

Her comments effectively ended breakfast table conversation. Lily and Constance left with Betty; Bob stayed with Jane.

The day wasn't as hot, but the air felt wet. The sky was milky blue, looking like condensed humidity. Betty looked up. "Rain predicted for tonight. We could use it." They walked in silence toward Main Street. She led them the few blocks to the church, then showed them a path around the side to the cemetery.

In the distance was a pale figure. It seemed to Lily that the figure was dancing or flitting about. When they moved closer it became apparent that the person was pulling up something, weeds or grass, and flinging it into the trees. "Damn it, she's at it again," Betty said before breaking into a run. Stepping onto the grass, Lily stooped to remove her sandals before following; Constance kept walking. When Lily came closer, she could see Betty speaking to an old woman. But when she caught up with them, she realized that the woman wasn't old.

The woman—Jonas' mother?—was white everywhere. Lily had never seen skin that pale on a living human being. Her hair was white, as were her eyebrows. She wore a man's v-neck undershirt over a skirt that at first glance looked white. At some point the skirt must have been blue denim, for the ghost of blue remained. Same with her faded eyes. Ghost, Lily thought. That's what Jane meant when she said they'd see for themselves. This ghost was all that was left of Lillian Atwood. Lily shivered, then squared her shoulders. Maybe Lillian Atwood had let the Atwood men consume her, but Lily Atwood did not have any intention of allowing that to happen to her.

"Lil." Betty put her arms around Jonas' mother to get her attention. The woman stopped flitting about. Betty led her to the bench in the shade, sat her down and kneeled next to her. "Lillian, there are some people here who you might like to meet."

The pale eyes seemed to come into focus, like a camera lens when the power is turned on. She looked down at Betty, reached out to pat her hand. Betty nodded toward Lily and Constance, who had stopped a few feet from the end of the bench. Lily took a cautious step forward, fearful that the ghost woman would skitter off like a startled cat.

Lillian's voice seemed to come from far away, perhaps from her husband's grave. "Do I know you?"

Lily came to sit next to her on the bench and took her hand between her own. The hand was cold and dry, strange on such a humid August day. "Mrs. Atwood," she began, but Betty shook her head. "Lillian. You know, my name is Lily."

"Joel called me Lily." The voice sounded hypnotized.

"My parents named me Lily," Lily said, adding a lie, "after an author whom they admired."

The voice came a little closer. "Author? Which one?"

"The author's name is Edith Wharton. My parents love her writing and that she made a life for herself when women weren't supposed to do that. She was very brave."

"Not me." Lillian Atwood turned to Lily Atwood. "I'm not brave."

"I'm not sure that I agree," Lily said in a conversational tone.

The older woman's voice became a shade more sure. "Joel says I'm a coward."

"When did he say that?"

"When I won't fight back."

"Hmm," Lily said. Panic was rising in her chest, yet she found such pity for what was left of this woman. Lily wasn't sure where her questions were coming from. She took a deep breath. "I've never found that it pays to fight a bully."

Lillian giggled. The sound chilled Lily. "Bully. No one ever dared called Joel that. But he was. Oh, he was. My bully. Always mine."

"Did Joel bully Jonas?"

It was as if the question popped Lillian like a balloon. She sagged against the back of the bench. "My baby. Where's my baby?"

"In Lakeland. That's just north of Chicago on Lake Michigan," Lily said matter-of-factly.

Those strange eyes turned toward Lily. "You've seen him?"

"I saw him yesterday." In the Guilford, Connecticut, jail, Lily thought. "He was fine. He'd taken a few days off and was just going back to work."

"Why doesn't he come to see me?"

"He sent me to see if it was okay, if you wanted to see him," Lily said, again wondering how she could do this, lie, or rather make up stories. Then she had the answer: this woman had been hurt so badly she had no strength left. Lily found that she, too, wanted to protect her. "In fact, I just learned about you."

Lily waited for her mother-in-law's inevitable question. After a minute of silence, it came.

"Who are you?"

"I'm Jonas' wife."

"He married?" She shook her head with such violence that Lily thought she might be having some sort of fit. Betty, though, merely reached over and placed her hand firmly on one white shoulder. The head-shaking ceased. "The only person he could marry was Maureen."

"Why is that?" Lily asked, forcing her voice to remain calm.

"Jonas knows." The faded face developed a coy expression. "So does Maureen." She stood up, stepping around Betty as if she, too, were a gravestone. "Besides, Jonas is dead. So that makes you a liar." She veered back to her husband's grave, patted it one more time, then walked off.

Chapter 34

Betty stood up and dusted off her knees. She turned to watch as Lillian faded into the distance. "For a moment there I thought she was going to snap out of it." She gestured toward the church. "We might as well go." She sounded defeated.

Constance asked, "Who is Maureen?"

"And why would his mother think Jonas could only marry Maureen?" Lily asked.

Betty walked back toward the church, taking the path through the tall bushes this time. "Lillian would only know about somebody local. At least, that's probably the case. You never know what information she absorbs and what she ignores. But I don't know any Maureen in Jonas' generation."

"What about the high school principal? Any possibility she might know?" Lily asked. "The woman with the red hair, the one who asked to see my identification. The school must have been pretty small when Jonas attended."

"Dorothy. Dorothy Cranmer. Never hurts to ask, I always say." Betty checked her watch. "Let me call her from the church office. She might be at home but she's probably over at the high school. Classes start in a few weeks, you know."

"How about we just go to the school?" Lily asked. "I'd love to see yearbook photos of Jonas."

"Sure thing. My truck's over by Jane's place. Think that dog of yours would like to go for a ride?"

"He wouldn't miss it," Constance said. "Neither would I. Can I sit in the back with him?"

"You'll have to, young lady. Front seat gets crowded with more than two people."

Constance grinned, then turned to Lily.

Lily was remembering that sometime in the past, when Jonas actually briefly showed anger, he'd mentioned the name Maureen. She remembered asking him who he was talking about. She also remembered him saying that once again she hadn't been paying attention, that he'd said something else entirely. Now Lily superimposed that conversation on what was left of his mother. There was bullying, she thought, and then there was bullying. Every generation improving on the previous one. She turned to Constance. "I'm really glad we came here."

Constance hung back, letting Betty get twenty feet or so ahead of them. "For a good time, visit Parthenon, Kansas," Constance cracked. "Home of superb fried chicken and extremely odd ducks."

"Do you suppose the son of a bitch is a bigamist?" Lily said.

"Not a chance. Way too smart for that, if he fooled you all these years. Plus, that poor woman is not a bitch."

• • •

Parthenon County High School featured all the dull institutional architecture from the late nineteen-fifties, with a brand-new dull twenty-first-century wing that blended all too well. Poured concrete, lots of vertical windows, walkways connecting corners of the four sides of the building, minimal landscaping. Lily counted three trees. Dorothy Cranmer met them in the front office, standing behind a battered wooden counter that reminded Lily of the one at her own high school. Today the principal was dressed in black linen pants and blouse, which made her red hair flame brighter than ever. It would be hard for any student to miss the woman when she was patrolling the halls. Assuming she did that. Maybe principals hid in their offices these days.

"Did you speak with Lil?" the principal greeted them.

Lily nodded. "How long has she been off in a different world?"

"Good question." Dorothy looked approvingly at Lily. "Why don't you all come into my office? I have the air conditioner cranked up to nuclear freeze."

Constance mouthed, "A sense of humor?" to Lily, who raised her eyebrows. Maybe.

The first thing they noticed in the principal's office was a rug in the same hue as her hair, with a geometric design in greens and blues and purples. It should have been blinding but in the high school set a tone of cheerful iconoclasm. Lily liked the woman immediately because of her crazy rug even while she suspected that that was the whole idea. "Wow. What a wonderful design," Lily said, sitting down on one of the chairs arranged around a more standard-issue wood desk.

"One of my students from maybe twenty years ago went into the carpet design business. One day I found this rolled up and leaning against my door, with a note thanking me for pushing her into art courses back in the day. This, apparently, was the bestseller that year. I keep it to remind myself that being pushy can sometimes be useful." She sat behind the desk, pulled out a drawer and propped up her feet. "Now, about Lil." She chewed the inside of her cheek.

"I'm thinking it was a long time before Joel was killed that she'd begun to lose her hold on reality. You have that feeling, Betty?"

The older woman nodded. "But when? Or maybe we just noticed it after Joel was killed and Jonas disappeared."

"She didn't have them to hide behind anymore, you mean?" Lily asked.

"More like they weren't blocking out her light anymore," Dorothy said.

Lily liked her bluntness, though she was willing to bet it wasn't always popular with, say, the school board or the superintendent. "When did Jonas, uh, leave town?" she asked.

"Right after high school. He graduated and left for college. Never saw him again. Never thought anything about it until Lil started saying he was dead," Dorothy said. "You all want something cold to drink? There's diet Coke in the office fridge." When everyone nodded, she buzzed the outer office and asked someone to bring it in. "When he didn't visit her, year after year, we finally just thought she was right, he was dead. Then someone ran across his obituary."

"Who? Who saw Jonas' obituary?" Lily asked.

It was Betty who answered, "Laurel. The librarian. Does that sound right?" She looked at Dorothy for confirmation, but the principal shook her head.

"I'm sorry, I don't remember." At that point an adolescent girl arrived with five cans of Coke bound together in plastic rings. "Got one for yourself, Ophelia? Smart." Dorothy pulled out cans and handed them around, giving the last one to the delivery girl, who scooted out the door as if the can were burning her hand.

"Ophelia?" Constance queried.

"Guess her parents weren't up on their Shakespeare," Dorothy said. "Nice folks, though. All I can say is they didn't go to school here."

Lily sat forward. "Dr. Cranmer, Jonas' mother said the only person he could marry was Maureen. Do you know who that is?"

"Call me Dorothy." She sipped soda, but for the first time since meeting them at the office door, Dorothy Cranmer was looking over their heads instead of straight at them.

"Dorothy." Lily used her teacher voice, the professional one that instantly pulled her students into line. This time, the principal met her eyes, though there was a slight smile on her face as if she, too, knew about summoning the teacher voice. "I've been married to Jonas Atwood for five years. Lately I've learned I don't know the man whose name is on our marriage license. Frankly, that scares me."

"He was stalking her in Connecticut," Constance put in. "Ended up explaining it to the police and the FBI."

"FBI?" Betty asked.

"Long story," Lily said, "but true. So far I've learned that his mother is alive, she thinks he's dead, and his father was murdered. Wouldn't you agree that these are things that, under normal circumstances, a husband would confide to his wife?"

"Of course," Betty said in a prim voice.

"What's Maureen got to do with this?" Dorothy asked.

"Well, I was rather hoping you could tell me that." Lily sat back, sipped Coke. If she were Dorothy Cranmer, she'd feel the pressure of three people staring at her, waiting for her to come up with a reasonable answer.

"Dorothy, give," Betty said. "No point in protecting Lil. She's the one mentioned Maureen to these young women."

"It's not Lil I'm protecting." She swiveled around in her desk chair to stare out the window into the muted afternoon sun. Her back to them, she tapped the edge of the Coke can on the concrete windowsill. When the tapping stopped, Lily knew she'd made a decision, but the principal waited another full minute before turning back. She opened what looked like an address book by the desk telephone, dialed—it was an old black dial phone—and waited.

When the person on the other end answered, Dorothy identified herself. "I know it's been a long time. Listen," she said hastily, "there are three other people in my office. One of them is Jonas Atwood's wife." There was silence. Dorothy turned back to the window, the telephone cord snaking over her shoulder. "Evidently. She says she saw him two nights ago." Dorothy picked up the Coke can and tapped again on the sill while she listened.

Lily thought she herself ought to be on edge, waiting to hear whether or not this Maureen person would talk to her. Because Lily had no doubt that's who Dorothy was talking to. She also had no doubt that if Maureen said she didn't want to see her, that she, Lily, would find another path. Often she'd felt this way about her research. Often she was disappointed. But it was the only thing in her life that she had ever felt sure about, except Nate, and at some point she'd just decided to enjoy it. Maybe that was a sign of maturity or maybe that she'd never grown up, that she was being cocky. But there it was.

"You sure about that?" Dorothy was saying. She turned back and eyed Lily. Lily didn't waver. "All right. Sure." Dorothy handed the telephone receiver to Lily. "Maureen wants to talk to you. Maureen Copeland."

Into the phone, Lily said, "Hello, this is Lily Atwood."

"So you were dumb enough to marry that charming snake," said a low-pitched voice.

"Yep, that's me, the local idiot," Lily agreed.

At her admission, the gruff voice laughed hugely, a guffaw. "God, I know that feeling. So, how long before you can get to Kansas City? We gotta talk."

"Are you free for dinner?"

"Sure. Come on by. We'll go out for barbecue. You like barbecue?"

"Doesn't everyone?" Lily said, though the only barbecue she'd ever had was what her father produced on the backyard grill. Which she loved. "I've got a friend traveling with me, and her dog. Do you know a place where we can stay?"

"Honey, you all can stay with me if you can stand it. Come on and we'll figure something out. One idiot to another, you know."

"I'm learning fast," Lily said. Maureen gave her directions from Interstate 35. The high school principal was back to staring out the window. Betty watched her with a worried look. When Lily put down the phone, Betty said, "Dorothy? Why don't you want this Maureen to meet Lily?"

"Some things are best left as they are."

"How do you know Maureen?" Betty was pushing against Dorothy's resistance, Lily could see, but didn't understand why. "Who is she?"

"One of my teachers, one of the best. Taught chemistry." Dorothy finally faced her old friend. "She must have taught your son, too. Didn't he take chemistry?"

Betty turned pale. "Mrs. Copeland? That's who Lillian was talking about?"

"Miss Copeland."

Betty started to ask another question but Dorothy held up her hand. "That's all I'm going to say. I'd rather Maureen did her own talking." With that she stood up and escorted the other women out of her office. Before she could shoo them out the door of the main office, though, Lily managed to ask, "After I've talked to Maureen, may I call you?"

Dorothy said, "Up to Maureen. This is her story."

Chapter 35

Betty drove them back to the bed and breakfast, Constance once again sharing the bed of the pick-up with her dog. When they arrived, she jumped down stiffly. "In my family, we say we have done something twice: the first time and the last time." She nodded. "I have ridden in the back of a truck twice."

"You want me to do the driving to Kansas City?" Lily asked.

"Not a prayer."

Lily and Constance quickly packed. They found Betty in the kitchen with Jane, who offered them lunch. "Since you're not staying for dinner, I hear."

"How very kind of you," Lily said.

Jane smiled at Bob, who sat at her feet panting. "How about you? A little more roast beef?"

"An offer he would never refuse," Constance laughed. "Do we get some, too?"

In answer, Jane pulled roast beef from the refrigerator and began slicing. Betty found bread. Without asking their preferences, she slathered mayonnaise on the bread. Soon, all four women were choosing roast beef sandwiches from a platter, while Bob, who had once again inhaled his, sat looking at them hopefully. Betty told the story of their morning with Dorothy Cranmer and the call to the mysterious Maureen. At that point, Jane looked up, an interested look on her face.

"Maureen Copeland? Sure, I remember her. She was a stunner."

"She was?" Betty said. "I don't remember that."

"Your son sure would," Jane laughed. Then she went back to her sandwich.

"So give," Constance said. "A stunner? What did she look like? My chemistry teacher—well, the only thing stunning about her was that she taught high school. Not any social ability except to frighten adolescents."

Jane ate a few more bites, then wiped her mouth delicately with the linen napkin. Lunch, even in her kitchen, was gracious. "Maureen Copeland was—is—tall for a woman, with endless legs. She had long black hair and really upright boobs."

Constance choked on roast beef, coughed, laughed.

"Seriously. The woman must have been at least a D cup. At first glance, she would have been more believable as a lingerie model. The high school boys wanted to bed her and the girls wanted to be her. Since she was maybe thirty, she was just enough older than they were to have authority and a certain, I don't know, glamour."

She didn't sound like Jonas' type, Lily thought, then caught herself. How would she know what his type was? All the women she'd known that he'd dated, including herself, were graduate students. If any of the women had had "upright boobs," they'd been covered by sweatshirts. Did women pay attention to what other women wore? Probably, just not Lily. Now she looked carefully at Constance. Her friend wore fitted denim shorts and a tailored white linen blouse. She could have been a gentleman farmer's daughter, with her mop of curls and tiny frame. Not to mention that emerald pendant she always wore.

"Did Jonas hang around with her?" Lily asked.

Both Jane and Betty shook their heads. "I don't really remember," Betty said.

"She'd moved back here from K.C. to take care of her mother," Jane said. "Little strokes, I think. Her father had died so there wasn't anyone else. Maureen was just so not small-town anymore. She wore sophisticated clothes and could get away with tight jeans. Most of the women in town her age had husbands and children. That was their job. Here was this career woman, even if her career was teaching, such a woman's job and all that. But you know, we all liked her. She'd done the right thing coming back to care for her mother. After a year or so of that, though, she began to droop."

Betty put in, "Her prettiness go, I don't know, less. She got skinny, like she'd forgotten to eat; her hair thinned, her skin turned sallow."

"Was that before or after her mom had to go into the home?" Jane said, offering around the sandwich platter. Constance took seconds and sneaked the remaining corner of her first sandwich to her dog. His tail whacked her ankle.

"You know, I just don't remember. My son graduated about then, my daughter got to be such a handful and Maureen Copeland just fell off my radar screen."

"But she was a nice woman?" Lily asked.

"Warm," Jane said.

"Caring," Betty added.

Lily asked, "How long had she been smoking?"

"Never saw her smoke," Jane said. "That's just her voice, like her mother's was, low for a woman. Same as Dorothy's voice, for that matter." She got up and cleared the table. When she didn't offer dessert or more iced tea, Lily took the hint.

"Well, we ought to be going if we're going to make it to Kansas City by dinner time," she said.

"Have you got our bill made out?" Constance asked.

Jane fished in her apron pocket and held out a piece of paper. Betty tried to take it but Constance got it first. "Jane was kind to take us on such short notice." Constance left the kitchen, returning in a moment with a check, which she handed it to Jane, who put it in the same pocket. "When we come back to Parthenon, may we stay with you again?" Constance asked. "I will be dreaming about your strawberry roll-ups and your Japanese flower arrangement. Where did you learn that?"

Betty's face softened. "I had Japanese friends in art school in Kansas City. You recognized the arrangement?"

Constance smiled. "So beautiful and simple. I looked at it and felt myself unwinding."

"Me, too." Jane held out her hand to Constance. "By all means, come see me again. Bring Bob."

But not me, Lily thought. And wondered why.

...

"I never knew any of his friends," Lily said.

They were heading east at seventy-five miles per hour on the Kansas Turnpike. The landscape was flat except for the tiniest rise far in the distance. Constance considered the possibility that she was seeing a heat mirage. Late afternoon sun burned through the passenger-side windows, pooling onto her face and shoulder. Bob draped over Lily like a dog-fur stole, his head propped on her arm. Constance had cranked the Subaru's air conditioner to "nuclear freeze"—she liked Dorothy's phrase—thinking that Lily must be overheated under all that fur. Constance could have sworn that Lily had been asleep, since her eyes were closed, head back against the headrest. "Jonas' friends, you mean?"

"Yes." Lily was silent for another mile or so.

"Did he have friends?" Constance prompted.

Lily said, "That's the thing. I don't know. He doesn't now. Or maybe he does and I don't know them." Bob stirred and she patted his flank with her free hand. "After we'd dated—God, that term seems weird to say—after he'd…"

Constance took her eyes off the road for a moment to check out Lily but couldn't tell whether she was happy or sad.

"Bedded me. Glazed my brain with sex." This time Lily shook her head. "Anyway, we stopped going out with the other grad students. I'd been friendly with a group of them, men and women. We'd get pizza or go out for coffee late in the day. Sometimes we'd get a glass of wine after we all emerged from our library carrells after sessions on our dissertations. Jonas would say that he didn't get to see me enough as it was, that he didn't want to waste time on other people. The others sort of faded out of our lives."

"Alden did the same. Controlling someone requires isolating her."

Another few miles flew by. The rise on the horizon began to look a bit like rolling hills. "Does northeastern Kansas have hills?"

"No idea," Lily said. "Why?"

Constance glanced at the compass that showed NE in green digital light from the bottom edge of the rearview mirror. "Well, we're going in the right direction."

"That's a switch." Lily's laugh sounded bitter.

"What is a switch?"

"That I might be going in the right direction."

"Lily, what are you talking about?"

Lily shifted in her seat. Bob shifted with her. His roast beef lunch had put him into a sound postprandial sleep. "You know, when Prairie Shores fired me, I didn't know anyone at school who would tell me why, what I'd done or not done, what the politics were that I'd missed. Academia is a who-do-you-know game. My closest friend at Prairie is a near-retirement biology professor. All he could do was guess. I don't know anyone else."

"You know me."

"But I had to get away from Jonas to meet you."

"Lily, what you are saying is that your husband is controlling and that he has been that way since day one."

Lily gave a quick nod.

"Did that not seem wrong to you?"

"Not until this summer. I never had lots of friends. In fact, the first time I had a clique to hang out with was in grad school. Before that, in high school and college, I was the oddball. I knew what interested me and went after it while the others were going after each other." She snorted. "I was a virgin before Jonas."

"Probably one reason he wanted you."

"What do you mean?"

"Are you sure you want to talk about this now, with me? Remember, I have never met Jonas."

"Yes. I'm sure. You know, I feel like beginning in about June, I've regained my peripheral vision. Like I can see around myself."

"You mean you have regained your perspective because you are away from Jonas?"

"Partly. But it's almost like I've gotten a pair of glasses. Things seem clearer. People."

"But what made you realize that Jonas had cut you off from your friends?"

"Betty and Jane and Dorothy. They've been friends for years, they know about each other and help each other."

"That kind of friendship is uncommon."

"I want it," Lily said. "I want friends. I liked going downstairs to the cafe this summer and knowing that Ed and the others would be sitting at their table in the window and that there was always a chair for me. Now I wish I'd gone more often. I liked it that Maria worried about me and made sure I ate well when she saw me. I want to worry about other people."

"Jonas?"

"I don't miss being manipulated into worrying about him and only him."

Lily inched over on her seat before gently sliding Bob's rump to rest in the cleared space. He resettled without waking up, curling so his head rested on her chest. She propped her chin on the dog's head, out of the hot light.

"Lily, why did Prairie Shores fire you?"

"Actually the department chair said that they'd reviewed me in advance and that tenure wasn't going to happen." Lily snorted. "That's before I knew my husband had fucked her to get her to do his bidding."

"But there must have been a committee. Why no tenure consideration, then?"

"No idea. I asked the one person on campus I thought I knew well enough and who might have known more, the dean of students. She said get out while the going was good."

"Let me get this straight," Constance said. She steered into the first curve the turnpike had offered in miles and miles. "You have been publishing about Wharton all along, right?"

"Of course. How do you think I got the NEH grant?"

"Good teacher evaluations?"

"Know what? I think they were too good. I like teaching and the students know it. But you and I both know the dirty little secret of college administration is that they don't value teaching, and if you do it too well you're regarded as a little nothing, someone who maybe should be teaching high school or junior college. Good teachers don't become campus stars, the professors that make colleges famous at least to each other. Those are researchers."

"But Lily, if your hunch about Wharton and James turns out, you will be famous."

"They don't know about my hunch. Only you do."

"Let me get this straight," Constance repeated. "You are publishing in respected journals and getting good teaching evaluations. You taught a course that no one else could teach. Yet they let you go?"

"After first having me interview my replacement, which they neglected to mention at the time."

"Does this not all strike you as irrational behavior on the part of Prairie Shores? National searches for new faculty cost money. New professors cost money until they begin to produce. It makes no sense."

Lily's chin rose. "No, it doesn't."

Constance thought that perhaps Lily was right about regaining peripheral vision. "What are you going to do about it?"

"The merest glimmer of an idea has come to me. It may be migraine aura, but nothing hurts. In fact, I feel better than I have in months. Years."

...

Northeast Kansas was hilly. The highway led them onto a bridge over a broad sweep of the Missouri River and past a sign for Kansas City, Missouri. Following Maureen's directions, they found themselves driving in an area of old houses and apartment buildings that would have looked at home in Lakeland or New Haven. They could have been in any midwestern river town, Constance supposed, but it also looked like any old New England town. Hills and big trees and the occasional brick-paved street. Then they got lost in a shopping area that looked Spanish, the stores upholstered in stucco and roofs of red tile. There was even a tall bell tower. "Ever been to Spain?" Constance asked Lily.

"No, just to England for some James research."

Constance pointed at the bell tower. "That looks like one I saw in Seville."

Lily pointed to a huge fountain with cast-metal sculpture horses galloping through water. "Where are we?"

Constance spotted a policeman directing traffic—the area seemed to lack stoplights—and asked for directions. He pointed to a steep hill. "Up there. Turn right when you get to the top of the hill. Keep going until you see some small houses facing a park. The houses all look alike. They used to be university housing, or something."

"University?" Constance asked.

"UMKC is right up there, too. University of Missouri at K.C." The cop turned back to his hand signaling, dismissing them. Constance did as he said and found six houses facing a spacious park. By her New England standards, the houses weren't small, situated behind deep front yards. Each was painted a biscuit color with brown trim. Maureen Copeland's house was on the far end. They parked in front, climbed a few steps from the street and another half-dozen steps to the front porch from the brick walk. Before ringing the doorbell, Constance turned around to look over at the park. Even on such a hot and humid afternoon, there was a breath of cool air coming from the thick stand of trees. A few tiny children played in a cleared area, watched over by a cluster of young mothers. Sounds of happy cries carried to the two women from across the street.

It was Lily who pushed the doorbell. Running footsteps could be heard from inside the house before the door was yanked open by a boy of about fourteen. He stared at Lily and Constance. "Who are you?"

Since Lily appeared to be struck mute at the sight of the boy, Constance asked, "Is this where Maureen Copeland lives? Do we have the right house?"

The boy turned and yelled, "Mom, ladies here to see you." He left them on the porch and disappeared up the staircase visible from the door.

Constance tapped Lily. "Are you all right?"

Lily swallowed then reached her hand to rub her eyes. She looked as though she'd seen a ghost.

Constance poked her. "What?"

"That boy." She swallowed again. "That boy looks just like Jonas."

Chapter 36

A tall woman wearing faded denim shorts and an orange tee shirt emerged from the back of the house. "Sorry about leaving you out there." She held open the screen door. "Come in. It's cool inside."

Lily stood where she was. "Who is that boy?"

Maureen hooted with the same deep laughter that Lily had heard from her on the phone. "You must be Lily, right?" She propped the screen door open with her back, reached out and took Lily's arm, pulling her inside. "That's my son, Peter. Yeah, he's the image of his father, isn't he? On the outside. I've been working since he was born to make sure the rest of him is as different as can be." She showed them through a living room to a cool windowed porch shaded by huge old trees. She turned to Constance, who had followed them through the house. "Didn't you say you had a dog?"

"He is in the car," Constance said.

"Lord, he'll broil alive out there. Bring him on in."

Before Constance left them, she saw Lily standing in the middle of the room as if all the air had been sucked out of her. Maureen was trying to lead her to a chair. "Honey, we've got a lot to talk about, but it isn't all bad," Maureen was saying. "Peter's a great kid and he knows I think so." For her part, Constance wondered just how many more surprises Lily could absorb. Perhaps that peripheral vision was a migraine after all.

...

Lily waited patiently for the room to stop spinning. She knew where she was and how she'd gotten there. After all, Maureen Copeland stood right in front of her, hands holding Lily's shoulders. "You all right, honey? Come on and sit down." Lily reached up and put a hand on Maureen's shoulder. The woman stood firm, shaking her long black braid so it slipped behind her back. "You feel like your world just slipped into a different axis?"

At that question, Lily snapped to and focused on the face that hovered above her. "How did you know?"

Maureen took Lily's hand and led her to a rattan chair cushioned in dark green chintz. "Happened to me about fifteen years ago. Been there, done that, got the son to prove it."

Lily sat on the edge of the chair. Maureen settled onto the sofa next to her.

Lily looked her over, as if she were a museum exhibit. The older woman didn't flinch. Her dark brown eyes, fine black brows, high cheekbones and olive skin reminded Lily of pictures she'd seen of the Native American women who'd run things while their men were away. Tough, maternal and absolutely beautiful. If her beauty had faded, as Dorothy and her friends contended, Lily couldn't imagine what she'd looked like before. "Why would you fall for an eighteen-year-old kid like Jonas?" Lily asked, then felt her face get hot.

Maureen's eyes crinkled when she gave that hoot of a laugh. "You cut right to the chase, don't you? Woman after my own heart." She stood up. "How about some iced tea?"

"Got anything stronger?" Lily said. She hadn't moved from the edge of the chair but now she could feel the cool of the cushion fabric under her hands. Reality was creeping back.

"I'll put something in the tea." Maureen left by a wide doorway set further down the room.

Lily allowed herself to slide back into the chair. She took in the room. The same dark chintz covered sofa and chair. The floor was polished light wood. Mini-blinds in a pale coppery color were pulled halfway down wide windows. Black and white prints that looked as if they might be by Thomas Hart Benton hung on the walls. There was a dark wood coffee table in front of the sofa. It was a serene space. Lily felt some calm seep in.

A paperback book lay on a corner of the table. She picked it up. *The Things They Carried* by Tim O'Brien, a book that had come out when she was in high school. She turned it over and read the back cover.

"It's pretty good," Peter said.

Lily started. When the boy took a step back, she was in familiar territory: getting to know another adolescent. Once a teacher, she thought, and said aloud, "I always meant to read this." The boy looked shy when she handed him the book. He turned it over in his hands. "Do you like to read?" She gestured toward the sofa.

The boy hesitated a moment before sitting near her. He said, "Yes," and looked as if he wanted to say something else.

Peter was already as tall as Jonas, which wasn't surprising, Lily thought, given that his mother must stand close to six feet. His hair was the same chestnut as his father's.

Lily had a hard time thinking of Jonas as a father. Jonas never wanted children. He'd made that clear to Lily before they were married. Then he changed his mind, expecting her to accommodate him immediately, as usual.

"I like to read," Peter blurted. "But..." He seemed to have run out of words again.

"I promise not tell anyone," Lily said. "I teach college students. By the time I meet them, some have decided that reading is okay, and some read only when they have to. The good writers, though, all love to read."

The boy nodded. His eyes were brown, though nowhere near as dark as his mother's. His brow, his chin, his nose were all Jonas'. But when he sat back on the sofa and stretched out his legs, Lily could see he would eventually be tall and rangy. Jonas would have been jealous. That thought must have made her smile because Peter smiled back. She pointed at the book in his hands. "What's it about? Besides Vietnam, I mean."

He thought for a long moment. "It's stories from the war. But it's hard to tell what's real and what's not. It's like the person talking isn't sure, himself."

"That's called the unreliable narrator, when you as the reader feel you can't trust the narrator's account."

"Unreliable. Yeah, that sounds right." He looked at the cover of the book. "It's on the reading list for school, which is why I got it. But I'm having trouble putting it down. It's like I can't get it out of my head."

"Because," Lily asked, leaning forward, "the author leaves so much up to you?"

Peter smiled again and his shyness evaporated. "Yeah, that's it. You know, everyone's always telling kids what to think and feel. But this O'Brien guy, he acts like he's talking to adults."

"He is. I'll bet he never expected his book to get adopted by schools. What year will you be in?"

"Freshman year of high school. It's going to be a pain being the newbie again."

Lily laughed. "Now you know how my college freshmen feel, only they're in worse shape."

"Worse? How can that be?"

"Just a few months before they land in my classes, they were high school seniors, stars in their firmament. They probably enjoyed healthy cases of senioritis. Then they get to college and haven't a clue."

"I don't know if I could go away to college." Peter's voice was low, as if he didn't want his mother to hear.

"Because?" Lily asked.

"I don't think I could stand cafeteria food all the time." He made a face.

"My students complain about it. Sometimes they even write in their journals about it. Doesn't make me want to eat with them." She grinned at him. "Of course, there is a solution to that problem."

"There is? What?" Peter sat forward, as if whatever Lily might tell him was of utmost importance. Jonas did that, too. It was part of his charm. Peter, though, looked not just attentive but hopeful, making Lily feel she'd better say something brilliant.

"Learn to cook."

"Yeah, but would there be a place to cook for myself?"

"If you can cook, people will provide you kitchen space, I guarantee you."

"Good." He sat back, looking satisfied. "Mom's teaching me. I make a pretty good broiled chicken, but my salads suck. The lettuce is always too wet."

"Make salads without lettuce."

His look said her banal comment sounded brilliant.

His mother came in, carrying a tray with four glasses of ice tea. "Oh, there you are, Peter." She set the tray on the table and pointed to the glass closest to her. "That one's yours. I left it plain for you." Peter walked behind Lily's chair to pick up the book and his iced tea. At the living room doorway he turned to say, "It was nice talking with you," and departed.

"What a great kid," Lily said. She felt buoyed by having Peter take her seriously.

"I told you all of it isn't bad," Maureen said. "I didn't feel that way when I found out I was pregnant."

Lily covered her mouth and leaned forward to see if Peter could hear them. Maureen said, "No secrets in this house. None. Peter knows who his father is, knows what happened, knows I chose to have him and love him. Not that that last part was a choice. Of course, he also thinks his father is dead."

Chapter 37

Right at that moment, the idea of Jonas dead held a certain appeal. Then Lily wouldn't have to figure out why he wanted his hometown to think him dead. Then she wouldn't have to figure out how he managed to pull it off without changing his name, without doing more than moving away. The thought of her husband made her body feel too heavy to move. But there was Maureen, an earlier victim of Jonas, sitting on the sofa a few feet from her. Maureen hooked a foot around the base of the coffee table, pulling it to one side. Then, as her son had, she stretched out her legs, sat back and sipped tea. Maureen didn't look as if she were too tired to move, though she had more reason than Lily. Or maybe not.

Lily sat up, her movements careful. She picked up the cold glass and sipped. Behind the taste of tea was a lemon flavor that was richer than lemon juice. "Lemon liqueur?" she asked.

"Limoncello. It's Italian, mostly sugar. If that doesn't do the trick, I'll pull out the hard stuff. But I don't think we're there yet."

A laugh bubbled up from Lily's chest, breaking through her inertia. "I don't know where we are. But I get to ask the first question."

"Why?"

"Because I found you?"

Maureen cocked her head, then nodded.

"What made you fall for an eighteen-year-old kid like Jonas?"

Maureen's gaze shifted toward the living room, where her son had gone. It came to Lily that Peter was four years younger than Jonas had been when he'd gotten Maureen pregnant.

"Fall for Jonas?" Maureen put the tea glass down on the coffee table but picked it up again a second later. "That's not what happened." This time she put the tea down and left it there. She turned on Lily. "Have you noticed that Jonas is a control freak?"

Lily jerked back before she caught herself. This woman wasn't angry at her. She wasn't angry at all. But her words cut. "Only recently. June, in fact."

Maureen looked at her in disbelief. "You're kidding. You must be oblivious."

"Until recently," Lily said. "June, in fact."

Maureen smiled. "Sounds like we've got some stories to tell each other."

"Okay," Lily said, "we agree that Jonas is a control freak. How did he take control of you?"

The older woman looked thoughtful. "There are some people who can sense the weak points in others. School bullies do that. Jonas wasn't a bully, don't misunderstand me. His talent was sensing the bigger picture of a person's life. He could tell when a person was in charge of her life or when her life had taken charge of her, leaving her weak and vulnerable."

Lily tried to connect Maureen's analysis to the Jonas she knew. Had she, Lily, been weak? Vulnerable? She'd never felt that way. It was more that Jonas had a plan that included her, a plan that settled an open question in her life. Though perhaps that was her weakness.

"I'd been teaching here in Kansas City since the time I'd qualified," Maureen was saying. "I had no interest in moving back to Parthenon. It wasn't as nice a place then as it is now. If you think of your basic dusty one-street rural town, that was it. A place to leave for good, visit at Christmas only if you can't think of a reason not to. But then my father died.

"My mother began to fail almost immediately, though looking back I think she probably had the beginnings of dementia while Dad was alive but he hid it from me." She ran her hand over her mouth, her attention somewhere outside the porch. "I'm it for my family. No siblings, cousins or other useful relatives. I was spending all my time on the Kansas Turnpike. When Dorothy Cranmer offered me a job teaching chemistry, I grabbed it. It just seemed like that would simplify my life." Her attention came back to the room, the Benton prints, the door to the kitchen. "I'd just bought this house. I don't know if you noticed, but there are only six of them. I always wanted to live in one. I had my dream job here in Kansas City, teaching honors science and chemistry, living in my dream house, even if I could barely afford furniture after paying the mortgage every month." She shrugged. "It took maybe five minutes to find a UMKC couple who wanted to rent it. I packed up and left in about ten minutes. Otherwise I knew I couldn't have done it, gone back to Parthenon.

"So there I was, teaching average kids in my old high school, spending evenings at the nursing home making sure my mom was fed and bathed and treated properly. I was on automatic pilot: when the alarm clock threw the switch every morning, I went into action. For me, action took the place of feeling, if not of thinking. I wore myself out every day. It turned out my mother didn't have Alzheimer's. She'd get these little strokes that were coming more and more often. Mom couldn't remember who I was. She called me Mama. It was like her memory regressed further and further, the forward parts cut off with a sharp blade. About six months before she died, she went from being a mean crazy old lady to a delightful child. I cried every night."

Without thinking about it, Lily leaned forward to take her hand. It was cool and strong. Maureen squeezed Lily's hand before gently removing her own.

"Jonas later told me he'd watched me all fall semester. Then he signed up for chem, which began in January. He wasn't an exceptional student, shall we say, and took to stopping by after school to ask questions. Before I knew it, he knew all about my mother. My treadmill of a daily schedule. Then one evening late he showed up on my doorstep. I was so tired it didn't even occur to me how inappropriate it was for a student to come to a teacher's house, not to mention for the teacher to ask him in. I gave him a Coke. He asked me about my day. He listened. He was the only one who listened, or the only one I gave the chance to listen."

"Having someone listen is addictive," Lily said.

"It's addictive," Maureen agreed. "It's comforting. It's soft and warm. It's sexy." She stopped.

"Suddenly this fairly average-looking kid…" Lily prompted.

"Yeah. He kissed me. I don't know where he learned about sex, but he knew his stuff. He became a necessity in my life."

"Then he was gone," Lily added. She knew how much Jonas liked to withhold that which he'd always before enthusiastically offered.

"Worse. He was still in Parthenon. It was the end of his senior year, he'd been accepted to that Ivy League-ish school out east and he had three months to watch me want him." This time Maureen took up her iced tea and drank half the glass before replacing it. "It was only years later that I got it that that's what he enjoyed the most. More than sex with an older woman.

"My mother died at the end of that July. I buried her in the graveyard behind the church that faces Parthenon's Main Street. All I can remember of the funeral was Jonas standing in the front row of mourners, dressed in black, watching me with this little smile. He left town a few weeks later. A few weeks after that, I realized that the reason my period had stopped wasn't because of all the stress I'd been under. I sold my mother's house and most of her possessions, told Dorothy I wouldn't be back to Parthenon High that fall and skedaddled."

She smiled for the first time since beginning her story. "Peter was born in December at Menorah Hospital, which used to be less than a mile from here. He was my Christmas present, the best one I've ever had."

Lily leaned toward her. "But you never told anyone in Parthenon?"

"Far as I know, no one there knew about Jonas and me."

"They don't," Lily said. "Well, Dorothy may have an inkling, but she protects you."

"I ought to invite her here for Thanksgiving or something. She's good people."

"When did you go back to teaching?" Lily asked.

"The following year. There was enough money left over in my parents' estate for me to take off work. I gave myself from the time Peter was born until the following August to figure out how to be a single mother. I thought if I could work that out then I could become a working mother."

"You learn a lot about kids from teaching," Lily said. "I'm an only child, too. My folks are dreadful parents, so it was when I became a teaching assistant in grad school that I started learning about kids, what they're about, what they respond to." She shut up then, embarrassed. This wasn't something that she'd talked about to anyone before except Nate. Certainly not Jonas. "Do you still teach chemistry?"

"Would you believe I'm an assistant principal?" She shook her head. "I don't know why I took my required graduate hours in administration. Soon as there's an opening for principal, I'm a shoo-in." This time her smile was self-deprecating. "Easier to pay the mortgage on a principal's salary."

"Or pay for college."

"Phew," she laughed, "you're right on the mark there." The laugh ceased. She leaned back on the sofa, arms crossed. "Okay, your turn. Why did Jonas arrange to be dead?"

"Uh-uh," Lily said, shaking her finger at Maureen. "Before we can figure out why we have to figure out how."

Maureen watched Lily for what seemed a long time. Lily struggled to meet her eyes. Finally Maureen said, "We?"

"You. Me. Constance."

"We," the older woman said. "'We' would make for a huge change in my life. Uh-uh. No way. I like it just fine the way it is."

Lily said firmly, "We. We need to figure out how Jonas pulled off having Parthenon think he's dead. We need to figure out where he figured out how to do that. Jonas is just not that original a thinker."

"Don't get ahead of yourself," Maureen said. "Seems to me you know my story but haven't volunteered yours." One eyebrow rose.

"How about I tell you on the way. How do you feel about Parthenon in August?"

"Why are you in such an all-fired hurry after all these years?" The other eyebrow rose.

"Let's say my husband has finally gotten my attention. He had to stalk me, lie to me about his family and maybe a couple of other more important things. He's up to something. We have to find out Jonas' story, and we have just a few weeks before I have a grant deadline and you probably have to go back to being an assistant principal."

Chapter 38

Maureen shook her head. "You don't need me for whatever quest you're on." When Lily made as if to stand, Maureen said, "Sit down. We're not done here."

Surprised, Lily sat, her body stiff. The affable woman had disappeared, replaced by, well, one tough broad. Lily smiled at the thought.

"What's funny?" Maureen demanded.

Feeling like a student caught without a hall pass, Lily invented an excuse. "You sound like my high school principal."

"What a surprise." Maureen didn't smile. "I answered your questions. Now I have some questions of my own. First, where did Jonas meet you?"

"Grad school. He was working on a Ph.D. in psychology. My area is literature."

Maureen sat back. "Holy shit." She stared at Lily.

To Lily, the woman's dark eyes looked horrified. "What? Are you all right?"

"Just bear with me a moment." Maureen leaned forward, forearms on knees. "Let's table for later consideration why a master manipulator like Jonas felt an advanced psychology degree would be useful. For now, tell me, did Jonas approach you first or did you approach him?"

"He went after me. Definitely. I kept fending him off."

"Until he wore you down."

Lily nodded. Where was Maureen going with these questions? But her mouth was set so firmly and her eyes glittered so brightly that the hair on Lily's arms stood up. "What? Why are you so angry all of a sudden?" Lily wanted to curl into her chair but straightened her back instead. Her tone matched Maureen's. "You're scaring me. Tell me. Now."

"Lillian Atwood, Jonas' mother?"

Lily nodded.

"She earned a Ph.D. in literature from the University of Kansas before meeting Jonas' father." Those black eyes shifted, appearing to look over Lily's head. But Lily knew she was looking inward, probing into the past. "His father was a charmer. Good looking, sexy. Joel Atwood had been through every woman in town. But as soon as he spotted Lillian, he wouldn't leave her alone. He got her pregnant, knowing her family would insist she marry him. Then he owned her. She had to depend on him. According to Dorothy, who could write the history of Parthenon, Kansas, Joel hooked that poor woman. He got her addicted to him and left her over and over. Each time she'd beg him to return. He got it all—every woman in town and Lillian. Joel turned her into the ghost you described. Jonas watched the whole drama. He idolized his father."

• • •

Constance opened the front door of the house, gratefully letting Bob and herself into the air conditioning. Kansas in August was no song from a musical, no matter what Rogers and Hammerstein thought. Bob's tongue hung out the side of his mouth and his curly blonde coat looked wilted. Constance set off in search of a bowl of water for him. She had started toward the sound of Maureen's voice in the sun room when she heard her say, "Lily? Lily? What's going on?"

Bob got to Lily before Constance did. Lily's face had taken on that pea-green cast that Constance remembered from two nights ago when they had found Jonas stalking her in Guilford. Bob jumped onto the chair to lean against Lily, his eyes focused on her face. Constance demanded, "Maureen, where's Lily's purse? Where did she leave it?"

Maureen leapt up and bounded out of the room, returning in seconds with the purse. Constance dumped the contents on the coffee table, grabbing the vial of pills from the mess. She handed a pill and the remains of the tea to Lily.

"No, I can't. There was alcohol in the tea. Can't mix the two."

"How much booze has she had?" Constance said to Maureen.

"Less than a teaspoon. I'll get plain water."

Constance thrust the pill at Lily. "Take it. We'll keep an eye on you. Otherwise the migraine will take hold."

Bob nudged Lily's chin with his nose. She held out her hand for the tablet. Maureen returned with a glass. Lily swallowed the pill, leaned back and closed her eyes. Bob leaned back with her, his head on her shoulder.

"Bob needs water." Constance pulled Maureen out of the room and into the kitchen. "What the hell did you say to her?"

Maureen's face had also turned pale, giving it a yellow cast. She sat down. "That Jonas' mother had a Ph.D. in literature, that his father turned her into what she is on purpose. That Jonas adored his father."

Constance was opening cabinets at random, looking for a bowl. Maureen ignored her or maybe didn't see her, since the other woman's head was in her hands. Finally Constance spotted a stainless steel mixing bowl, which she filled with water. On her way past Maureen, she said, "Migraine. It comes on her like this. It looks worse than it is."

Maureen looked up. "She seems like such a tough little thing."

"She is, though she failed to realize it until recently." Constance led the way out of the kitchen.

Lily still leaned back in the chair, eyes closed. Her color didn't look much better but the fact that Bob had relaxed his vigilance and leaned his head on her shoulder communicated much to Constance. She put the water on the floor beside the coffee table. Bob hopped down and took a long drink before returning to Lily's side. Lily said, "It's okay," before opening her eyes. To Constance, she said, "What were we talking about in the restaurant the other night that set me off?"

"We were debating, as I recall, why Jonas picked you instead of a rich woman like me."

"Jonas didn't care about money," Maureen said.

"He does now." Lily sat up. "He spends every dime we make."

"Which is why I think his sudden departure from Prairie Shores is significant," Constance said. To Maureen, she said, "This woman is one of the best researchers I have ever met when it comes to the lives of dead authors. But she is missing something crucial in the story of her own life."

Lily giggled. Constance frowned; Maureen cocked her head. "You know," Lily said, "the doctor told me to figure out what triggered my migraines."

Maureen moved behind Lily's chair, her hands on the chair back. Over Lily's head, her eyes met Constance's. "Peter's been wanting to visit my home town."

Constance said, "That child's face will raise a lot of questions in Parthenon, Kansas."

Maureen shrugged. "I can handle it. So can Peter, I expect."

Lily added, "So can I."

When Constance restocked Lily's bag, she removed a few migraine tablets without Lily's noticing and wrapped them in a fresh tissue. Later she put them in her own bag, just in case.

Chapter 39

They left the rental car in Maureen's garage. Maureen drove them in her white Ford Explorer, Constance in the front passenger seat, Peter scratching behind Bob's ears in the backseat, with Lily leaning her head on the dog, eyes closed. By the time they'd cleared the Kansas City suburbs, Lily began to feel better. They'd caught the headache before its tentacles could claw their way in. She opened her eyes cautiously to the afternoon sun. Her sunglasses cut the glare enough to make it bearable.

"You okay?" Peter asked. "Mom said you have a colossal headache." He kept his voice low, and Lily suspected that his mother had also told him to be quiet and not bother the sick lady. She sat up and smiled at him, joining him in his rhythmic scratching of Bob's head.

"I'm all right now."

"I overheard most of what you guys said out on the porch."

"I thought you might," Lily said. "At your age, I did the same thing. Otherwise you never quite know what's going on in your life."

"Mom tells me everything. But sometimes not right away."

"You think she waits until she feels you can handle the information?"

He ducked his head. "Yeah. That's it."

"But most of the time, you're just waiting for her to get around to telling you."

"Yeah," he repeated. "So can I ask you a question?"

"May I ask one first?" Lily said. The two women in the front seat were talking, not paying any attention to what was going on behind them, or perhaps they couldn't hear anything over the road and engine noise.

Peter said, "I guess."

"What did you already know that your mother and I talked about?"

The boy looked out the window at the flat green and tan landscape. It was an event when a tree whipped by. Without looking at her, he said, "I knew about my father getting Mom pregnant with me. I knew my grandfather had been murdered and that nobody ever figured out who did it."

"Did you know already what we said about your father?"

Peter turned and looked her in the eye. "My mother said he was charming, that everyone loved him. But she said it turned out he couldn't be trusted. Is that true?"

Lily kept herself from blinking, unwilling to break eye contact even from behind dark glasses. Peter was trying to figure out who and what he could count on, where he was safe, how far he could go. A lot of her students were like Peter, even though they were at least four years older. "In my experience, it's true."

The boy chewed his lip. "You married my father."

"Yes. Five years ago."

"So he's not dead."

"Very much alive, as of a few days ago. I didn't know his hometown thought he'd died until I went there yesterday."

Peter chewed his lip again, then seemed to consciously stop, as if he'd been told not to do that. Instead, he propped his chin on Bob's head. The boy gave Lily a considering look.

He's debating how much he can ask me, she thought. How much I'll tell him. Despite his resemblance to Jonas, she found herself caring for this boy. He was not a Jonas, Jr. He was what Jonas could have been in different circumstances. Though on the face of it Peter's life as the fatherless child of a single mother should have been rockier than that of Jonas, who had known and lived with—on and off—both parents. "You know what I tell my students?" she asked him.

"Your college students?"

Lily could tell that he wanted to be treated like a college student. She nodded.

"What do you tell them?"

"There is no such thing as a stupid question. That if they ask a question and I don't know the answer, I'll tell them that, too." She waited to see if she'd been right about his wanting to ask something. She thought he'd want to know why his father had disappeared. She couldn't have been more wrong.

"Do you think I'm like him?" His voice was so low she could barely make out the words.

"You look like him." She thought there might be tears welling up in the boy's eyes before he turned his face away. "I recognized you right away this afternoon. But other than that, you couldn't be more different."

He didn't say anything.

"Your father is a handsome man. But you're old enough to know that outside looks don't necessarily reflect the inside of a person, what someone has to offer other people."

"So how'm I different from him? From my father." Peter had pulled the dog toward him, so the word "father" blew through Bob's fur. The dog licked him. Briefly Lily wondered why Bob treated Peter as one of his own people. Had Constance introduced the two while Lily was fending off migraine?

"Your father is, well, he seems to be missing some things in his personality. I'm only just now figuring that out." What that said about her, Lily preferred not to consider just yet. "You're empathetic. He's not. It's a crucial difference."

"What's empathetic?" She barely caught the words, spoken as they were into the dog's back.

"It means you can tell what other people are feeling and, more importantly, that you can feel what other people feel and care what they feel. Your father cares only about what he wants."

When the boy turned to her, in his expression Lily caught a glimpse of what he would be like as a man. His mouth was set, his chin firm. He suddenly seemed someone not to tangle with, someone like his mother who commanded respect. "You don't love him," he said. "You regret marrying him." His eyes opened wide. "Oh, jeez, I'm sorry. I shouldn't have said that." The kid Peter still was had returned.

"I don't mind," Lily said. "That's what I'm talking about, empathy. You picked up on my feelings. See?"

"I'm not sure I like it."

Lily leaned over to pat Bob on the head, which put her hand near the boy's chin. When she sat back, Peter was watching her, more with interest than embarrassment. "Not sure you like being empathetic?" she asked.

"Yeah."

"Ignorance is bliss?"

"Mom says ignorance is dangerous."

"No kidding." She sighed. "You don't have a choice about being empathetic or not. It's what you choose to do with the information you're sensing that's important. My rule stands: all questions are reasonable ones."

"Okay, then when did you figure out that you didn't love my father?" He used the words of the fourteen-year-old with the directness of the man. Lily didn't have any experience with boys his age, but she thought he might well be mature for a soon-to-be high school freshman.

"I haven't felt right around Jonas for some time now. He did something mean to me that I found out about in June. Then I spent the summer away from him. Then it turned out he was stalking me."

"When he could have just called you or something?"

"Exactly." Except she'd routed his calls to voicemail. But still.

"Then when Mom told you about what my grandfather did to my grandmother, why did you turn green?"

His question blindsided Lily. Oh, yes, this young man had empathy and to spare.

When Lily didn't answer immediately, Peter said, "Was it because you feel like my father is trying to do the same thing to you?"

"Yes. I felt stupid not to have noticed."

"But you don't have any children."

"I—" Lily started to say. Could she tell him? Should she?

"If you don't have any children, then how could my father do that to you?"

"You mean control me?"

He nodded.

Lily found that she'd caught her top lip between her teeth. She let go, but her teeth insisted on clenching as her hand drifted toward her waist.

"You said there's no such thing as a stupid question. That you'd tell me if you didn't know the answer." He was leaning back against the car window, arms crossed. Both he and Bob watched her.

This was an important question for him. "Are you sure you want to know?"

He looked scared but said yes.

"Jonas—your father—began insisting that we begin a family last year. Around Christmas he got his way."

"You don't look pregnant." Peter's face and ears turned red.

"Early in March I lost the baby." This time the tears were in her eyes. "It was a boy."

"I'm sorry. I shouldn't have made you answer." He shook his head, eyes wide, looking scared.

Lily forced herself to smile. "No, you were right. We all have to stand by our words." She swallowed hard. "Here's the thing. Your father was angry that I lost the baby. He insisted we try again as soon as possible."

"Oh," Peter said. "Oh. Got it. No empathy." He frowned. "You could say he's consistent, though."

"He's what?" Was this really a fourteen-year-old?

"Consistent?"

"What brought you to that assessment?"

"He knows what he wants and goes after it. If what he wants happens to be a person, he doesn't care what happens to the person. Look what happened to my mom. Look—there's me."

"Yes." This boy was way ahead of her. "And?" she asked.

"Well, and he chooses really strong women and fools them."

Miles ahead of her.

They'd pulled into a rest stop. Maureen and Constance were turned toward them.

"You lost your child," Maureen said.

"I would have been next," Lily said. "He intended me to be Lillian."

"Yes," Maureen said.

Chapter 40

"What are you talking about?" Constance said.

"Lily was talking about my father because I asked her," Peter said. "If he's not dead, will I meet him?"

Maureen and Lily looked at each other. It seemed to Lily almost as if they suddenly shared parenthood of this young man. Lily raised her eyebrows, and, still facing Maureen, cocked her head slightly toward Peter. Maureen frowned but nodded slowly. To her son, she said, "Could you handle it if your father asked you to do something that you didn't think was the right thing to do?"

Now it was Peter who took his time answering, eyes on his mother. Finally, he said, "Do you think I know the difference between right and wrong?"

Without hesitation, Maureen said, "Yes. But sometimes adults do things that seem right at the time but in fact cross the line into wrong. Do you think you can tell the difference?"

"I don't know," the boy admitted. "But I have to try."

"Yes," Maureen said again, "you do. Are you ready to find out how your father fooled everyone in his hometown, including me, into thinking he was dead?"

"I think," Peter said, once again scratching Bob behind the ears, "that why he did it may be what's important." Then he shrugged. "You know, it didn't make all that much difference to me thinking he was dead, because one way or another he wasn't around for me."

Bob whimpered to be let out of the car, bumping his head against Peter's hand. Constance clipped on the leash and handed it to Peter. The boy solemnly escorted Bob out of the car. The women watched him for a second before getting out themselves.

Lily was thinking that Peter was perhaps too wise a child for his own good. He obviously sensed other people's reactions and emotions, ones that he hadn't had to deal with himself and might not yet be equipped to deal with.

But what he had said was exactly true. It was more important to understand why Jonas needed Parthenon to believe him dead than how he'd accomplished it. She needed to know both why and how. It was as though she were armoring herself in a hurry. The four of them would stay the night in Parthenon, then she and Constance would be going to Lakeland. She wasn't looking for a confrontation with Jonas. But it was imperative to find out what he was up to.

Which reminded her. Lily looked at her watch; it was after six o'clock, and still hot as hell. She pulled out her cell phone, not really expecting to find a signal out here in the middle of nowhere. But somewhere in those wheat fields a farmer must have leased land for a cell tower, because she was able to reach Bethany's home number. A man answered the phone, which for some reason surprised Lily until she remembered that her student lived at home. Calm, she told herself. "May I speak to Bethany?" she said while relaxing her shoulders and neck.

"Who's calling, please?" the voice demanded.

"Lily Atwood."

"Does my daughter know you?"

"Yes. I was her English professor."

"I never heard of professors calling their students."

This wasn't the first time Lily had heard a parent say something like this. Usually when she had to call a parent, it was with bad news about a student who had disappeared from her class. If the dean of students didn't know anything, Lily would call home to find out what was going on. "It happens all the time. Didn't I meet you when Bethany came for her scholarship interview two years ago?"

"Short woman? Long black hair? Black dress?"

"That's me. You have a good memory."

He laughed. "You were the only woman who interviewed Beth. Wait a moment while I get her."

"Hello? Is that you, Dr. Atwood? Why are you calling? I mean, I'm thrilled that you're calling and all, but—"

"Why is your professor calling not once but twice in two days?"

"Well, yes."

Lily wanted to warn Bethany to stay away from Jonas, in case he took it into his mind to visit her again. In case? She shook her head to clear it. If Maureen was the first, then Lily was the second, and it looked as though Bethany was the third. Jonas was getting older and the women he chose were getting younger. She had to find out what was going on and why. In the meantime she didn't want Bethany to be next.

"Dr. Atwood? Are you still there?"

"Do you remember when I called you last time that I asked you about the man you wrote about, the one who showed up at your pool?"

"Sure. Why?"

"Has he been back?"

"I haven't seen him. Why?"

"Because I've discovered that he's a stalker," Lily said. "I don't know why he's stalking you, but I know he is."

"Stalking me? You mean he came to the pool to see me? Me?" The girl's voice had thinned. "Oh my God." The last three words were muffled, as if she'd clamped a hand over her mouth to keep the rest of the house from hearing.

"I'm sorry to frighten you," Lily said, then changed her mind mid-sentence, "no, I'm not. I want you to be wary."

"You want me to be afraid? Dr. Atwood, right now I feel like running or hiding under my bed. My heart is racing."

"Oh, hell, I'm sorry. I should have told you this face-to-face, but it couldn't wait." Lily stopped to think. Scaring the girl was the wrong way to go about this, when what she needed was for Bethany to think rationally. "When you're in your hometown, you feel safe, right?"

"Sure. I know everyone, everyone knows me. The place is so small we all watch out for each other." She took a long breath. "But right now I feel like he could be looking in the windows. He's out there, right?"

"No, he's back in Lakeland." Lily hoped that was the case. Bethany caught her out.

"How do you know?"

"Because the police put him on a plane to Chicago last night. No, night before last."

"I hear you can drive from Chicago to here." The student's voice was angry. Lily couldn't recall her ever employing sarcasm before.

"I know him." *No you don't*, Lily's mind lectured her. *You don't know the man you married.* "Until I tell you otherwise, I want you to make sure that he doesn't have the chance to talk to you alone. If he comes to your pool again, make sure to join that crowd of young mothers or that Cary is there." She paused. Speaking more softly, she added, "I'm serious, Beth. This isn't a story. This is real life."

There was a long silence. Lily looked around for some wood to knock on.

"Should I tell my father?"

"Is he the sort of man who will stay calm, who'll stand by you?"

"No, he won't stay calm, but yes, he always stands by me. I'll ask my mom how to tell him. He needs to know. Maybe a family conference. We do that for something important. Dr. Atwood, who is this guy? How do you know him? How do you know he's stalking me?"

Lily knew she had to answer. When she opened her mouth nothing came out. She cleared her throat, looked up at the sky, which was a blue so bright it seemed to have lavender in its depths. Over by the rest stop's little brick building, Maureen and Peter were talking. Constance had walked Bob into the shade of a handful of trees near the sign that said "Dog area." A week ago she didn't know two of the humans or the dog, yet suddenly all were necessary to her life. Oz, she thought. If I ever get a dog, I'll call him Oz. In Hebrew, Oz meant brave.

"The man who is stalking you—his name is Jonas. Jonas Atwood."

She heard a gasp.

"Isn't that your husband?"

"Yes, but how do you know that?"

"I saw him once at Prairie Shores, coming out of your office."

"But I don't recall Jonas ever visiting me in my office."

"Oh, you weren't there. But the department secretary greeted him when he passed her desk."

"Had he been in my office?"

"Must have been, since he was coming out of it. In fact, he locked the door."

"Where…" Lily started to ask, but Beth interrupted.

"Your husband is stalking me? How do you know? Oh, wait, because he came here, he came to my pool. But how did you know it was your husband? How did he know where to find me? How would he know my name?"

"He worked in the college's finance office until October of last year."

"So much for the privacy of student information," Bethany said, sounding more adult and in charge than Lily had heard her before. "That explains how he found me. But how do you know he was looking for me? That he didn't just happen to drive through town, raising money or something?"

"He had your picture on his cell phone. It was the screen wallpaper."

"Oh. My. Lord."

"Bethany, it would have been better to tell you all this in person," Lily repeated, "but I was worried that he'd get to you before I did."

"Dr. Atwood, I'm not only telling my family, I'm telling the police chief."

"A wonderful idea." Lily was petrified at the thought.

"He's my uncle."

"Even better."

"Dr. Atwood, is it dangerous, knowing you?"

"Me, no. Jonas, yes. Yes, it is."

"How awful."

Lily could only agree, but merely said, "Beth, call Cara and tell her all this. She has experience with this sort of thing. And she has a good sound head on her shoulders."

"I've already told her about the guy. Now we can connect the dots."

Excellent, Lily thought. The two working together created a strong fortress against the Jonases of this world. "Beth, I'll call again tomorrow."

"Checking in?"

"If you don't mind."

"I'll call you every day. How's that?"

"A weight off my mind." She could have bitten her tongue as soon as she mouthed the cliché. A weight off her mind, sure, because she'd transferred part of the weight to this nineteen-year-old girl.

"You know," Bethany said, "I was getting really bored here and a little, I don't know, bothered because I could never be alone. Now I'm glad I'm home." She laughed, much to Lily's surprise. "No problem, Dr. A, arranging for a bodyguard around here."

"You'll be all right?"

"I'll be all right," but her voice had turned shrill. "Whether my father will let me return to a college that gave my information to a stalker, I don't know."

"Remind your father that the stalker has moved on to another college."

"Yeah, like that'll make a difference." She sighed. "Okay, here goes. Talk to you tomorrow, Dr. A."

• • •

This time the text message Jonas received read "Get your ass home. Urgent." It was from the phone of Audrey King.

Now there was a name out of his past, one full of the best connotations. His father had introduced Audrey to him when he was fifteen or sixteen. He'd brought Jonas up to the loft in the house Joel had designed, the loft that truly designated Joel's house as a bachelor pad. There was this gorgeous woman, maybe ten years older than Jonas. She looked him over carefully before she told Joel, who was standing behind him, "He'll do. Now get out of here."

Jonas had no idea what was going on. He turned his head to ask, "Dad?"

"Stay here with Audrey. She needs to teach you a few things."

"Like what?" There was a swishing sound. His attention shot back to the woman. Had she done what he thought? No way.

"Jonas?" She turned her back to him. "First thing you learn is how to undress a woman. Unzip me."

Jonas' hands shook so hard that he grabbed the zipper pull too hard, almost toppling her over on him. Her laugh rang out. "All right. Let me show you."

She ran her hands over his chest, unbuttoning one button after another but so slowly, too slowly.

That was half his lifetime ago but he remembered every second. So Audrey wanted his ass back in Parthenon?

Chapter 41

Jane Budd appeared delighted to see Constance and Bob while treating Lily and Maureen like strangers. Peter seemed to mystify her. She understood that he was Maureen's son. What she didn't seem to want to understand was that there was a reason he looked just like Jonas Atwood. "But Jonas is dead," she said more than once.

They were all in Jane's kitchen, which was so large that four humans and one canine didn't begin to crowd it. She sheltered behind her butcher-block and marble-topped kitchen island. Constance, who had called ahead to make sure that Jane could house them for the night, stepped over to her. Reaching up to put an arm loosely over the older woman's shoulders, Constance said, "But you know that Jonas is alive. That is why we came here in the first place."

"What do you want from me?" Jane blurted before covering her mouth with both hands.

"Not to upset you," Constance said so softly that Lily could just hear her. "Would you like to show us to our rooms?"

The look on their hostess' face said this was the last thing Jane wanted to do. What she said was, "You know that none of the bedroom doors lock?"

"Is that important?" Maureen asked.

Jane started, as if Maureen were a statue that had suddenly found speech. The older woman darted glances around the kitchen, seeing everyone watching her, including boy and dog, who had settled onto the floor next to the table. She smoothed her gray hair into place, saying, "Oh, what am I saying? Of course I'm delighted that you're all here. Follow me. Constance, would you like the same room you had last night, the one that leads to the garden?" When Constance nodded, Jane bustled out.

Bustled, Lily thought, that's a word that Edith Wharton would use, something she'd probably seen many times, what with women then wearing long skirts. The verb bustle was onomatopoeic and the noun described that dreadful padding over the fanny that was fashionable when Wharton was young.

Jane wore the same denim skirt as before—evidently washed, since it was flour-free—but it seemed to Lily that she should be wearing a shirtwaist and long skirt with a chatelaine, a chain holding a bunch of keys around the waist. I must be getting tired, she decided, my mind is wandering.

Constance had dropped back to Lily. "Is she not something out of a romance novel? Is there not something mysterious about her?" she murmured.

"I was just thinking she's an anachronism."

Constance chuckled. "Mrs. Danvers?"

"Let's hope not. Otherwise doors without locks could be a problem."

"Not with Bob around."

"Can I bunk with you?"

"Sure. The room has twin beds," Constance said. "You scared?"

"Uneasy. Jane's giving me the creeps. Lately, that's saying a lot."

Walking down the hallway, Constance said, "My family's housekeeper when I was little actually wore a chatelaine. Now I wonder where she got it. It must have been a pretty valuable antique."

"Your family had a housekeeper?" was all Lily could say.

"Of course, the current one wears jeans and a tee shirt," Constance went on. "Looks pretty good on him."

"Him?" Lily said. Constance rarely gave glimpses into what her home life had been like growing up. Lily decided her friend was trying to distract her.

"Him. They pay him more than the Beinecke pays me. He earns every penny."

"Constance, what would it take to convince a small town like Parthenon that a former resident had died?"

"Later. After dinner. How is your head?"

"Fine. Where's your sense of urgency?"

"One step behind my growling stomach. When was the last time we ate today?

When Lily couldn't answer, Constance said, "This morning. Here, out on the porch. Give me the line about armies fighting on their stomachs?"

"Armies travel on their stomachs," Lily automatically answered.

"Close enough. Food first. Then we shall marshal our forces."

⋯

Jane offered to make dinner but at Constance's urging the others opted to repeat their fried chicken dining of the previous night. Bob was duly installed on the restaurant's front porch, this time with a plate of leftovers lovingly provided by the kitchen staff. The hostess again offered to keep an eye on him, commenting that he seemed such a sweet and well-behaved dog. Then she seated the four of them at a table looking out over the Japanese garden. Peter asked if he could explore the garden for a few minutes, and Maureen said yes, be back in ten minutes. The boy carefully checked his watch before heading out the door.

"Okay," Maureen said, "we have ten minutes to figure out our plan of attack."

"How would Jonas manage to convince a whole town that he's dead?" Lily asked.

"It's the why that bothers me more," Maureen said.

"Was there a hometown newspaper eleven years ago?"

"The *Parthenon View*," Maureen said. "It came out twice a week. Everybody read it for the social notices and obituaries."

The waitress brought a round of iced tea. Constance took a long drink of her tea before asking, "What kind of social notices?"

"Who went to whose house for dinner, what the churches were doing, the garden club, that sort of thing," Maureen said. "There wasn't much in the way of hard news. The only murder I can remember reading about was Jonas' father's, and I don't remember much of that, since it happened about the same time my own mother was dying." She thought a moment. "Jonas's father was killed after school was out that spring, about a month before my mother died." She shook her head. "Though other than Jonas, I only vaguely knew who the Atwoods were, just the sort of information that floats around a small farm town."

Through the window Lily could see Peter inspecting the garden's little wooden bridge. "Jonas' obituary must have run in the newspaper. Would that have been enough to convince the town? Did the town need convincing?"

"If his mother believed him dead, that would be sufficient," Constance said.

"Even though his mother was so detached from reality?" Lily said. "Who would have told his mother?"

Maureen thought about this while drinking her own tea. She drained the glass before signaling the waitress for refills. Her stomach growled audibly. "Some bread would be nice," she said, and repeated it when the waitress came by. The waitress offered muffins or biscuits.

Constance insisted on both. She smiled at the young woman. "We have driven to Kansas City and back today. No food since breakfast."

"Oh, wow, I'll bring you guys a couple of baskets. Butter and honey, too." The girl raced off.

"She would last about ninety seconds in New Haven," Constance said.

"Offering two baskets of free food? No kidding," Lily said. "The college students would be climbing over each other."

"Remind me not to move to New Haven," Maureen said.

"Actually, I like Connecticut," Lily said. Thinking of her conversation with Bethany, she added, "Guilford is the only place I've ever felt protected outside of my uncle's studio. And at the Beinecke, thanks to Constance."

The waitress returned immediately with a basket of warm biscuits and another basket of muffins. She pointed to the muffins. "The orangey ones are carrot, the others pecan. Sweet. Not the biscuits. I'll go see what's happening to your dinners."

Maureen devoured two biscuits while Constance worked her way through a carrot muffin, all before Lily could decide what to eat. Constance solved the problem by dropping a pecan muffin and a pat of butter on her bread plate. "Eat this before it gets cold."

"Betty," Maureen said while reaching for a muffin. "Betty's the one who always seemed to watch over Lillian. Betty would tell her. Or maybe the bank manager."

"After dinner, let's pay a visit to the newspaper," Lily said.

"If anyone's there," Maureen put in. "Though it's a daily now."

Lily said, "Someone will be there. Then we'll find Betty."

Maureen looked over Lily's shoulder.

Peter appeared at the table. "Hey, how come no one told me about biscuits?" He made a face at his mother. "You know I love biscuits."

Lily pushed the basket toward him. "Eat up. Good chance of more where those came from." She smiled when the boy put three of the five remaining biscuits on his plate, devouring the first one plain while buttering the second and slathering honey on the last.

Chapter 42

Maureen watched her son eat. They had matching metabolisms. Both could eat constantly and not gain an ounce. He was growing up so fast. She felt a burst of love and pushed the rest of the biscuits toward him. Here was this child who could have ruined her life and instead had become her life. In a few years he'd be off to college.

She had wanted to make sure that she wasn't one of those mothers who hovered around her adult children because she hadn't figured out anything else to do with her life. That's why she made sure she was on track for the next opening for high school principal. At heart Maureen wasn't particularly social, but she'd made a point to know her principal and the other vice principals well. She'd have plenty to keep her busy when Peter left home.

Now he caught her watching him and stopped with a mouth full of biscuit. Maureen's throat felt tight. She worried what this unplanned trip to a town she'd always avoided would mean to her son. Of course he was afraid of the unknown. At his age, she would have been stunned by fear if her parents had suddenly changed course. Change frightens children and animals, she reminded herself. She smiled reassuringly at her son, who resumed his attack on the biscuits. But under the table her foot tapped.

The others talked and planned. Maureen found herself viewing them with detachment, a stance that she knew only too well. She remembered that when she was renting out her Kansas City house when her mother was dying, she felt distanced, as if she were watching but not actually participating. This is what happened when life overtook her. Now here she was having dinner with two women she hadn't known this morning. In Parthenon, the place she'd sworn never to visit again.

It didn't look much like the town she'd known. She thought of the house she'd grown up in, the high school she'd attended and where she'd taught so disastrously. No, she corrected herself, the teaching wasn't a disaster. Dorothy Cranmer, the principal back then, thought she'd been the best chemistry teacher Parthenon High had ever seen. Dorothy had been so insistent that Maureen stay that Maureen had finally given her a few hints as to why it was imperative that she leave. Dorothy had backed down. They exchanged Christmas cards. It wasn't until Maureen had been named vice-principal of the Kansas City high school that Dorothy had stopped her annual job offers. Until then, she'd tried everything to lure Maureen back. At one point Dorothy had gone so far as to convince the board of education to update the chemistry lab where Maureen had taught.

High school chem labs didn't really need updating, in her experience. What the students needed to learn was so basic that the information behind Chemistry 2 and advanced placement chem was decades old. Her current school was flirting with the idea of teaching physical chemistry but she doubted that anything would come of it. That was college-level material. Most students stopped after Chem 1 and the periodic table of the elements. Hell, she thought, that dated back to, what, 1869 .She'd always loved the periodic table. It was so certain. A given in every chem classroom was Dmitri Mendeleev's baby, the pull-down map of the chem world.

Lily. Long black hair like Maureen's own, but otherwise there was nothing to connect them, she thought, except Jonas. She'd stopped caring about Jonas when he'd smiled at her in that malignly knowing way at her mother's funeral. It was as if the funeral had officially marked the end of two lives, her mother's and any she had in Parthenon. Switched off. Gone dark. She still had the best part of Jonas, his son. She'd never told him she was pregnant, never had the chance. Not true, she corrected herself. She knew where he'd gone to college. She could have tracked him down. If she'd been in the least bit interested in having him know.

So why, she asked herself, was she here? Why did she care to help Lily Atwood?

Because Jonas had lied to them both.

Yes, but...

But there was more. She looked down at her plate. There were two more pieces of chicken there. She couldn't remember eating the first one, but her stomach wasn't insistent anymore. She picked up another piece and took a bite. It was crisp, warm, salty and sweet all at once.

If she preceded Lily in Jonas' life, then who came before her? Was there a pattern? Had he taken control of her for those months not so much because she was vulnerable, as she'd always thought, but for other reasons as well? She thought of the boy who had listened so well and appeared tuned in to her feelings. What had she known of him?

A memory came back with that vividness of a morning dream, in full color. That first night Jonas came to her door. She'd asked him why he was there. He'd said, "I need your help." She must have been about to close the door—she was tapped out helping others, between her mother and her classes—when he said, "Actually, you need me." She let him in.

But she'd never asked him how he'd known. That he'd been right was all that was important at the time.

How had he gotten Lily to open the door to her life? Did he convince her, too, that she needed him? How did he know? Did he research people or was it instinct?

She shivered.

She looked again at her son. He was listening to Lily and Constance. They, in turn, were talking about Lily's research. Lily caught her eye then looked pointedly at Peter. So they'd changed the subject from his father on purpose to settle him down. It must have worked, because he'd eaten all the chicken and vegetables on his plate. Lily offered him the last piece of chicken from her plate and he took it.

"Are you all finished?" she asked.

"Can we have dessert?" Peter wanted to know.

"How about we go out for ice cream in awhile. When you're actually hungry."

"I'm still hungry," he protested.

"Come on, everyone. We're going for a drive." Maureen pulled the keys out the pocket of her denim shorts and rattled them in her hand.

"To the newspaper?" Lily asked, pulling out her credit card. She slapped Constance's hand away from the check. "You may be rich, but I'm not destitute."

"You're rich?" Peter said. "Cool. Is it fun?"

"Fun?" Constance looked thoughtful. "Sometimes. Mostly I have found it is about independence."

That was enough to distract Peter from the disappointment of skipping dessert. After Lily paid the check, they retrieved Bob from the porch and got into the car.

"How far is the newspaper?" Lily asked as they pulled away from the restaurant.

Maureen shifted the car into drive. "It's in the other direction."

##

The high school was dark. Maureen had stopped by Dorothy's house for a key to the science wing. The principal was so stunned at seeing her former teacher that she'd given her the key before asking for an explanation. "I've got an idea," Maureen had said. "I'll explain later. About everything." She pulled the red-haired woman into a hug. "It's all right. Everything's all right," she reassured her. "It was the right thing to do, putting Jonas' wife in touch with me."

"You trust her?"

"I think she's guileless. That might be why Jonas could fool her into loving him. Or at least having him. Until recently she has been too unsophisticated." Maureen held her palm up. "We'll talk later. But you did the right thing to call me."

Dorothy wrapped her arms around herself as if she were cold on this steaming night. "The new science wing is on the southwest corner. You'll see, it's poured concrete. That key opens the plate-glass door that faces the running track."

The new wing was lit by bright lights powered by motion sensors. Maureen turned the key in the lock, which opened easily. They stepped inside the school. It smelled of floor polish and pine cleaner. She gestured for the others to stay inside the door while she went a few yards down the hall. She sniffed—only more pine. A few more yards down there was another hallway. Standing at the corner, she sniffed again. Now she caught it, that chem lab odor that no amount of cleaner could completely defeat. She gestured for the others to follow.

"Did you teach here?" Peter's voice rang off the walls.

"In this wing? No, it was built after I left. The school's about twice as big as it was when I was here."

Her nose led her to a laboratory. She felt for the light switch, flipped it and headed right to the front of the room. Yes, there it was. She reached up and hooked the black plastic ring, pulling it. The periodic table of the elements covered the wall. It was a particularly beautiful version, the colors vivid.

"Mom," Peter said, "a periodic table? Now? This is why you brought us here?" There was a hint of protest in his voice, which meant he was getting tired.

Constance and Lily looked tired, too. Both had taken front-row seats. Lily was redoing the knot in her hair, Constance fingering her green jewel pendant. At her son's words, they leaned forward, their willingness to be surprised written for her on their faces.

"Bear with me for just a few minutes."

She was so tall she could reach the top of the chart. She pointed to the right side of the table, where the element squares were red and yellow and neon pink. "When Mendeleev started assembling this table in the nineteenth century, not all the chemical elements were known. Zinc was one of the known." Her finger moved over two squares. "Arsenic was another." Her finger traced up one square and over another to the right on the map. "Aluminum was a known element." Her finger skipped down two squares and stopped at the square labeled In. "So was indium."

She backed up to lean against the teacher's desk, which was where it always was, in front of and to one side of the periodic table. "Here's the thing. When Mendeleev put together his table, he figured out that there had to be other elements out there. Why? Because the chemical weights and reactions predicted a pattern. If zinc weighed sixty-five and arsenic seventy-five," she was back at the map, tracing across the fourth row, "and if aluminum and indium had similar reactions when combined with hydrogen," this time her whole hand slid down two rows from Al to In, "then there had to be elements in between.

"He was able to go through and say what the properties of an unknown element were, what its weight would be, how it would react with other elements, its melting point, what salts and oxides it would form, based on what he knew about its upstairs and downstairs neighbors on his table. At the time he was writing, there was a raging debate about whether atoms were real or just theoretical aids for conducting chemistry. Now we know that everything in the chart is determined by the constituents of atoms."

"Mom!"

Lily ignored Peter's outburst. Her eyes narrowed. "What's important is that the known was sufficient to predict that there was some specific unknown to be found. Sounds like my research."

"Or any research," added Constance.

Maureen nodded. "Actually, it's more than that. It was enough to predict details about the unknowns before they were discovered. Other chemists discovered those missing elements."

Lily strode to the blackboard and grabbed a stick of chalk. "Okay. We know that Jonas pursued Maureen and left after that was successful." She wrote in capital letters JONAS then underneath MAUREEN. "We know that seven years later he pursued me. Successfully." She made a face as if biting a lemon, but wrote in the number seven and then her name:

Maureen 7 Lily

"If we know that these elements exist…" Lily knocked on the blackboard with her knuckles.

"There must be more," Peter added.

"Who came before Maureen? Who is between Maureen and Lily?" Constance said.

Lily had stepped back to look at her timeline, her periodic table of Jonas Atwood. "There must be an element after me. Jane Hardy." For Maureen's benefit, she explained, "My former department chair. She and Jonas, uh, got together to arrange that I lose my job." She added Bethany to the board.

"Nope, doesn't make sense," Maureen said. "I was older than Jonas. You're his same age. Bethany is, what, nineteen?" Lily nodded. "No, there has to be someone between you and Bethany. Or maybe Bethany doesn't fit the chart."

"Sometimes the ninja aim in one direction to hide that they're really going another way." Peter popped up from his seat to demonstrate the ninja move. He looked like he was dancing.

"Maybe," Lily said. "But he did stalk Bethany."

"Maybe," Maureen said, "it had something to do with the reaction between the two of you."

Constance was the only one still sitting at a student desk. "Lily is his first failure."

"No," Maureen said. "Jonas had no concept of failure. The Jonas I knew, the teenager."

Lily stared straight at the periodic table, but Maureen could tell she wasn't seeing it. Her silence lasted long enough that everyone turned toward her, including Peter. Finally she nodded. "Jonas creates failure around him. It must make him feel stronger. There has to be some reason why he arranged for my dismissal from Prairie Shores, since it cut our joint income by almost half." She tapped the pointer. "Jonas perceives failure, just never as his own." Her smile was rueful. "When we were talking in the Guilford jail, he tried to make me believe his being there was my fault. I'm sure that my not buying it didn't sink in." Lily nodded again. "When he doesn't get what he wants, he acts like the discussion is finished, but then a day or a week or a year later, he'll start the discussion over, as if we'd never talked about it in the first place."

Maureen remembered that about Jonas. "So you're a new chemical reaction, one Jonas is incapable of predicting," she said. "No chemical element repeats in the periodic table, but there's no reason why Lily cannot become a new element in Jonas' table."

"We are missing one major piece of the puzzle," Constance put in. "If when you left there were only a few hundred dollars in your joint checking account, how is Jonas paying for airline tickets and meals?" To Lily, she said, "Credit card?"

Lily blushed. "I canceled all of our joint cards the day I saw the video of him with my former department chair." She held up a hand to Maureen. "I'll explain later."

Peter said, "It's okay. I'm old enough to understand."

"It's so wrong, what your father did. I'll tell you about it another time. Would that be acceptable?"

Peter nodded.

"Then," Constance continued, "there is a financial aspect to the mystery of Jonas. Possibly why he left your college in such a hurry."

"Possibly why he went to a place with much deeper pockets," Lily said thoughtfully. She patted the periodic table. "I'm beginning to like Mendeleev. What's his first name?"

"Dmitri," said Maureen.

Peter asked, "Mom, were you thinking about this at dinner?"

"Sure, why?"

"Because you were eating chicken. I didn't know that you could think about more than one thing at a time."

"It is a female thing," Constance explained.

"Could I learn it?"

"If you hang around with grown women enough, I suppose you could," his mother said doubtfully.

"Did Jonas hang around with grown women?" Lily asked.

"Could he have spent time with Jane, our innkeeper here?" Constance asked. "She acts like a skittish cat every time his name is mentioned. She avoids looking directly at Lily. There must be some sort of history there, because with everyone else she is gracious."

"She wouldn't look at me, either." Peter picked at a thread hanging from the edge of his cutoffs. "I mean, right from when she first met me. It wasn't like I had a chance to do something wrong."

Maureen walked over to him and put her hand on his head. When he looked up at her, she saw the confusion on his face and her heart hurt. She sat down next to him. "Peter. You know you can call this off any time. We can come back to Parthenon when you're older, when you're ready." She was afraid she'd become so carried away with meeting Lily and finding out about Jonas that she'd forgotten the most important person was her son.

"I know, Mom. You always said you'd take me when I was ready. But you know," he picked at the thread again until she pulled his hand away to enclose it in her own, "I always wanted to come. It was you who wasn't ready."

Maureen stared at him and, before she knew it, could hear herself laughing. "Oh, lord, out of the mouths of babes and all that."

"Mom, I'm not a baby." His dark eyes flashed; at that moment he was more boy than man. What an age, fourteen, Maureen thought. His whole personality is changing the same way his voice did.

"Well, then you're too damned perceptive for your own good." She leaned over to hug him. Her boy allowed her the hug.

"Jane wouldn't look at you, either." Peter leaned in to look at his mother's face. "I can't believe you missed that, too."

Constance cleared her throat. "If I may make a suggestion? About a course of action?" She tapped her watch. "It is after eight. Unless we intend to stay here more than one night, perhaps we should each take a specific task. I suggest that I speak with Jane. She seems comfortable with me."

"If you're going to do that, Peter and Lily better stay out of the way," Maureen said. "Suppose we go to the newspaper office and see if they'll let us look at back issues."

"You want to find out why Jonas told the town he was dead?" Lily asked. "That just requires finding his obituary, if there was one. I've got another idea."

"If you're talking about looking into how his father died, don't you think that could wait until another time?" Constance said.

Lily took out her cell phone. "I want to see the police file on Joel Atwood. Primary sources are always best."

"How are you going to pull that off?" Maureen said.

"Well, you know what E.M. Forster wrote." Lily punched in a number and walked a few yards away.

"I think," Constance explained, "she means his well-known note before the beginning of *Howard's End*, the one taught in every intro to lit course: 'only connect.' That now is the time to use her connections."

"Who would that be?"

"My guess is her friend Ed, the Guilford cop."

• • •

Lily heard Constance tell the others what she was doing while she dialed Ed's home number. Those last few days she and Constance had spent with them in Guilford, Ed, Donna and Larry had made her feel part of another family. She'd never felt that way inside her own nuclear family, nor in college, grad school or at Prairie Shores. It would never have occurred to her before that calling someone for assistance, especially late evening, would be anything but an imposition. Ed answered with "Lily? Where are you? Are you all right?"

"Hi, Ed. We're in my husband's home town. Turns out the town thinks he's dead. His father was murdered when he was in high school."

Ed whistled. "That guy's some operator. How do you think he did it?"

"We think he probably manipulated the rumor mill."

"No, I meant how do you think he offed his dad," Ed said.

"No, he couldn't have—he adored the man."

"Don't know much about murder statistics, do you? Most times it's a loved one who does it."

She shivered. Married to a murderer? Don't think about it, she told herself. Facts first. Comfortable, comforting facts. "Listen, do you think you could call the local police department, get them to share what's in their file on the murder? Maybe you could tell them about Jonas' peculiar behavior, that you're looking into his background and turned up the fact of the murder and want to know more. Would that work?"

"How would I have turned up the fact of the murder?"

"Jonas' full name is Joel Jonas Atwood III. Which means there's a murdered man with his same name. Would that do it?"

"Yup. Hold on." A minute later, he said, "Okay, got my notebook. Where is the hometown?"

"Parthenon, Kansas."

"Get back to you soon as I can," Ed said. "Could be right away, could be a while. Chances are if it's right away, the cops aren't interested in handing out info."

"Would it be better if Donna or Larry called?"

Ed laughed. "No way. Cops hate the Feds. Me and Donna and Larry are the only known exception to that rule."

Chapter 43

Constance found Jane on the front porch in one of the wide chairs, her head back, bare feet propped on the hassock. Her eyes opened when Constance lowered herself onto the chair next to her. Bob looked at her, tail wagging, but wouldn't move from Constance's side. "Where are your friends?" Jane asked.

"At the newspaper office."

"There wasn't an obituary on Jonas Atwood. Just Joel."

Jane's small talk had evaporated. Constance peered at her face. The only light on the porch came from a wall sconce above and behind Jane, casting her in shadow. "We have tired you. Perhaps Bob and I should go on to our room and leave you to relax."

"That's not necessary. I don't think I can sleep, anyway, after seeing that boy. He is the very image of Jonas Atwood." Jane pointed with her chin toward a side table. On it was an open bottle of wine and a half-empty goblet. More glasses were arranged on a silver tray. "Help yourself."

Though she wasn't interested in wine, Constance poured herself a small amount. Jane seemed to want to talk. A quiet listener in the shadow outside of the circle of dim light might be all that was necessary for Jane to tell her story. Constance herself had often talked like this to Bob. She slipped off her shoes and stretched out on the wicker chaise. Jane sipped wine and looked out into the night. Constance heard crickets ticking and the hoot of what might have been an owl. Bob shifted position, his nails clicking on the polished floorboards.

Softly, Constance asked, "What did Joel Atwood look like?"

Jane tipped her head back against the chair. One hand rubbed throat and chin. Her answer was so long in coming that her words seemed to wake Constance. "Like his son. Like Jonas." She swallowed more wine. "If they stood next to each other, Joel and Jonas and Peter, they'd look like the same man at different ages."

As if no woman were involved in their conception, Constance thought.

"But Joel..." Jane carefully placed her wineglass on the table next to her. "Joel." She leaned back again, this time stretching her legs out to prop her feet on the hassock. "Joel knew how to make a woman feel wanted, to feel alive in the way only a woman can." For a few moments the only sounds came from the crickets. "None of us had any doubt why Lillian let him come and go as he pleased. Just as long as he came back, every now and then, to remind her how, well, how alive she could be, that would be enough."

Somebody did not feel that way, Constance thought. Otherwise the man would still be alive and able to stand in that three-generation portrait Jane had sketched on the night air. He sounded like the town tomcat. But then Lily—the younger Lily—maintained that Jonas was charming, which Constance couldn't sense from the only time she'd seen him. Jonas struck her as manipulative and self-centered and a facile liar. Inside her head, Constance chided herself. After all, she'd only seen the guy from a distance on the Guilford Green. Too far away to feel any chemistry.

"That's why I helped them that night."

Jane's listener held very still.

"That awful night." She sat up in the chair and clutched her arms to her abdomen. She rocked. "When Jonas showed up here, all he had on was a pair of track shorts and running shoes. His chest looked just like his father's had at the same age. His face looked just like Joel's after, well..." Her hand went up and stroked her neck again. When she spoke next, her voice was so soft that Constance could barely hear it over the crickets. "All he said was 'I need you.'"

Like she'd been programmed, Constance reflected.

"He drove me to the parking lot behind the high school. His father's car was there, all by itself. The keys were in it. Jonas drove it to Joel's house. I drove Jonas' car." Now her hand gripped her thigh as she rocked. "That wonderful house. Empty. Jonas didn't tell me where his father was. I think I knew. There was a spot of red on Jonas' running shorts, near the pocket. I noticed it when the dome light went on when I opened the car door. Then he drove me home."

Constance tried not to move, mentally relaxing the muscles in her legs and feet. It seemed Jane had finished talking. The silence lengthened. Bob sighed. Even the crickets had bedded down for the night.

But Jane wasn't quite out of words. "I know you're here. I know you're listening. It's time. When you came back with the child I knew it was time."

Constance stirred, thankful that she could move again. "Time?"

"For the truth to come out. It's time to break the silence. Silence can be the biggest lie of all, you know. We owe children more than that."

"Peter."

"Peter. He has something his father and grandfather never had. They had charm, sex appeal, they had that ability to read what you need and give it to you. I hope the grandson doesn't have that. It's too dangerous."

"What does Peter have that Jonas doesn't?" Constance slid to the end of the chaise, closer to Jane.

"Transparency. I think that's what I mean. He is what he seems to be, not what he thinks you want him to be. It's a kind of goodness."

"Honesty," Constance suggested.

"Yes." Jane subsided back into her chair. Again she took up her wineglass. This time she drank deeply. "Honesty. The relief of it."

Chapter 44

It turned out that the night editor of the Parthenon newspaper had been one of Maureen's students. "Maybe your worst student," the woman admitted. "Luckily I rarely need chemistry to get the paper to the printer on time."

"You never know when it might come in handy," Maureen said. Peter rolled his eyes at his mother's comment. The night editor smiled politely. When they'd told the editor they wanted to research a murder and a disappearance that took place over a decade before, the night editor lit up. "Sounds like a story."

"Maybe," Lily cautioned. "But not for right now." She'd leveled a teacher look at the editor, who was about her own age.

"I have lots of patience," the woman said. "For a journalist. You learn that real quick in a small place like this. Especially since the computer only has issues back five years. I'll have to show you how to use the morgue." She pointed at Peter. "That's what we call the room where old papers are stored."

"Dead papers," Peter said.

"Yeah," the editor laughed, "dead but not buried."

Lily left Maureen and Peter digging through back issues. She walked the few blocks to Jane's inn, climbing the front steps in time to hear Jane say "Honesty. The relief of it." She paused to listen for a minute. When there were no more words from the porch, Lily opened the screen door and, turning, closed it quietly. Her eyes, accustomed to the dark from her walk, saw Jane lying back on a chair, legs stretched out. The older woman looked deflated, flattened. Then Lily spotted Constance sitting up on the chaise. Bob was lying alertly at her feet. Constance put a finger to her lips and patted the cushion next to her. Lily sat.

Jane opened her eyes and regarded Lily. She straightened her back, squared her shoulders. "Where are the others?"

"At the newspaper offices, looking for stories on Jonas and his father."

"His death." Jane's voice was firm.

"Joel's, yes. And a report of Jonas'."

Constance leaned down to pat Bob, who had ooched over in that dog way to lie in front of both Lily and her. "Did you hear anything about the police report?"

"Yes. I'll know more once I locate a fax machine."

"There's a fax machine in my office, next to the kitchen," Jane said. "Would this be the police report on Joel's murder?"

Lily nodded.

"In some ways, I've always wanted to know what the police knew. In more ways I didn't want to know anything." She pushed herself out of the chair. "Not knowing anything turned out to be quite difficult. Come with me."

Jane walked briskly across the porch and through the front door of her house. Lily hung back. "What's happened? She seems not to hate me for the moment."

"The full story later. For now, you need to know that Jonas turned to Jane for help the night that his father was murdered. She was the one who drove his father's car back to his father's house."

They were trailing behind Jane. Lily grabbed Constance's arm. "Is she the missing element?"

Constance pulled Lily along. "You mean with Jonas? No. Her affair was with Joel. She still seems to miss him, sexually. As it were."

Lily laughed nervously. "As it were? Constance, sometimes you are so an Edith Wharton character."

They found Jane inside the door next to the entrance to the kitchen. "Here," she said, and pointed to the small black machine next to the telephone. "Here's the number." She handed a slip of paper to Lily. "May I read the report when you get it?"

"Of course." Lily took the proffered number. Jane turned to go. Lily put out her hand without actually touching Jane. "Please stay."

The older woman's face relaxed momentarily. She gestured Lily to the chair behind the desk. Lily shook her head. "Let me make a phone call. Then would you handle the fax?"

In response, Jane sat in the the desk chair, back straight.

Lily used her cell to phone Ed and give him the fax number. "Do I want to know how you got this report?" she asked him.

"The case is old but it's still open. Seems that the Parthenon cops are interested in any help to clear it off the books. Read the file. If you have any questions, talk to this guy." Ed gave her the name of a Parthenon policeman. "He's the old guy on the force, the one who's the walking history of the place."

"Does he know you're passing the report to me?"

"I told him that you were cooperating with me. That way, it sounds like I'm in charge. Act like the properly submissive little woman if you talk to him, okay?"

Lily thanked him. By the time she'd clicked off the cell, Jane's fax machine announced incoming. The three women watched it. Lily counted the pages as the machine shot them into the bin: twenty-three. Was that enough for a murder investigation? The fax chattered into silence. Jane took the pages, squared the stack and handed it to Lily. Lily read the first page and the second, passing each to Jane when she'd finished. Constance had moved next to Lily, reading along with her.

The language was stilted yet in its own way vivid. The report described the scene of a June night fifteen years before. There was way too much detail, but what it came down to was that the weather was perfect: upper sixties by the time the cops arrived at the scene, low humidity. The writer's implication was that such a perfect night was rare. All over what was then a little town, people were out, strolling with children to buy ice cream from a truck, sitting in the park, just taking advantage of the freedom the weather offered before the heat returned to trap them inside.

The police, too, had been out and about. No one had thought to check at the high school. Graduation had been the previous week; summer school classes didn't begin for another week. The buildings were shut down tight. But the running track had been prepared for summer gym classes, the cinders refreshed and spread evenly. The track then was where the new science wing was now, from what Lily could tell, right behind the high school, just beyond what had been a stand of trees.

It was the janitor who had called the police. While rechecking a lock on the side door, he saw a car drive off just as he pulled into the school parking lot. No, he hadn't seen the car close enough to identify it. But since it had been there, he thought maybe he'd check the other doors, too. All were locked. It was such a beautiful night that he decided to take a nostalgic walk around the track. In his time, he'd been on the high school track team. That track meant good times to him. Then he saw the body under one of the trees. It looked like some guy asleep. But when the janitor got close he could see that one leg of the guy's khaki pants was wet with blood. He touched it. The blood hadn't begun to dry. At that, he ran back to the school, let himself in and phoned the police.

Lily handed the next few pages on to Jane. The police determined that the victim was Joel Atwood, age forty-three, Parthenon citizen. In fact, he was the local agricultural agent and a member of the board of directors of the town's bank. In the little town, he was Somebody. What the janitor hadn't noticed in his haste to get away from the body was that there was a knife sticking out of the side of Atwood's left thigh.

"He bled out," Jane said. "I knew that. Now how did I know that?"

"It is in this report," Constance said. "Information flows through small towns, in my experience."

"Could be," but Jane sounded doubtful.

The knife turned out to have belonged to the victim and the only prints on it were his. It was a combat knife Atwood had bought from a military surplus store just outside of town. That kind of knife opens in one smooth motion with what amounts to the push of a button. Oh, it was perfectly legal, not a switchblade. What would the local ag agent and bank director want with one? No one knew, except that he'd been stabbed with his own knife.

The only other evidence was partial footprints around the body. It looked as though someone had come along with a broom and swept the dirt and leaves and cinders. Other footprints came from running shoes, lots of them, as was to be expected next to the running track.

How had Joel Atwood gotten to the high school? His car was parked in his garage; his house located so far out of town in the other direction that it was unlikely he could have walked to the high school without anyone seeing him. He'd have to walk right through town, right by all those people out to enjoy the evening. The only fingerprints on his car's steering wheel were from Atwood and his son, Jonas, who was known to drive the car occasionally. Jonas was home with his mother. The parents were separated, having lived apart since the boy's birth. The mother, Lillian Atwood, insisted that her son had been home all evening.

The police kept probing. A man killed with his own knife? Could it have been suicide? Suicide by knife is rare, the report noted, and is almost always done by men who stab themselves in the chest, not a femoral artery. Joel Atwood's latest girlfriend, whom he'd called that afternoon, attested that Joel seemed to be his usual self. She had come to his house to meet him at ten o'clock that night, as they'd arranged. Instead of her lover, she'd found cops waiting to interrogate her.

"After that," Jane added, "she tried to go back to her husband. He divorced her. She left Parthenon, though eventually came back."

They finished reading the faxed report. Jane slumped in front of the fax machine. Lily and Constance sat on the floor, since there were no other chairs in the room.

"Jane, tell Lily what you told me."

Jane's voice suddenly sounded like that of an old woman. "Jonas came over here that night. He drove me to the high school. He drove Joel's car to his father's house, parked it in the garage. I followed in Jonas' car, then he drove me home."

Lily pushed herself off the floor. Everything hurt, her joints, her heart, her head. But she had to know. "Jane."

When Jane raised her face, Lily could see tears leaking into deep grooves around her mouth—wrinkles that Lily hadn't noticed before that moment. "Jane. Did Jonas kill his father?"

The older woman's head moved back in forth in slow motion. "He only had this tiny spot of blood on his shorts."

"He could have changed his clothes before he got to your house."

Jane's head was still shaking, denying. "He was covered with sweat, his hair plastered to his scalp, he smelled of sweat."

Constance stood up to walk around behind Jane. Head tilted to look Lily in the eye, Constance asked, "Jane, what was Lillian like fifteen years ago? Was she like she is now?"

"Yes."

"Then how could she insist that Jonas had been home with her the night his father was stabbed? That's what the police report said and they believed her."

Jane turned her head away from them, looking out the office window, past their reflections and into the dark. "Lil could be lucid. She could be made to be lucid. Joel had that effect on her. I saw it."

"But Joel was dead." Lily leaned closer. "There's no mention in the report of Lillian Atwood acting crazy."

"Jonas." Jane stopped.

"Jonas, what?" Lily demanded, voice rising. Then repeated, "What?" more softly.

"Looks like his father. Has the same voice."

...

Constance helped Jane upstairs to bed. Instead of Jane worrying about Constance's comfort, she allowed Constance to fuss over her. Obediently she took off her apron, skirt and blouse, and allowed herself to be helped into pajamas. Constance pulled back the light covers, finding herself yanking hard to loosen the sheets from the tightly-made bed. Jane stretched out, hands folded on her chest like a corpse arranged in a coffin. In the soft light coming from a lamp on the corner of a tall dresser across the room, Constance thought she saw color in the woman's face. She looked relaxed, as if she had shed a heavy burden.

By the time Constance came downstairs, Maureen and Peter had returned. They all turned out to walk Bob, much to his delighted relief. Then Maureen called a conference of war in the kitchen, as far away in the house as they could get from Jane's room.

"What's to talk about?" Lily said. "We know the details of what happened the night Jonas' father was killed, but not the why or who. In other words, nothing essential." She was pacing the kitchen, followed by Bob. Every time she turned, the dog turned with her, occasionally allowing himself to bump her with his nose. When he did that, she absent-mindedly reached down and smoothed his head.

Maureen was keeping an unobtrusive eye on Peter. After all, Joel Atwood was his grandfather. The boy seemed more worn out than agitated. "Did you want to go to bed, baby?" she said softly.

"In a couple minutes." He looked around, spotted the cookie jar. "Do you think it would be okay if I took a cookie?"

"I'm sure Jane won't mind. Just be quiet about it."

Peter crept to the counter, opened the jar in slow motion, and pulled out two huge cookies. He put the top back on the jar, brought the cookies to the table, and repeated his silent movie performance, pouring milk into a glass. The three women watched him, all trying not to grin. After he'd eaten, he went to bed.

"Any way we could get Lillian Atwood to talk about that night?" Constance said. "Any way we could snap her into reality?" She brought the cookie jar to the table, then went to the refrigerator for milk. She and Maureen had milk and cookies.

Lily hated milk, but took a cookie. She ate half of it, then put it down on the scrubbed table. "I have this crazy idea." She picked up the cookie again and bit into it.

After a minute of nothing but the sounds of crunching and sipping, Maureen said, "So give. What's your crazy idea?"

When Jonas was courting her, he was always telling Lily stories, case narratives. He'd figured out right away that he could capture her attention with a story, especially one that had elements of pure conflict. All the stories seemed so unlikely to Lily, that people would actually do such things outside of the fiction. But she listened. Because he was breaking client confidentiality by telling her, Jonas claimed she never remembered the stories. After assuring him she did remember and hearing over and over how she was wrong, she finally let him believe what he wanted to. It was just easier.

She started to tell the other two women about the case where a psychiatrist at a large mental institution suspected that a patient had been abused by a family employee. The patient refused to talk. Her doctor got to know her visitors—mother, father, older sister. He'd talk to them, ask about their day, really listen to them, until they became comfortable enough to tell him family stories.

One day the mother mentioned how his patient's former governess had dropped by to find out how her ex-student was doing. "Such a caring woman," the mother had said. "She took such good care of my daughter, turned her into a lady. Before that she was quite the tomboy." How did she do that? Mother shrugged delicately, implying that that wasn't her responsibility. But right then the older sister added, "Got her to lose weight, too. What Mother didn't say was that she was a fat tomboy." The doctor suggested the governess visit his patient. With him right there.

The governess did visit, a few days later. How, she asked the doctor, should I greet my former student? Well, he said, how did you usually greet her? "I went into her bedroom and yanked off the covers. She was so lazy, you know," the woman said in a coy voice.

"Every morning?"

"Of course. Consistency is key when dealing with children."

"How old was she when you first went to work there?"

"Twelve."

"Then what would you do?"

"Why, get her dressed, of course."

"This is usual for a governess?"

"It is for me."

She would put the girl in a shower, first hot, then cold, holding her firmly. Then she'd dress the girl in what she, the governess, thought was proper attire for a young woman of breeding. Starched little dresses with elaborate collars, the sort of thing guaranteed to make a fat girl look like an overgrown baby. Then she'd take the child to the park for exercise. "She'd play nicely with the other children while the nannies and I chatted."

The other children were toddlers. His patient must have been bored out of her mind.

Then came lunch, "a little steamed spinach and boiled chicken, you know."

What subjects did the patient excel in?

"Subjects?" The governess looked mystified.

"History? Mathematics?"

"Oh. Well, she'd read all afternoon. I don't know what exactly."

"What were you doing while she read?"

"Watching her."

From the next armchair, the governess would literally watch the girl's every move. All day every day, the girl got no privacy, including when she used the bathroom. Not surprisingly, she was ecstatic at the end of each day when her parents and sister came home to release her from governess prison. But then the parents went to Europe and the sister to college, and guess who took over the girl's complete care?

The doctor said, "Let's go see your girl. Start her day the way you used to."

The governess marched into the patient's room, doctor right behind her, and snatched off the bedclothes. The doctor gave the girl a nod and the thumbs-up gesture. She stared at him for a moment, wordless as always, then sat up, put her legs over the side of the bed, and hauled off and slapped her former wardress across the face. "Now get the hell out of my life." It was the first time the doctor had heard her speak. He tossed the governess out of the room, and he and the patient got to work.

"Did he cure her?" Constance wanted to know.

"According to Jonas, the doctor treated her as if she were a torture survivor. As I recall, Jonas thought that was a little over the top."

"Not going to happen," Maureen said. Her rough voice could cut diamonds.

They looked at her. She was shaking her head at them. "No. Don't even think it. I will not expose him to that."

Lily propped her elbow on the table and her chin on her palm. "Are you—"

"No," Maureen hissed. "No and no and no and no."

Constance watched the two of them, looking lost. "May I join in this conversation?"

Chapter 45

"Tell your friend she's crazy," Maureen said, voice soft in warning.

"All right. Lily, you are crazy. Now, will one of you tell me what we are talking about?"

But neither of the others spoke. There was a long and uneasy silence.

Peter came back into the kitchen wearing pajama bottoms and what was left of a tee shirt, saying, "Mom, I can't sleep," before noticing the tension in the women's posture. He looked from one to another, and finally said, "What's going on?" in his man's voice. He strode over to the table to stand between his mother and Lily. "What are you fighting about?"

"Nothing," his mother said.

"You," Lily said.

"Oh, good heavens, now I get it," Constance added.

"No," Maureen said to the seated women. "That's final."

Peter took a chair next to his mother, turned it around and sat on it, arms folded on the chair back. To Lily it seemed as if the man that Peter would be was once again back with them and, for now, in charge. "Mom, you're refusing to consider something that involves me. Don't you think you owe me the courtesy of letting me in on what that might be?"

"Lily has a very bad idea," Maureen said in that parental tone of finality.

"About me?"

"A very bad idea," she repeated.

"Lily?" He turned to the woman he'd known for a less than a day.

"This is between you and your mother," Lily said.

Peter leaned his shoulder against his mother's. She allowed herself to rest against him. "Mom, it's time for you to let me in on your decisions about me. You know, before you make them."

She turned to look at him, taking in his adult demeanor. His hair stood in wet spikes, his tee shirt gapped open at one shoulder seam and the pocket was mostly ripped off. Lily thought he looked like a man who'd accidentally put on his child's clothes in the dark. Then he hugged his mother, and the kid was back. "Mom, tell me."

"She wants you to pretend you're your grandfather."

Peter reeled back as if he'd been struck. "Grandfather? How could I—Wait, do I look like him?"

"Jane says you and your father and grandfather all look like the same man at different ages. Looked, I guess," Constance said.

"Okay, back up." The man was sitting with them at the table again. "Why would I pretend to be my dead grandfather?"

Lily reached towards Peter, palm flat on the table, fingers open. "To see if you could shake your grandmother into enough clarity to remember what happened the night he was murdered."

"No way," Maureen said.

But her son's face shone with curiosity. "How would I do that?" he asked Lily.

Over his mother's interruptions, she reviewed the bare facts of the night of the murder: body at the high school running track, grandfather's car at his house, his own knife in his thigh. "Your grandmother insisted at the time that your father was home with her all that evening. The police reports make her sound quite sane."

He sat back. "Wait. She's insane?"

"She lives in her own world," Maureen said. "Always has, long as I've known her. She drifts, doesn't usually make sense. Lily says she's like a ghost, and it's a pretty accurate description."

"But why—?"

Lily said, "Jane told us tonight that your grandfather could always get Lillian to focus, that it was something like behavioral conditioning. After he was killed, Jonas could do the same thing because he looked and sounded just like his father."

Now Peter sat and thought. He shook his head a few times. The glass he'd used earlier in the evening stood on the table near Constance, who slid it across to him, along with the milk carton. He filled the glass, sipped, thought, sipped. Then he put the glass down, centering it in front of him. "I've never met my grandmother. Let's go see her tomorrow."

"The murder took place in early evening," Lily said.

"We'll go in the morning. If it's my face she's going to react to, then it won't matter what time it is."

"Peter, I don't think you're ready for this," Maureen said.

"You know that book I've been reading, Mom? About the soldiers in Vietnam? I don't think anybody's ever ready. You know, you do what you do. Maybe learn from it, maybe not."

"Is this where the parent starts learning from her child?"

He shrugged. "Any more cookies in that jar?"

Peter left the kitchen, followed closely by Bob. Constance seemed to be analyzing her dog's behavior. Maureen thought Constance had been about to get up and follow the pair before changing her mind. "Is there something bothering you about Bob?" Maureen asked.

"It's interesting that until the last few days, the only person he ever bonded with was me. When Lily showed up, I had to tell him firmly that she was a friend before he would give her a chance." She pushed the crumbs together on her plate before adding, "He took to Peter instantly. When he met adolescent boys before, he kept his distance." She smiled ruefully at Maureen. "My guard dog has connected with your son."

"But something's on your mind," Maureen said.

"Bob is worried about Peter," Constance replied.

"The boy's had a lot thrown at him today," Lily said. "I can imagine some of what's going on in his mind."

"Like what?" Maureen demanded. It offended her that Lily seemed to presume to know her son. Peter was hers and hers alone.

Lily paid no attention to Maureen's bristling. "Like, who is he? Up until my showing up on your doorstep, you were your son's only family. Right?"

Maureen nodded, suspicious.

"Today he learned that his biological father is still alive, married to me. I don't know what that makes my relationship to Peter. Then just now he learned that his paternal grandmother is also alive." She leaned back in her chair and frowned at Maureen. "From my earliest memory, I've been outside of my parents' life. The two of them formed a tight pair, and I was kept outside of their circle. Separate. My grandparents were also distant, and died when I was in high school. That's when I found my Uncle Nate. He's my only real family. Until I married Jonas. Though Nate never really trusted him."

She made a shooing motion with her hand, as if swatting a fly. "But that's neither here nor there. What I'm getting at is I can imagine Peter's confusion, trying to digest everything he's learned about his family. He's at the age where he's the center of the world, you know. That's his perspective. His world was pretty set. Not now. Now he's wondering who he is."

"Don't lecture me about adolescent psychology. He's my son."

"Yes, above all things. You've made him what he is. Nature and nurture and all that. But what might he become?" Lily shook her head at Maureen, who was again ready to interrupt. "You and I know he'll become the wonderful man we're already seeing little glimpses of tonight. But what does Peter know?"

"Shifting sands," Constance said.

"Definitely," Lily said.

Maureen got up to go after her son. From behind her, Constance said softly, "Let Bob do his thing. He is quite good at encouraging clear thinking."

"A dog?" Maureen said. "I don't think so."

"My uncle says that some things a man has to do for himself," Lily said.

Maureen turned around to glare at them. "He's not a man. He's a fourteen-year-old boy."

The other two just watched her. What were they waiting for? Maureen wondered. She chewed the inside of her cheek. "He's a boy," she repeated. Lily shrugged. Constance raised an eyebrow. "He may be trying to be a man, but—"

Lily suddenly nodded. "Yes, it's that 'but' that my students so often have trouble with. Growing up is no mean feat these days. There's no official ceremony that announces you're a man or a woman. You're expected to mature, to suddenly be a responsible human being. To know who you are."

"When the sands are constantly shifting," Constance put in.

"Ain't that the truth," Lily said.

Maureen sat down on the edge of her chair. "You two have never had children. You don't know anything about child-rearing."

"Absolutely," Constance agreed. "But hang out in academe for a while and the lessons are forced on you if you pay any attention at all."

"If you care at all," Lily added.

Constance said, "Adolescents take the caterpillar-to-butterfly cycle to new lengths, but the metaphor stands. Unless I miss my guess, that boy in there is beginning to get the idea what wings might feel like."

"You mean he's ready to fly out of my nest?" Maureen said.

"Perhaps I should have said what wings might look like. He is glimpsing his adult self."

"And he's scared shitless," Lily said. "Not something he wants his mother to see."

Maureen sat back in her chair, arms folded. "You two are beginning to scare me. Like you're something out of a Greek play, the chorus telling the audience what to expect. You going to give me the line from *Medea* next, about how thankless having children is?"

"Let Bob do his thing," Constance said. "Skip the analysis."

"Can I eavesdrop?" Maureen said.

"You could, but that would be cheating," Lily advised. "He'll tell you what you need to know."

...

The next morning, Peter called a conference on the front porch before breakfast. Lily found herself partly amused but mostly impressed at his taking charge of a string of headstrong women. It couldn't be easy for the diffident boy she'd met. She and Constance put down their coffee cups and followed him, the dog at his heels, down the cool hallway. His mother, however, was not amused at her son. Her lips were set in a tight line, her eyes darker than ever.

"Mama bear," Constance whispered to Lily. "Watch out."

When they got to the front porch, Peter was standing in front of the side table. Constance and Lily sat on the couch but Maureen was already talking to her son. "Peter, what's going on?"

"Mom, do you trust me to tell the difference between right and wrong?"

His question evidently blindsided Maureen. She frowned. Peter gave her a sad smile, as if disappointed in her reaction. She straightened to her full height, forcing her son to look up at her. "You know I do. I've always trusted you. That's why I've always told you everything. But you're still a boy. Since adults aren't always doing what they seem to be doing, I worry that you can't tell the difference."

He stuck his hands in the back pockets of his shorts. Lily noticed that he'd put on an actual shirt, one with buttons down the front and a collar and no apparent holes. With his hair combed, he looked quite presentable. Like Jonas on stilts. "That's fair," he said. "But I think sometimes you have to let me make my own decisions and follow them through."

The two of them acted as if Lily and Constance weren't in the room. It was fascinating in a way, Lily thought, being given the chance to see a boy tell his mother that it was time she allow him to make his own mistakes. A lesson in parenting for all of them. Maureen dropped into a chair, eyes never leaving her son. She frowned, smiled, then looked for a second as if she might cry. Finally she gave her shouting laugh. Her son looked relieved rather than insulted. "You get it?" he asked.

"Well, you push, I pull. That's what mothers and sons do. But, yeah, I think I get it. When were you going to spell it out for me? Now, for instance?"

"You ready?" he said.

"Well, babe, ready as I'll ever be." She sat back, stretched her feet out onto the hassock, and gestured to her son to say his piece.

"Okay, well, after you guys—ladies, I mean—told me that I looked like my father and grandfather, that scared me. I mean, one got murdered and the other abandoned my mother when she needed him."

"He never knew I was pregnant. Maybe I should have told him," Maureen said.

"Oh, I know that. That you didn't want to wreck his life, or have him wreck yours. Then he died. Supposedly died. That's not what I'm talking about. Mom, I'm not judging you. Okay?"

"Yes, Peter," she said.

"Lily says I look like him but that I'm not like him on the inside. But still, you know, he's my father. Maybe I am like him, maybe I can't help being like him."

"Not a chance," Maureen said, voice firm. She leaned toward her son. "You are so different from him. That's not something you need to worry about."

"But it is. It's me we're talking about here. You know how you read about twins who grew up apart but end up doing the same things, working at the same sort of jobs, taking up the same hobbies? You know, some things you can't get away from."

"Did we forget that half of your genetic material is from yours truly?" his mother said. "So, what's really bothering you? Let's talk about stuff we might actually have a shot at taking control of."

Evidently this last was a regular phrase in the Copeland household, because Peter nodded. Worry only about what you might control? There's a concept, Lily thought, that would save a lot of emotional energy.

"Okay," he repeated. "Here's the thing. I want to meet my grandmother. But I don't want to, like, surprise her, try to get her to say something. If she does, well, she does. But I just want to go there and be me."

"Fair," his mother said. "And?"

He took a deep breath before saying fast, "I want Lily to go with me."

"We'll all go," his mother assured him.

Peter was shaking his head. "No, just Lily."

Oh, lord, Lily thought. "Maybe I should leave?" She started to get up off the sofa but mother and son waved her back.

"Why Lily?" Maureen asked, her voice too quiet.

Peter dropped down on the foot stool, shifting his mother's legs with his in a move that also seemed a regular occurrence in the Copeland house. He leaned toward his mother. "Here's what I've been thinking." Bob padded up to join the boy. "I told Bob last night. He said I had to sleep on it. But I still want to do it this way."

Maureen glanced at Constance, who shrugged.

"You and my grandmother aren't really connected. I mean, she probably knows who you are, but that's it."

"Actually," Lily said, "your grandmother told me that the correct person for your father to have married was your mother."

That stopped the boy. He swung around to look at Lily. "She knew?"

"It would appear to be the case," Lily answered.

"Holy—"

"Watch it," his mother warned.

"—guacamole," he finished. Then sat in thought, hand on Bob's head. "That changes everything. Mom, you and I gotta go see my grandmother."

"Leave Lily and Constance here?"

"They should come, but wait outside."

"What do you think?" Maureen consulted the other adults in the room.

"Sounds like a plan," Constance said.

"Works for me," Lily added. "Just take good notes. What about Bob?"

"He'll wait with you," Peter said.

"Thank you," Constance said. Lily looked at her, thinking that she was being sarcastic, since her dog seemed to have changed allegiance. But she was quite serious. When Maureen and Peter left the room, Constance told Lily, "Bob's got a sister who's about to have puppies. Either I'm starting over with a puppy or Maureen is."

"You'd give him up?"

"It's up to Bob. I hope he chooses me."

Lily couldn't believe Bob would leave Constance. Right now, Bob knew Peter needed him more than Constance. Now, how do I know that? she wondered. What do I know about dogs? Well, one thing, maybe. "Let's talk later, but I think I'd like one of Bob's nieces or nephews."

"Along with the trainer I went to in New Haven? Then you'd get nature and nurture, which about covers it." They were following Constance's dog, Maureen and Peter out to the white Explorer parked in front of the inn.

"Constance, I've got to confess, I'm glad it's Maureen that's going to see Jonas' mother. That woman frightens me."

"Have you considered the possibility that the whole ghost thing is an act? That there is a real Lillian Atwood underneath that she doesn't want anyone to see?"

Lily stopped at the front gate and turned on Constance. "You must be joking. No one can keep up an act for, what, more than twenty years?"

All Constance said in reply was, "Jonas."

• • •

Lily held onto Constance's arm. She felt as if her world had shifted into focus. The part of her that was straightforward and unimaginative didn't want to believe that someone could keep up an act year after year. But the part of her that had studied and analyzed others' imaginations thought, yes, it was possible. The difference between person and persona. Wharton wrote about it all the time, the difference between what a character might actually be and what he or she—mostly she—wanted New York society to believe. But it took so much energy to put on an act all the time. Look at the protagonist of *House of Mirth*, who faded into death.

What was the line, what you see is what you get? That was her, Lily knew. But Jonas?

Constance was saying, "Lily. Are you all right?" She'd pulled her arm away and was shaking Lily gently by the shoulders.

"But it would take so much energy," Lily said.

Constance picked up her thought. "Acting a part?" She started to pull Lily toward the car, but Lily dug her heels in. "People do it all the time," Constance said. "You should meet some of my ex-husband's relatives. Right out of your Wharton novels. Or how about all those phony doctors or investment gurus or fake Du Ponts who end up in *New York Times* exposés after their masquerade ends."

"We need to discuss this with Maureen before they go over there. Now." Without another word, Lily dashed to the car, where Peter and the dog were already in the back seat. Maureen, about to shut the car door, turned in time to see Lily waving both arms at her. It was so unlike the undemonstrative college professor that Maureen ran to her. "What's wrong?"

"Have you ever talked with Jonas' mother?"

Maureen shook her head. "Why?"

"Maybe Peter was right, maybe it should be me who goes in with him. At least I've seen her act. Constance said just now that this whole ghost thing, this poor-Mrs.-Atwood-who-has-lost-her-reason, might be an act. It's hard to believe anyone could keep that up for a couple of decades, but if it is an act—"

"Then that drifting old lady—who, come to think of it, can't be more than sixty years old—is desperate to hide something," Maureen finished for her. "Peter might be in danger."

Constance joined them. "Lily's husband evidently plays a different role for each audience. It is possible that he learned it from his mother. Perhaps his father. In any case, he is so good at role-playing that he fooled Lily for a number of years."

"That wouldn't take much," Lily said.

"Actually, I should think it would take quite a lot," Constance said. "You are in fact quite acute, though you are also accustomed to being told you are not."

Lily laughed. "By my mother, in fact."

"Point made," Constance said.

Maureen rocked back and forth, heel to toe, considering. "All right, then, I have a question. Do you think Lillian Atwood would put on her act in front of Peter?"

Constance answered, "The idea is that Peter's resemblance to his father and grandfather will shock his grandmother into being herself. Whatever that might be."

"It's a risk," Lily put in. "If she's invested so much energy into hiding her real self, what is it that's so important to hide from public view?"

Peter spoke up from right behind his mother. "I'm going to see her. Mom, you're going with me. Come on." He turned back to the car, where Bob waited for him.

The three women watched him. Lily asked Maureen, "What do you think?"

"That I wish we'd stayed in Kansas City." She took a deep breath. "He's going to meet his grandmother whether I want him to or not. So let's control what we can. I'll go in with him. You two stay close, eavesdrop if you can. Bring Bob."

Lily pursed her lips, shaking her head no, then said, "You're right." Then suggested, "Police?"

"It would ruin the effect," said Constance.

"Peter won't wait for them," Maureen said.

"Go, then," Constance said. "With great care." But when Maureen turned to go, Constance gripped Lily's wrist. "We will watch through the windows or front door. Then you will join them to see if your mother-in-law snaps back into character." She released Lily's wrist.

She's done this before, Lily thought. What Lily didn't know about Constance deepened each day. "Did it work before, surprising someone out of his persona?"

"It worked." Constance's face was grim. "*Her* persona."

Chapter 46

Jonas' mother lived in a small white two-story house a few blocks off Main Street. The house needed painting. However, someone had swept the front porch, the windows looked clean, and a little garden of multicolored celosia and dusty miller surrounded the foundation. Not particularly difficult to keep up, Lily thought, but weed-free. The question was did Lillian Atwood do for herself or was this more evidence of the quiet care of Betty and the other women.

She, Constance and the dog waited on the porch, well away from the door and windows, while Peter rang the front bell. His mother towered behind him, one hand on his shoulder. When there was no answer after a minute or two, he rang the bell again. He waited calmly, hands in his shorts' pockets. In his place, Lily doubted she could have stood so quietly. Again there was no response to the bell. Peter pulled open the screen and knocked on the front door. It wasn't until he'd knocked a second time, using the "shave and a haircut, two bits" rhythm, that the door pulled open. Lily got the feeling that the older woman had been standing behind the door, waiting for some signal.

Dressed in tattered gym shorts and a tee shirt whose "Parthenon Track Team" logo was just readable, Lillian stood looking at her grandson. Her colorless face took on a look of wonder with a touch of triumph. "I knew you'd come," she said.

"I'm Peter Copeland," he said, putting out his hand.

"I know," she said and stepped back to invite him in without shaking his hand. When his mother followed, Lillian said, "Welcome to my house, Maureen. I've been wanting to meet you for many years. My son spoke well of you." After Maureen and Peter went inside, Lillian took a step outside onto the porch and looked straight at Lily, Constance and Bob. "Come in out of the heat. We have so much to talk about." She went inside.

"Maybe you were right," Lily said to Constance.

"I certainly do not see a ghost," Constance said. "Though that in itself is disturbing."

Inside it was cool but bright, shades and curtains drawn back from all the windows despite the day's heat. A faint scent of lemon oil colored the air and, as they went further into the house, baking. Lily sniffed. Sugar cookies?

Peter's grandmother seated her guests in a room fitted as a library. Light wood shelves filled with books lined all the walls, over and under windows, right up to the doorway. Lily said, "May I?" and her mother-in-law nodded.

The books were fiction, from the classics to that year's hottest bestseller. Lily spotted *Pamela*, considered to be the first novel written, all of Jane Austen, all of Edith Wharton, even a copy of *Tristram Shandy*. "Did you actually get through *Tristram*?" Lily blurted out, then felt herself blush. She'd never managed to finish the book, no matter how often she tried, and felt somehow a failure for it.

Lillian laughed. "It's a bugger, isn't it? But it's amazing what you can accomplish when you're left alone. Make yourself comfortable, please, while I get the iced tea."

"Did you know we were coming?" Peter asked.

"No, dear. I didn't know. I hoped. I knew you were in town asking questions, I assumed looking for your past and mine. Under the circumstances, I couldn't very well chase you down."

"What circumstances?" he asked.

"We'll talk. Would you like to help me bring in the glasses?"

"Sure." The two went through the doorway, turning left down the hall.

When their voices faded, Lily said, "Person? Or persona?"

Constance, too, investigated the shelves before taking a seat in a well-worn arm chair.

"Who does she remind you of? Or maybe I should say, what?"

"A retired literature professor. Someone who has spent a lifetime doing exactly what she wanted, to read." Lily spotted John Updike's *Rabbit, Run*, which turned out to be a first edition. A few shelves away, she took out a hardback copy of Hemingway's *The Old Man and the Sea*, only to discover that it, too, was a first edition. Some of these books were so valuable that they should be locked away in a rare book library.

She was kneeling to pull out a book from a shelf at floor level when Peter returned carrying a tray of glasses, followed by his grandmother, who held a large plate of sugar cookies. They put them on the coffee table. Peter stood up, looking uncertain. "Sit here," Lillian suggested, pointing to a corner of the sofa. She sat in the opposite corner facing him. Maureen pulled a chair near her son, while Lily and Constance took armchairs. Bob looked between Peter and Constance, choosing to sit by the latter. Constance looked pleased if a bit surprised.

"Now you," their hostess said to Lily, "I met in the cemetery the other day. You are my son's wife?"

"Yes." Lily stifled her next word, which would have been "ma'am."

"Please introduce me to your friends."

"This is Constance Cordrey," Lily said. "We met when I was doing research at the Beinecke."

"Yale, yes," Lillian said. "I've never had the pleasure of seeing it in person but I've seen pictures. Quite a place."

Constance said, "I think so. This is Bob, my dog. And Peter's."

Peter's smile looked like the sun outside. "You think so?"

"Bob thinks so, which is the important point."

Lillian began handing around the iced tea without asking if people wanted it. Then she handed the plate of cookies to Peter. "Do the honors, please."

Everyone took one cookie before Maureen handed the plate back to Peter. He looked a question at her. She said, "Ask your grandmother."

"Eat them all," she said. "There are more in the kitchen." She looked around at her guests. "Now, may I assume that you're wondering why I acted the way I did in the cemetery?"

"And everywhere but here, or so we're told," Lily said.

"It's a long story but a short one," she said.

"Tragic?" Lily asked.

"In the sense that Aristotle meant, yes."

"What's that mean?" Peter asked.

"That a man is brought down by his own weakness," Lillian answered. "Aristotle referred to it as the tragic flaw. Your grandfather and your father owned—own—such flaws."

Peter turned white. "Me?"

"No," his grandmother said. "That's why I've stayed out of your life."

"Until now," Maureen said.

"Oh, no, my dear. Today is the exception. I am—" She took a long hungry look at her grandson. "I am poison."

She shook her head. "Poison isn't quite the right word. You'd think after all these years I would have settled on the word." Her eyes went blank and for a moment Lily thought she'd disappeared to again become the wraith of the graveyard. She must have felt Lily's apprehension because she again shook her head. "Poison will do. In any case, after prolonged contact with me, men who look like you" she pointed at Peter "go bad. Rotten fruit." She put down her iced tea. Her mouth pursed as if she'd bitten into that fruit. That's when it occurred to Lily that she hadn't touched her grandson.

Lillian suddenly stood up, caught the crumbs falling from her lap and dusted them onto her cookie plate. Then she threaded her way around the coffee table and beside Lily to the front door, which had been left open. Now she looked out the screen before closing the door and locking it. When she turned to find all eyes on her, she shrugged. "I would prefer no one overhear. The church women have gotten into the habit over the years of dropping by to check on me." As she returned to the sofa, Lily noted that she had a long stride, long legs that looked much better than Lily's would ever look in those old track shorts. Jonas' mother must have been a beauty. Now her hair was pure white, still thick, brushed back from her high forehead and caught in a rubber band at her collar. The elegance of her hair contrasted with the web of lines emanating from the corners of her eyes and nose and across her forehead. Odd, because the skin of her arms and legs was quite taut.

"I will tell my story and you will listen. Then you will leave and I will become that unfortunate Atwood woman again." She didn't wait for them to agree, instead directing her grandson back to the kitchen for more cookies. "You'll find chocolate chip ones and peanut butter. Bring them all." When he was gone, she fixed a look on Maureen. "He is fourteen?"

"Yes, almost fifteen."

"It is acceptable that he hears a story that refers to sexual attraction?"

"Fine with me. I doubt that he'll be either embarrassed or titillated," Maureen replied. "If that's what you're asking."

"Yes." Lillian gestured at the books surrounding them. "So much of what's real in life involves sex, whether or not the act itself is involved." The woman was quite unembarrassed by her words. Lily wondered what she had been like as a teacher. Had she taught? Lily put the question and received a nod in reply. "As a teaching assistant in American literature at the University of Kansas when I was working on my doctorate."

"Did you like teaching?" Lily asked.

"Indeed. In front of a classroom of young men and women was where I felt most comfortable. Talking with young minds about books." Her eyes followed Peter as he carried in a platter piled high with cookies. The care with which he held it seemed to entertain her. Before he could offer it around, she cleared a space on the table in front of his end of the sofa, leaning out of his way when he bent to put it down.

Lillian Atwood swept her small audience with a thorough glance before asking, "Is everyone comfortable?"

Lily nodded, the other women smiled, and Peter bit into a chocolate chip cookie. Bob had stretched himself across Constance's feet, eyes closed. For a few seconds, the only sounds were crunching and the whir of air conditioning.

Lillian leaned back, crossed her ankles and gazed over their heads toward the light glaring through the broad front window. Her hands clasped across her flat abdomen. "I grew up in Parthenon in the 1950s and 60s. It was little more than a farm town then. The high school was only a few years old when I went there. But the teachers were good. I was always most comfortable reading a book or sitting in a classroom. My parents, your great-grandparents," she smiled at Peter, "were teachers. Your great-grandfather taught mathematics and coached the high school baseball team before becoming the elementary school principal. Your great-grandmother taught sixth grade her whole life, not quitting after I was born, as most young women teachers did back then."

Reading was a way of life in Lillian's house, she continued. It was only natural that she would go on to university. But money was tight, so she moved no farther from Parthenon than to Lawrence and the University of Kansas—KU—one hundred miles to the east. It was enough, though. She majored in English and minored in history—"any literature major will tell you that you need to know history to really understand what you are reading"—coming home for occasional visits during the next eight years.

"I must have known Joel Atwood, since we were the same age in a town with just one grade school and one high school, but he never made an impression on me." When she met him at KU while finishing her doctoral thesis, it was by chance. Joel had graduated from the large state agricultural university, Kansas State, four years before with a degree in land management. He was visiting a potential investor in a land deal, a KU English professor who was land-rich in his home county in western Kansas. The professor made a point of introducing Joel to his fellow citizen from Parthenon, Lillian Stone.

"I was deep into revisions on my dissertation and really didn't want to be pulled away, but that professor was one of my thesis advisors."

"Whom you never, ever want to alienate," Lily put in.

Obediently, Miss Stone, as this professor called her, reported to her advisor's office. There she met a young man of her own age and her own height, with chestnut hair worn fashionably long, dressed in a blue suit and cowboy boots. "His eyes were blue, your father's hazel, yours brown," she said to Peter, snapping them all back to the present. "It didn't occur to me at the time that he'd chosen his shirt because the color, delphinium blue, made those eyes look deeper, somehow prescient. The reason it didn't occur to me is because I had not known any men who paid that much care to the specifics of their appearance. My father went out every morning clean, neat and pressed, and wore his clothes until they no longer fulfilled these requirements.

"After my advisor introduced us, Joel looked at me with his theatrical eyes and said, 'Thank you for introducing me to the woman I'm going to marry.'

"I thought him an utter fool." Immediately after meeting him she excused herself and returned to her office and dissertation. Over the next few months, Joel Atwood would appear with flowers or chocolates. When she didn't respond to those standard gifts of romance, he began asking her out for coffee. She refused, not wanting to be dragged away from her writing. He tried having her advisor pressure her, but the advisor merely laughed, telling Joel to wait, or so he reported to Miss Stone.

Joel researched Miss Lillian Stone. He read the articles she'd published in academic journals. Then he began to send her books. Not just any books, but first editions of the books she'd referenced in her published work. That got her attention. She still made him hold off until her dissertation was finished and she'd successfully defended it. When she went on her first date with Joel Atwood, her title was Dr. Lillian Stone. Given her publishing track record and her high marks from her students, KU had offered her a position as assistant professor. She was on her way to a life doing just what she'd always wanted, reading and teaching.

In her book-lined living room in Parthenon on a boiling day in August thirty-four years later, Lillian Atwood paused to sip cold tea. Her eyes swept the shelves containing her most precious possessions. She held onto the glass, allowing condensation to drip over her hands, then replaced it on its saucer. One hand gestured widely around the room. "You'll find everything about human nature here, if you pay close enough attention.

"Evidently I had become distracted, because Joel caught me completely off-guard."

She expected to date the man a few times, then go back to her work. She was twenty-six years old and a virgin, regarded as a confirmed spinster. What she didn't see was that she was beautiful and apparently unattainable, an irresistible combination for Joel Atwood. He was a man accustomed to getting what he wanted, a man who sought particularly that which appeared impossible to acquire. So, yes, he took the spinster on a chaste date. Then a second date and a third. When she was ready to call a halt, he kissed her neck, next to her collarbone.

The white-haired Lillian fingered the spot, just over a small scar. "I had never been kissed that way. Oh, I'd read about it in my books, but those were stories. Joel kissed me, then sent me away. When next he asked me out, I went, despite my better judgment." He took his time, but eventually Joel bedded Miss Stone. "I found out for myself what the books were trying to describe. Words can call it exquisite, they can refer to 'addicting' and 'clouds the mind,' but doing and reading are not the same." She raised her eyebrows at Maureen, as if to ask permission to continue her tale. Maureen nodded and gestured for her to continue.

"Did you know it's possible to become pregnant after just one act of sexual intercourse?" Lillian queried her listeners. Everyone nodded, including Peter. "I must have known, but it simply never occurred to me that it might happen." In Kansas at the time it was possible to find a doctor who would perform an abortion, but Lillian didn't take that route. "Unmarried pregnant assistant professors were simply unacceptable almost four decades ago." When Joel pressured her to marry, she gave in, ungraciously. Their families held a large wedding, Dr. Stone became Dr. Atwood, wearing a gold ring to legitimize her expanding waistline.

Then two things happened. Her dissertation advisor, now her department chair, suddenly decided she should take a leave of absence. She subsequently discovered that he had caved in to Joel's demand that he do so, partly because he was an old-fashioned man who felt women should be with their children and mostly because the land deal with Joel had been so lucrative that the department chair wanted in on the next deal. Jonas was born and Lillian Stone Atwood fell in love with her son.

"I meant to go back to work once he was in kindergarten, just as so many women intend. I cared for him and cuddled him throughout the day and read the rest of the time. Meals would get on the table, laundry and housework would get done, but for the life of me I cannot remember doing it." In the meantime, Joel reintroduced Lillian to sex. For the first time in her life, she was leading a life of the senses rather than a life of the mind. "It was intoxicating. I became drunk with it." Joel wrote a letter to that department chair saying Lillian had decided not to return, and signed her name. When he told her what he had done, she did not object.

"He had what he wanted. Me, yes. A son, yes. But what he had schemed for was control over me, the one person no one thought he'd be able to control. To the town, he was Alexander the Great. Then one day he moved out of our house.

"To me, he was the Roman general who sacked Carthage and then sowed the land with salt." She looked around at us. "Hyperbole, yes. But then we are all the center of our own histories. I should have let him leave. I should have taken Jonas and gone home to my parents. They were ready to welcome us. In retrospect, had I left to rebuild my single life, I would have gotten Joel back, because he would have pursued me to reassert his control. But I was addicted, thinking as addicts do only about my next fix, and my substance of choice, sex with my husband, was offered just often enough to keep me hooked."

Joel Atwood built his bachelor dream house out on the edge of town with the money that just kept rolling in. He never brought up the possibility of divorce and neither did Lillian. They led separate existences, with the occasional overlap. Because Joel doled out attention to his son sparingly, Jonas regarded him as he would a celebrity. His father embodied his model of male perfection. When Lillian tried to show him a view of reality, Jonas turned on her. "By the time he was fifteen years old, I knew my son would be just like his father. Controlling. Acquisitive. Selfish beyond belief. With enough charm for a dozen men. I became afraid of my own son. I waited for the day he would leave home for college.

"I made one crucial error."

Jonas' grades were good enough to be admitted into any college. But his father made too much money for him to get any financial aid, even student loans, unless he declared himself independent. That Jonas would not do. Lillian had never saved anything from the money Joel gave them. There didn't seem to be any point. But one night he came over to tell her that he hadn't any intention of paying for their son beyond age eighteen. "He told me I should have thought of that. It was the kind of unreasonable thing he loved to say, knowing that I had no way of fighting back. It meant the ugliness with Joel and Jonas would continue unabated in my life."

She turned to Maureen. "I knew what Jonas had done to you," she said. "He did it on purpose, repeating what his father had done to me, to prove he could do it. His father was amused. You were in fact part of his decision to try to keep the boy around to ape him. But if Jonas had stayed in Parthenon, he would have tortured you, and you would have become captive because of the child."

She shook her head so violently that Peter leaned toward her to help, but she held her palm up to ward him off. "Not again. The ugliness had to stop." She took a deep breath.

"There's something that I left out." She looked at her hands, now clasped tightly over her breasts. Without looking up, she said, "It embarrasses me still. Joel had introduced a new element to our sex. Pain. He liked causing me physical pain." When she looked up, tears filled the crevices next to eyes and nose. "A few days after announcing that he wasn't supporting Jonas beyond high school, Joel bought a knife. It must have been a whimsical purchase, because it was a combat knife, bought from some dreadful man who ran a military surplus store outside of town. Joel could open it in one smooth motion. It was sharp as a razor, the kind of blade that cuts you painlessly. Before you know it, the cuts burn."

Her lip curled. "The first night he had it, he kissed me here," again her hand went to her collarbone, "and cut me here," her finger moved to the scar on her neck. "He called it a little reminder of him." She swiped at her eyes and face with an impatient hand. "That pain burned away my addiction. I saw clearly. My husband was a reptile. His touch repelled me."

Lillian sat up, back rigid, hands on her knees. "What I am about to tell you —" Her hands sought each other, but she pulled them apart by sheer force of will. "I want you to know it. Let me tell it. Then you do what you think is right." One hand started toward Peter. Again she pulled back.

"By this time, Jonas had graduated from high school. He'd been accepted to Middlebury College in Vermont, a fine liberal arts college." She looked directly at Maureen. "I could tell you were pregnant."

Maureen interrupted, "Then you realized before I did."

"I was paying attention, something that I had failed to do for too many years. Before I noticed your condition, I had hoped Joel might kill me with that fool knife. But now I had to do something. What, I didn't know, but for once I had to act rather than merely react."

Now her hands clasped so tightly that her knuckles reflected the white of her hair. "Jonas had been a star of the track team. It was one of the things that got him into college, got him a scholarship. I'd never seen him run. By the time he joined the varsity team, I rarely left the house." One hand plucked at the shorts she wore, and Lily realized with a start that they were Jonas' old clothes. "I wanted to see him run. He loved going out to the high school track. Back then it was just beyond a grove of trees behind the main building. He thought of it as his track. He felt free there and I wanted a memory of him enjoying his freedom." She shook her head again. "I didn't particularly like my son but I dearly loved him."

She opened her mouth as if to speak, then closed it. Lily wanted to reach out and hold the woman, this woman who would have been such a wonderful mother-in-law in another life. Although she didn't want to hear what Lillian had to tell them, she knew she had to hear it.

"I think one of the church women gave me a ride out to the high school. Dorothy, probably, because she was the one who had taken me on as her particular responsibility, even though she had enough on her plate as principal of the high school. When I got through those trees, I could see Jonas flying around the track. He was running so fast it wasn't possible to see his feet as they hit the ground. He flew past me once, twice, three times before he noticed me. I waved to him but he didn't wave back. He seemed to speed up, if anything. But on his next circuit, he slowed down considerably and appeared to be looking over my shoulder. I turned and there was Joel. Before I could say anything, he had that knife out, point at my throat.

"I reacted before I could think. Self-preservation lies somewhere in the autonomic nervous system. Before that night I would just freeze when he hurt me, trying to will it to end. Not this time. Maybe I had made a decision subconsciously, maybe I picked up on Joel's real intention this time. I spun around, catching him by surprise. We were face to face. He held the knife in his fist." She mimed his action, elbow at ninety degrees, knife held firmly out. "He thrust it towards my neck, grinning at me the whole time. He assumed that I had no strength, that I was merely the woman that he'd carefully worn down day after day. It was a reasonable assumption. However, if you push and push at something, the pushing strengthens it. I lashed out with my forearm, catching his wrist. It surprised both of us when I whipped his arm down. The blade of the knife sliced into his thigh."

She swallowed, her face taking on a greenish tinge. Maureen leaned forward and slid the glass toward her. Lillian drank down half the tea. "Blood spurted everywhere. I've since looked it up. The knife must have slashed his femoral artery. I started to unbutton my dress, intending to use it as a tourniquet to slow the bleeding. But Jonas was there."

She gulped what tea remained. "He said, 'You're disgusting. How can you think of sex when he's bleeding. Get away from us.' He pushed me hard, throwing me down. I think the fall must have knocked the wind out of me because I blacked out. The next thing I knew, I was in the back seat of Jonas' car. He drove home—this house—pulled me inside and hissed at me to stay and act crazy. Then he left."

Her eyes filled with unshed tears. Her hands relaxed on her knees as she sank back onto the sofa cushions. "I killed Joel. I lost Jonas, if I'd ever had him. It would have been much easier had the knife gone into me. But if it had, the evil would have been visited upon the third generation."

Peter's face had gone sallow, his eyes wide with shock. Lily hadn't noticed that both Maureen and Bob had gone to him. Maureen sat on the edge of the sofa, both arms pulling her son to her chest. Bob was sitting on Peter's feet, eyes watching Lillian intently.

It was Constance who broke the silence. "Actually, you might well have saved Joel had Jonas allowed you to apply the tourniquet. You reacted logically, in self-defense. It was Jonas' behavior that altered the ultimate outcome. You wounded your husband but your son killed his father."

"No." Lillian's voice was strangled. "No, I killed him. After years of analyzing the event, I realize I meant to."

Chapter 47

No one spoke. Peter patted his mother's shoulder before gently freeing himself from her hold. Bob remained at his knees. Lillian's back remained rigid, arms wrapped tight around her chest. Constance wore the analytical look that Lily recognized from working with her at the Beinecke, when Constance had told Lily she knew all about what Lily was searching for.

Lily felt protective. Many of the books surrounding them told stories of victims, from Wharton's Ethan Frome, who set events in motion that sealed his fate as prisoner of his own house, to Updike's Rabbit, prisoner of his own past. Up until that very moment, Lily had felt kinship with these characters. But now, now, she wanted nothing to do with them. Enough, she thought, impatient. Lillian Stone Atwood refused to take charge until it was too late. She, Lily Atwood, was ready. "Enough," she said aloud.

"Indeed," Constance agreed. "Look at the facts. Your husband wanted to kill you. You defended yourself. Your son let him die."

"I killed him," Lillian said. "That's all you need to know."

"When I was in high school at the same time Jonas was," Lily said, "CPR was a required course. It was for Jonas, too. He told me." He hadn't, but Lily didn't care.

Lillian sat forward. "Was it?"

"It was," Maureen said. "I know that for a fact. Every junior was required to take the Red Cross course and pass it. Athletes had to take the course as soon as they hit junior varsity. Jonas must have taken it by sophomore year, two years before the, well, knifing."

Lily continued, "Jonas knew about tourniquets. He could have used that shirt you're wearing to at least try to save his father. Why didn't he?"

"Shock?" Lillian said, voice now wavering. She pulled at the shirt so hard a bra strap showed.

"If he was in such shock, how did he manage to throw you in the car, drive you home, and get Jane to drive his car to his father's house?"

Lillian's mouth opened but nothing came out.

"Surprise," Lily said. "Jane talked. Everyone apparently is tired of this whole charade. Even—"

Peter interrupted. "I have a question." He got everyone's attention. "How did my father convince the whole town that he was dead? And, you know, why?"

"Out of the mouths," his mother muttered.

"Stop it," he said, and his mother sat back, surprised. "I am not a child. Finding out about this is why we're here." He turned to his grandmother. "Do you know about my father?"

Her head was bowed, but Lily could have sworn there was a little smile on the older woman's face. Her hand dropped the shirt and relaxed in her lap. Without looking up, she said in a quiet voice, "I told people that Jonas' college had contacted me." Her chin rose, and yes, she was smiling. "It was my first bit of storytelling, with me as author. I let it be known in bits and pieces—the story told by the crazy lady in odd moments of lucidity, you know—that my son had been killed in a fiery car accident. There were no remains."

"What happened if Jonas returned to Parthenon?" Lily asked.

"I knew he wouldn't. He knew his presence would stir up interest in his father's murder. It was, as my students would have phrased it, a safe bet."

"But why did you start the rumor?" Peter demanded. His dark eyes narrowed. "What was the point?"

"Remember, I love my son. I wanted him safe even though that meant keeping him as far away from me as possible. If he were dead, any police investigation would die with him. The police never suspected me, probably because they thought I was useless as a human being. I made sure of that."

"Why didn't you leave town?" Maureen asked.

"To go where?" Lillian said with some tartness. "Do what? Be Dr. Lillian Stone Atwood? She died sometime in the last century, killed by her first and only husband."

"Plus, you liked being a victim," Lily challenged.

Lillian stood up and took a step toward her. Lily stood up as well, but the other woman stopped, all color drained from her face, her eyes no more than pale slits. She felt behind her, finding air, stepped back, found the sofa and collapsed onto it.

"It was what Joel always wanted me to be," she said. "But what I discovered after that June day was that I liked being angry. It is my anger that has kept me alive. It gives me the same feeling sex used to. A victim? No. An addict? Oh, indeed, to this day. I am in love, and I make very sure to stoke my anger every day. Without fail." Now those eyes glittered.

Lily assayed the idea that her mother-in-law really was out of her mind, but couldn't find gold in it. Lily's life story overlapped Lillian's just enough that anger seemed a quite reasonable and sane response. Lily intended to use her anger rather than indulge it. She had had enough of victims, especially herself.

"You are angry at yourself, are you not?" Constance said, in a bored voice.

If she was trying to provoke the older woman—and Lily suspected she was—it worked. Lillian Atwood jittered to the edge of the sofa. "Who are you to judge me? You've never been a victim, you with your fancy necklace and fancy dog."

Without moving, Constance said, "You do not know anything about me. I have been a victim. I am not impressed." Bob abandoned Peter for his mistress, taking up guard stance between Lillian and her. His ears laid flat, eyes fixed on the potential attacker.

"You've never murdered anyone." Lillian's shout brought her off the sofa and two steps toward Constance.

Constance rose also. Bob growled. Constance tapped him on the head. When he glanced at her, she shook her head. He sat on his haunches, still watchful. "Neither have you murdered anyone. If that is what you regard as your life achievement, you fool yourself."

Unblinking, Constance stared at Lillian. Her green eyes glowed, a pink flush colored her cheeks, and her curls seemed to electrify. Bob's rumbling growl broke the silence. Lillian turned as pale as the ghost she'd played for so many years, and swayed. Peter broke away from his mother and got to his grandmother in time to catch her as she fell. He carried her to a chair, sat her down and pushed her head towards her knees. "Grandmom, wake up. Come back." She moaned. Becoming aware of her grandson's arms, Lillian tried to push him away. He held on.

Peter turned to Lily, his face implacable. "You have to fix this."

"I intend to," she replied, equally implacable.

• • •

Constance gathered the iced tea glasses onto the tray and took them into the kitchen. Lily followed her. The high color in her friend's face had faded, but those eyes still sparked. Lily asked, "Why are you so angry?"

"Why would I not be?" Constance found dish soap, filled the sink and began washing glasses. "I hate it when people waste their lives." She rinsed a glass, put it in the drainer next to the sink, and glared. "We only receive one life. Here is this brilliant woman who allowed some fool to completely derail her one life.

"You know what makes me mad?" Constance was slapping the dish cloth against the edge of the sink. "Instead of taking charge after her husband moved out, instead of getting support from her parents and telling her department chair that her husband forged her signature and that the chair better do something about that or she would let people know what a sexist pig he was—this was at the height of the women's movement, you know—" Constance put down the cloth and took a breath. "She gave in. She never fought back. I cannot tolerate such cowardice."

By this time Lily was leaning against the kitchen door frame. "You're projecting," she said.

"Of course I am projecting, Dr. Freud," Constance snapped. She rinsed the iced tea pitcher and began opening cabinet doors. In the cabinet next to the refrigerator she found a jar of Nestea. Holding it up to show Lily, she said, "A Nestea woman." She shook the jar. "Maybe there is hope after all."

"That there's something there behind the act?" Lily said.

"Oh, something is there." Constance measured tea into the pitcher, turned on the cold tap and added water. "It just needs to grow a backbone."

"It is possible," Lily's voice was soft, "to kill someone but to leave them alive. To murder without a death. My father-in-law killed my mother-in-law. Her remains sit in the next room."

Constance dried her hands on the dishtowel. "Those remains?" Constance nodded in the direction of the living room and Lillian Atwood. "Killing her killer would have been self-defense. Who knew that better than Jonas, who observed the whole process?"

"Yes, I've thought of that." In a louder voice, Lily said, "Bring the tea. Did you notice any paper around here?"

"I keep a pad and pen in my bag. I left it inside the front door."

Peter appeared next to Lily. "What are you going to do? What do you need paper for?"

Lily slipped her arm through his. "We are going to construct a plan. First we figure out what we need to know, then we determine how to find that information. Believe it or not, I have a doctorate in doing just that. I am an expert at investigating." Her laugh was dry. "Just ask your father."

Chapter 48

After the wide-open space and saturated blue of the Kansas sky, the tight bungalows and dim strip malls cluttering the gray of Chicago's northwest side felt claustrophobic to Lily. Constance drove the rental car from O'Hare to Lakeland, with Lily navigating from the passenger seat; Bob sat on the backseat, keeping an eye on his women. It was raining steadily, late-summer rain that hints of autumn around the Great Lakes. Windshield wipers beat a steady rhythm, but neither Lily nor Constance were lulled.

"We meet your uncle first?" Constance asked.

"He's got the key to the new locks on our—my—apartment. We have to see him first."

"Tell me about him."

Lily had spent enough time with Constance to understand she wasn't making conversation. Constance asked questions because she wanted to know answers.

Lily needed to think about the question. How do you describe a given in your life? That person you could always rely on but who rarely intruded? She pictured Nate Miller. "Well, he's tall and lanky. For that matter, so are my parents. I take after my paternal grandmother, who was short, too. Anyway, he's a cabinetmaker. Wait until you see what he builds. They're works of art. He's got a waiting list of customers that's a couple of years long. People plan their renovations around Nate's work."

Lily directed Constance to turn left at the next light.

"He never tried to turn you into a woodworker?"

"By the time I found Nate, I was already on the road to literary research. He had to fight his family to do what he loved. He always told me that I should go ahead and do what I loved. It's tricky enough, he said, to find out what that is without fighting other people's ideas. But if you can find it, then you never work a day in your life. He was quoting someone, but I can't remember who. Steinbeck, maybe. He loves Steinbeck." She turned around to pat Bob. "We never had a dog. Don't know why."

"You never wanted one?" Constance asked. She adjusted the windshield wipers one notch faster.

"Not until now. Now I can't imagine life without one."

Constance laughed. "Just wait until you get to house-train a puppy. Go through two or three levels of obedience training. There will be days when you long for life without one."

"How about we just let Bob train my puppy?"

That stopped Constance's laughter. "If you get a female, you know, he just might help out."

"Have his nieces and nephews been born yet?"

"A month ago. I called the breeder yesterday. She says she still has the runt of the litter, a female."

"Just like me," Lily said. "Runt, I mean. My parents never got around to the rest of the litter."

"Well, I asked the breeder to hang onto the pup until she heard from me."

"She'll do that?" Lily turned toward Constance.

"Sure, I put a deposit down on her for you."

Lily thought about that. "Thank you. Now I have something and someone to look forward to when this is all over."

"This will never be all over," Constance said. "You must know that."

"Resolved, then. So I can see the next phase of my life."

Constance said, "Choose carefully."

"You chose well," Lily said.

"I was lucky. Like you, I have work that I love." She stopped for a yellow light. "What does your uncle think of Jonas?"

Lily pictured the closed expression her uncle reserved for his nephew-in-law. Had he always looked that way?

Nate was a reserved man. His best friend, after his wife, was an architect who had built a low-slung house overlooking a bit of Lake Michigan beach on the very northeast point of Lakeland. The house was hidden from the road. It was like a wonderful secret, which is why Nate had designed and crafted built-in shelves and tables that folded up behind wall panels, carrying the secret through to the interior design. Walter, the architect, had figured out a way to package Nate's designs and sell them to other architects and interior designers. That's where the money had come from for him to buy his studio and house. He and Walter sometimes acted like a couple of spies dreaming up their next caper. When Nate and Walter were together, Nate's face was alive and open, the way it was with her and his wife and, lately, Cara.

But not with Jonas. Ever.

She related this to Constance, who mulled it over while she drove through Prairie Shores. Lily directed her to Nate's building, down the alley next to it, and into the small parking lot in back, next to his van. She wondered where Cara was, since her car wasn't in the lot. Constance switched off the ignition.

They sat in silence. Rain beat steadily on the roof. Bob yawned with excitement and pushed his wet nose into his owner's hair. She turned to Lily. "Are you ready?"

At the sight of her uncle opening the back door, Lily felt a lurch inside, a burst of love for this man. "I'm ready. It's time to listen."

"To your uncle?"

"Yes, something I should have done six years ago. Also for me to talk. To tell him, as he would say."

Constance reached over the seat and opened the car's back door from the inside. "Hurry quick," she told Bob, who hustled out into the rain to find a bush. The women dashed through the open door to the workshop, Bob right behind them. "Wait," Constance told him. She took him outside, had him shake out his wet coat, then brought him back. By that time, Nate Miller had a clean shop towel held out to her. She dried the dog before standing up and holding out her hand. "Hello, I am Constance Cordrey."

Nate took her hand gravely, then looked down at her other companion. "Who is this?"

"Bob, my dog." Bob looked up at Nate, tail still. Lily stepped forward. "Bob, this is my uncle. He's a friend. Friend." The dog's tail went up but didn't wag. "Nate, would you hold out your hand, please?" Nate did so, palm down in the dog-approved manner. Bob stepped forward to sniff the hand while Lily repeated, "Friend." Nate kneeled down to Bob's level. His action seemed to decide Bob, whose tail wagged.

"A watch dog, I take it?" Nate said. "Not a bad idea for a young woman these days." He looked at Lily as he said this. Her returning smile was sad but firm. Nate said, "Good." They were still standing in the rear of the shop, under the overhang in the loading area Nate had built to take in wood and send out his finished art. "Come in. I've closed the cat in Cara's apartment. Would you like some tea?"

Lily led the way into the familiar light and dry warmth of the studio. It was scented by the wood, with the occasional fruit note of resin and sour note of glue. Lily's second home. She headed right for the chair where she'd read all the books from the biography section of her high school library, in alphabetical order. She remembered Clara Barton and Florence Nightingale. Mark Twain. Benjamin Franklin. When she finished all the biographies, she felt bereft until a librarian introduced her to the fiction section, ushering her into a world she'd never left.

Her uncle offered Constance the rocker, one of his first creations. The wood was bumpy and imperfect but the chair much more comfortable than it looked. He handed them mugs of tea and put out a bowl of water for Bob before joining them. "All right, tell me."

Lily and Constance told him everything, from the moment that Jonas had shown up in Guilford to their meeting the day before with Jonas' mother in Parthenon, the return drive to Kansas City with Maureen and Peter, another hitched jet ride from KCI to O'Hare.

When they were done, he put down his empty tea mug on the floor, then sat tapping his fingertips to his chin.

Lily broke his reverie. "You never liked Jonas."

"True."

"But you never knew why."

"Also true. It was just a feeling. My wife told me over and over it was because I could never accept that any man was good enough for my Lily."

Lily felt herself flush and glanced out of the corner of her eye at Constance. Those green eyes were looking at Nate Miller approvingly. Lily grew even warmer. "Why did my mother like him?"

"Does she? Hard to tell what or who she likes. I assumed that she wanted you to have a real life outside of your books. Jonas was the only man who ever got your attention. It was his persistence that your mother admired. Plus that dangerous charm that he so relies on. From what you're telling me, persistence has worked for him with women in the past. This Maureen."

"You'd like Maureen. Peter—well, Peter is a wonder. Fourteen going on fifty."

"That's that age," Nate said.

"It is also Peter," Constance said. "He is something special. I can say that since we are in no way related. Consider it an objective view."

"Hah," Lily said. "You love him because Bob does."

"My dog has objective good sense," Constance said.

Nate cleared his throat. "I changed the locks the night you called me from Connecticut. Jonas showed up late the next day, pounding on the studio door. I didn't answer. When he telephoned, I told him what I'd done and why, that he'd find his belongings in boxes on the loading dock back there," he pointed to the rear of the store. "He came for them immediately. Took your car, of course. Nothing I could do about that."

Lily shrugged. "Now he can make the payments. I don't care."

"What did you do about your bank account?"

Lily looked at her hands. "There wasn't much in it. When he moved to Lakeland from Prairie Shores, Jonas took to spending all the money we had. Expensive clothes. Expensive toys, that camera and stuff." She looked up to find her uncle's eyes looking at her sadly. "Yes, and lots of restaurants I didn't go to with him. Business meals, he said, but I never saw any reimbursement." She stopped Nate's question with her hand. "It doesn't matter. When I got the grant money, I opened my own account at your bank. I gave your address here at the studio for the statements. I was thinking at the time that the grant money was mine, not his. But maybe subconsciously I was thinking it also wasn't his to spend. When he heard about the money, it was too late. I was on my way to Yale for the summer. Out of his sight."

"I think it made him angry," Nate said. "Right after you left, your mother called to say the downstairs tenants complained about him stomping around upstairs in your apartment, banging doors and drawers. After a while it went silent. We haven't seen or heard from him since. Did he leave town?"

Lily blanched. "Oh, no. I forgot. Bethany." She pulled out her phone and clicked on the contact. "Is Bethany there?" Lily sucked in her lips and clamped down. "All right. Thank you. I'll try her on campus." She punched the cell phone buttons hard. "I'm looking for Bethany Dwight. Have you seen her? She did? When? What did he look like? Listen to me. No, listen to me. Call campus security. Now. That man's dangerous. I don't care if he was your professor. He's not now. Good." She closed the phone. "Bethany went off with Jonas." She stood up. "She's smarter than that. What the fuck is going on?"

"Police?" her uncle asked.

She shook her head.

"Where are you going?" he asked.

"Prairie Shores. The campus."

He stood up. "My van's out front." He looked at Bob. "Coming?" To Lily, he said, "You can explain on the way. Seems like you left something out."

. . .

They looked for Jonas and Bethany in what Lily called his "known hangouts." First at the cafe in the student union; next, the mezzanine of the library, then the porch of the English department, which Lily regarded as a long shot. But its corner was dark and secluded. No go. Where, Lily thought, would Jonas take the girl? Out of sight. She asked her uncle to park the van on the far north end of campus and took them for a walk south along the lakefront path. On their right were low green hills rolling away from the lake, which churned gray on their left. The rain had lightened to fine mist, the breeze freshened, and the sky to the northwest showed a hint of blue. The four of them, including Bob on short leash, moved quickly but silently. Finally, in the distance at a curve in the path, in the precise spot Lily anticipated, they saw the pair.

Constance started forward, Bob straining at his leash. Lily pulled them back, hand on Constance's arm.

"Let's watch."

"She's in danger," Nate objected.

"I'm not so sure," Lily said. She put her finger to her lips. They moved a few feet closer.

Just then Cara joined them silently, finger to her own lips. She nodded to Nate and knelt to let Bob sniff her. When Lily crouched next to her, Cara whispered in her ear, "We planned this, Beth and me. Enough was enough."

While they watched, Jonas reached to put his arm around Bethany's shoulder. She spun like a dancer just out of his grasp, then stood there watching him, mouth closed, head cocked as if to say, 'your move.' Jonas moved closer to her, talking. Every time he moved within three feet of the girl, she floated away. She was keeping him out of her personal space. Lily admired her for it. Part of Jonas' method was to breach a woman's space so often that she felt comfortable with him there. Next he'd get her talking so he could do his beguiling listening act. Bethany stopped him before he could start any of his moves. When he waited for her to say something, she waited longer.

Bob began to get restless and Constance led him back up the lake path. To Nate, standing next to her, Lily whispered, "Go with them."

He didn't move.

"So Jonas won't see you. Please." Lily leaned into Nate's shoulder, feeling safe and protected for a brief moment before pulling away and gently pushing him. She felt him turn, felt the cool air chase away his warmth. She didn't take her eyes off her husband and his latest target. She moved closer, straining to hear their words. When Bethany spotted her, the girl nodded her head slightly toward Lily, as if she'd been waiting for Lily to be her silent audience. Because now she became the aggressor.

Bethany poked her index finger hard into Jonas' chest. He stepped back. She followed, finger cocked as if it were the barrel of a gun, punching him below the breast bone, right in the soft spot above the diaphragm. This way she brought him towards Lily, unseen behind his back.

"Now you'll listen to me, Professor Atwood."

"Jonas." His voice flowed like oil. "We talked about calling me Jonas."

"You talked. Now you'll listen."

Jonas smiled. He wanted the girl talking. He took a step closer to her, only to have her steely finger ram again into the center of his chest.

"You," Bethany jammed him again, "will cease to stalk me. Now."

Jonas' smile was gentle, as if handling a nervous mare. "Stalking? Hardly—"

She cut him off, poking him again in the same place. Jonas flinched. Lily guessed that he was developing a nice bruise right in that spot.

"I have photos of you coming up to me in those ridiculous swimming trunks at the pool. I have photos of you in the town cafe. I have statements from the people you asked about me. All of this is on file with the local police."

Jonas shook his head. "I doubt it."

"You don't know much about small towns, do you?"

Lily watched for a response from Jonas denying that but there was nothing.

"The police chief is my uncle. His deputy is my brother."

Jonas started to reach for the girl again, noticed her rigid hand and changed his mind. He shrugged. "You led me on, young woman. You told me to come to see you."

Bethany laughed. While she laughed, she gazed at the spot just below Jonas' belt, the spot that she'd described in some detail in that email to Lily from the swimming pool.

The back of Jonas' neck turned bright red. What Lily knew and was afraid that Bethany didn't was that when Jonas flushed it was from anger, not embarrassment. She'd seen him strike out in anger, most recently at the Guilford police station. She took another step forward, but Bethany saw her and shook her head.

"Prove it, you perv. While you're trying to prove that I led you on, know that my uncle and brother have spoken to the Prairie Shores police, campus and town. Cop to cop, you know?"

"You little bitch," Jonas said, aiming the flat of his hand at the side of the girl's head. Bethany danced out of the way, toward Lily, forcing Jonas to turn and face his audience.

"Well, well, well," he said, "if it's not my Lily. Our lady of the changed locks. My wife," he said to Bethany. "My dear wife. Legally bound." His hand shot out to grab her, but Lily copied Bethany's move, dancing out of reach. To Bethany, he said, "You can leave. You've served your purpose. You too," he pointed at Cara.

Until Guilford, not once since Lily had met Jonas had he ever tried to physically hurt her. The slaps aimed at Bethany and her were new. Something had changed deep down in this man, some tectonic slip of the plates of his personality. That slap signaled that Jonas was ready to change course. Like his father's combat knife had signaled Lillian Atwood.

"I believe, Mr. Atwood," Bethany said, her voice dripping sugar, "that your presence is the unnecessary one. Dr. Atwood and I have so much to talk about." Lily and Cara came forward and stood shoulder to shoulder with Bethany.

Jonas looked around him with exaggerated care. "What, no pet cops around, dear wife? Or an ill-behaved dog?"

This time it was Lily who didn't respond to his verbal jabs.

"You didn't need to change the locks on our apartment, you know."

"You should have signed a lease while you had a chance. The apartment belongs to my parents. They can do with it whatever they want, whenever they want."

Damn it, she'd slipped into his talking trap. Now he was smiling, contented, like the cat who had trapped his mouse and was looking forward to playing with it.

"I've filed a police report," he said, and waited.

Knowing what had happened in Parthenon, not to mention Guilford, Lily knew Jonas would avoid the police. She smiled widely enough that she felt her cheeks wrinkle. Got you, she thought.

Lily had to hand it to Jonas, he didn't look in the least bit worried or embarrassed or even perturbed. He put his hands in the pockets of his suit pants, eyes sliding back and forth over Lily to Bethany and Cara. One hand came out to rub his chin. He looked delighted. "Lily." His voice fondled her. She felt stripped. "Later, I expect," he said, before heading down the lakefront path toward campus. Lily heard him whistling. She scrubbed at her arms. "Bethany, why did you go off with him?"

The younger woman suddenly drooped. Lily led her to a nearby boulder and sat her down. "Why?"

"I'd had enough of him. The constant hovering, his turning up just to show his face. Cara understood. We choreographed this. But," she held up her index finger, "I called my uncle, told him what was happening, that if he didn't hear from me in an hour to call the cops here." Bethany took out her cell phone, said "Uncle Jack" loudly and listened. "I'm fine. No, really. Yes, he knows we've built a case against him. He'll back off now."

Lily took the phone from the girl's hand. "Hello, Chief Dwight, this is Dr. Lily Atwood." She listened, eyes on the lake, now blue with whitecaps. "Also the Lakeland police and the Guilford, Connecticut, police." She waited while Bethany's uncle emptied his worry onto her, then said, "I'm not done with my husband yet, sir. If necessary, when I get my plan underway, may I call on you for help?"

Chief Jack Dwight said, "Yes, but keep my niece out of it."

Lily handed the phone back to his niece, who listened patiently before saying, "Uncle Jack, do you remember when I took all those dance classes? The self-defense class? Yes, well, I'll handle this myself. You just be there to back me up in the next scene." She rolled her eyes at Lily. "I was your little girl. Now I'm your big girl. Love you," and she clicked off. "What plan? What can I do to help?"

"You're not exactly the girl Jonas thinks you are," Lily said.

"Lord, I hope not. That would be pretty pathetic," Bethany said. "Didn't I see you with some other people? A dog? A blonde dog?"

Lily and Cara grabbed the girl's hands to pull her up off the boulder. They set off on the path, in the opposite direction from Jonas, towards Nate's van and the blonde dog, who now came running towards them.

Pathetic, Lily thought. Well, she had a few surprises in store for Jonas, beginning now. Her next stop but one was the dean's office. With Bethany. Research was all well and good, but the best kind of research often required a little leverage. Jonas, bless him, had given them more than a little.

. . .

After Constance had introduced Bob to Bethany, they joined Lily and Nate in a strategy conference at the van. For the first time, Lily briefed Bethany on how her favorite professor came to leave Prairie Shores College.

"That witch Hardy fired you. Cara told me," Bethany said. "Though why she couldn't just sleep with your husband and leave you alone… Oh, never mind, probably because you're a human being and she's some sort of preprogrammed robot. Did you ever notice how she never looks at you when you're talking, looks over your shoulder instead, as if eye contact is bad luck or something. Have you met the new guy they hired to teach bibliography? Maybe Hardy has the hots for him."

"As she did for my husband?" Lily was leaning against the van's front grille, facing the lake. "I recommended the new guy for the position. Jane neglected to mention that it was for my job. In fact, she told me the department was expanding."

Her uncle raised his eyebrows. Constance began to laugh but caught herself. Bethany frowned, saying, "Dr. A, not a chance the English department expands. Science, sure. Maybe even poli-sci. Religion. English? Get real. No one on campus understands most of the English faculty. Deconstruction. Textual analysis. Everyone outside thinks those people ran off the rails somewhere a few stations back."

Constance's composure cracked and she laughed so hard that she sounded to Lily more like Maureen. Nate was laughing, too. Lily recalled more than one discussion with Len, her close friend in the biology department, when he made fun of pronouncements made by one member or another of the English department. "I guess I should have checked that a new position was really being funded, huh?" Constance's expression turned from merriment to something too close to pity for Lily's taste. "Well, all right, how about I consider these past few months a much-needed reality check?"

"Fine," Nate said, reaching to hug her. "Tell me, what's your next move?"

"First a stop to see Len. We haven't touched base since the day I was fired. Then Bethany and I are going to see the Dean of Students."

"We are? Why?" Bethany asked.

"Because you're going to tell her all about how one Jonas Atwood has been stalking you. Then I'm going to tell her what she can do to keep that bit of information out of the news and, possibly, off the police blotter."

Nate had let Lily go, stepped back and looked at her with narrowed eyes. Then he nodded.

Constance said, "We are coming, too," gesturing towards Bob.

"Of course," Lily said.

"A dog? In Dean Minton's office?" Bethany asked.

"Sure. Wait and see what happens when we refrain from telling Bob that the dean is a friend."

"Go for the gold, baby," Nate said, and opened the van's door. "Come on, I'll give you a lift to the biology building." To Cara, he said, "Then you and I better go back to the workshop and release Izzy. He's dying to know what's been going on without him."

...

Given the oddments usually to be found in and near Len Altawa's office—live rodents in a maze, dead salamanders, vials of fruit flies—Lily thought it better to bring the good biology professor outside to them. She went in to fetch him, finding him in his laboratory among the bags of Purina fruit fly chow. "How you can stand the smell of this stuff and still love to eat is beyond me," she said in greeting, tapping his shoulder.

The white-haired professor turned his ruddy face toward her, broke into a huge smile, and pulled out the white earbuds. It was only then that Lily noticed the iPod clipped to his worn leather belt. "Where'd you come from?" he cried at the same time she said, "Where'd you get that?"

"Ladies first," he said.

"Remember I told you that I got that Humanities research grant?"

"You did? That's wonderful, unbelievable, when does it start?"

"Len, I forgot to tell you." She softly smacked her forehead.

"Nope. Last time we talked was the day Hardy dropped her bombshell on you."

"Can you finish up here in a hurry?"

"That's what teaching assistants are for." Len leaned around a partition and called out something. A graduate student appeared and took over. "Come on," Len said to Lily, "let's get away from the smell of fly chow and you can catch me up."

Lily told him she'd spent the summer in and around the Beinecke, then rushed on to tell him about Jonas; about Maureen and Peter; about Jonas' lies and finding him hounding Bethany less than thirty minutes before. She finished the story on the front steps of the biology building, with Constance and Bethany adding bits, and Bob watching over them.

"Sounds like you lived years this summer," Len said. "So you probably want to know what I've managed to glean about why Jane Hardy pulled that stunt on you." When Lily started to say something, he waved her to silence. "Not a whole lot. Except that the timing was interesting. She gave you the good-bye and good luck speech in early June, the day grades were due. Well, seems that one of the assistant vice presidents for academics had given notice, oh, maybe a year ago. Two department chairs applied for the job. Raise in salary, no teaching, cushy offices, hobnobbing with the great and near great. Perfect for social-climbing faculty. That's our Jane. But she was up against strong competition—you know that guy in political science who manages to bring all those big names here. Jane had to prove she was strong enough for the job. Well, she got the job. The poli-sci professor got a promotion to full professor. Everyone's happy. But someone in administration is really, really happy that Jane got rid of you. Since you publish regularly in the good journals, your students love you, and your classes get bigger every year, I'm thinking getting rid of you served some other purpose here."

"Jonas," Lily said.

Len turned toward her. "And?"

"I'm guessing something about college donors. I'll be finding out." Lily clasped Len's hand. "Thank you. I promise I'll keep you posted." She stood up, dusting off the seat of her jeans. "You wouldn't happen to know anyone over in the development office, would you?" She stretched an arm down to give the older man a hand, but he stood up without her help.

"Someone who might have worked with Jonas? Didn't you know anyone?"

"I had my head in the sand."

"No more?" Len asked, but he was looking at Constance and Bethany. It was Constance who quite firmly shook her head. "I know someone who just retired from there." He turned to climb the steps to the building door, but over his shoulder he called, "I'll call you soon as I find out what you need."

"He's a real person," Bethany said. She looked at Lily and flushed. "I mean, here's this distinguished professor, he's got an endowed chair and all that but he's just like my grandfather. You know, my grandfather loves me and would do anything for me but he doesn't take any shit, either." She chuckled. "He raises cattle and pigs, so he's pretty much an expert on manure."

Lily thought that if Bethany had let on what she was really like back when she was interviewing for the presidential scholarship, she, Lily, would have voted for her. Now she was relieved the girl got the money without her vote.

"So do we go see the Dean of Students now or wait and see what your Len comes up with?" Constance said.

"Now. While this afternoon is nice and fresh in Beth's memory."

"Like Grandpa's pig lot: stinky," the girl put in.

They walked down the steps to the sidewalk that cut across the center of Prairie Shore's main quadrangle. Bethany was in the high spirits of someone who has faced a fear and triumphed. It wouldn't do them any good for her to show the dean how good she felt. When they came to one of the many benches that graduating classes had bequeathed to the college, Lily asked Bethany to sit down for a moment. She did, but bounced in her seat. Lily looked down at her and frowned.

"Bethany, please listen to me for a moment. The fact that Jonas stalked you all summer is serious. If your uncle wasn't police chief, if your boyfriend hadn't been at the pool a couple of crucial times, if you were the soft sweet girl Jonas thought you were—"

"I'd be in real trouble," Bethany interrupted. "Yes, I know." Her voice was quiet. She stopped bouncing. "Are you worried that he'll try the same thing on some other girl?"

"That's his history, what we discovered when we went to his home town." Lily sat down next to the girl. Gazing straight ahead at the campus where she had thought she'd teach forever, she told Bethany what they'd learned in Parthenon, Kansas. Lily told her everything, with Constance adding bits of information. When they were done, Bethany's expression was grim, mouth tight.

"He could be dangerous." She sat up and squared her shoulders. "I've been way too full of myself, haven't I? That's what my mom always says."

"My mother has always said I'm oblivious to what's going on around me and that I'd better not be. She was right. So, yes, maybe your mother knows what's she's talking about. I think you have reason to be proud of yourself. You handled Jonas perfectly. However, when we track down the dean, don't let on. I need information out of the dean. I want her to be worried about you, so worried she'll forget to hide what she knows."

Lily's phone rang. The biology professor had information, of the extremely useful variety. Perfect timing.

Chapter 49

No one tried to stop them walking Bob through the administration building's front door, though almost every student they passed stopped to say hello to him. His tail stayed up but he looked wary, game, yet on his guard. When they stepped into the Dean of Students office on the second floor, the dean herself, Diana Minton, a skinny woman whose black suit looked too large, was leaning over a clerk's shoulder, looking at something on a computer screen. After a glance up at Lily, she frowned, said something to the clerk before heading to the rear of the outer office. Lily called, "Don't try it, Diana."

The dean turned, arms crossed. "Try what, Lily?"

Rather than answer, Lily ushered the others toward the dean. Bob got to her first. When the blonde dean tried to back away, he growled. When she held her hand to him, he growled. When Lily came up to them, he looked at her expectantly. She merely patted him on the head. Smiling at the dean, Lily said, "Let's talk in your office, Diana."

"I have a meeting." She nodded toward the clerk, who agreed but looked embarrassed.

"Sure do," Lily said. "Let's begin." To Bob, she said, "Herd." He looked at her quizzically for a second, then turned and nipped at the dean's heels, effectively herding her into her own office.

"He never learned that command," Constance said sotto voce.

"Your dog's a genius. Roll with it," Lily said.

"The new Lily," Constance whispered.

"Nope, same old me." But inside the dean's office, it was Lily who sat Bethany and Bob next to the desk. Constance settled onto a sofa at the back of the office, next to a large box of tissues. Lily leaned against the window behind the dean's desk chair. She introduced Bethany to Minton, who claimed to remember her.

"Lily," Minton began, but Bethany interrupted her.

"Dean Minton, I'm trying not to involve my father or my uncle, the police chief, in what just happened." No doubt about it, Bethany could think on her feet.

Lily wouldn't have thought it possible for Diana Minton's pale skin to get any whiter.

"Police chief? Where?"

"In my hometown."

"What does that have to do with this college?" Minton demanded. She leaned across the desk towards the student, putting more space between her back and Lily.

"The man who has been stalking me began here, then turned up in my home town. That's over a hundred miles from here." Bethany continued over the dean's attempt at retaking the conversation. "I'd think you would want to know how he got my home address. Because, you see, he didn't follow me home from here. I would have known."

"How?"

"My uncle is the police chief." Bethany's tone was that of patience.

"In a rural town? So what?"

"He retired as a major crimes detective in Chicago before returning home. Does that make him more credible to you, Dean Minton?" She bent her head close to the dean. "Seems to me that this college should be worried about its students' welfare."

Lily still couldn't believe this was little Bethany. The baby had grown up over the summer.

The dean must have been thinking along the same lines. She leaned back in her chair, fingers tapping on the armrest. "Who is this stalker? Actually, how do you know he's stalking you?"

"Diana," Lily said from behind her, "cut the crap and listen."

"Lily, we don't owe you anything," she blurted, not turning around.

"What an interesting comment," Constance said from her corner.

"Who are you?"

"My name is Constance Cordrey. Of the New York Cordreys. Real estate, you know." She peered down her nose at the dean, as if the woman were her personal servant. Lily hadn't seen her pull that stunt until now, but it was a good one. The dean sat up straight, staring at Constance, then at Bethany in something close to fright. When her gaze settled on Bob, she said, "That dog can't be in here."

"He belongs to me," Constance said.

The dean looked caught, head swiveling between Constance, Bethany and the dog. Finally she relaxed into her high-backed leather chair, after first looking over her shoulder. Lily caught a glimpse of the good humor that had attracted her to Diana in the first place. "All right, everyone, what's going on?"

"Perhaps you remember Dr. Jonas Atwood?" Bethany asked.

"Of course. He's Lily's husband. He's—" but Minton stopped.

"He worked in development here at Prairie Shores before moving on to Lakeland University," Bethany said. "Which must be how he got into this college's computer system and found my home address. Because not two days after my Dr. Atwood," Bethany smiled at Lily, who gestured thumbs up behind Minton's back, "went to Yale in June, her husband showed up at our town swimming pool. I'm the lifeguard, by the way."

Minton swiveled around to look at Lily. "Yale? You went to Yale this summer? But we fired you."

Her use of 'we' interested Lily, but she only said, "More on that in a minute, Diana. Stay on track, here." She gestured for Bethany to continue.

"Dean Minton, just now Jonas Atwood cornered me up by the rocks on the lake path. He was closing in when these folks," she swept her hand around the office, "showed up. My Dr. Atwood," this time she nodded toward Lily, "has been watching over me. She was the only one, the *only* one, on this campus to know that her husband was stalking me. The *only* one who cared, even though she doesn't even work here anymore. Here's my question: What are you going to do about that?"

"Do about what?" Minton demanded. "I can't get Lily's job back."

"For heaven's sake, Diana, get with the program," Lily said. "What are you going to do about Jonas being on your campus?"

"Well, the same thing we did before, get rid of him." Minton suddenly looked frightened. As far as Lily was concerned, Minton had just confirmed her assumption.

"Didn't seem to take though, did it?" Constance's voice was dry and cold.

"Dean Minton, do I need my uncle in here to get the whole story, or can we just take care of this here and now?" Bethany glared at the dean, shaking her head. "Enough of the bureaucratic hoohah, okay? You all fired Jonas Atwood then fired his wife."

Minton started to object but Bethany rolled on. "Why did you get rid of him?"

"That's none of your business."

Bethany stretched her hand out to Lily, who passed her the cell phone over Diana's head. She dialed. "Uncle Jack? No, I'm okay. Listen, we're with the dean of students. She's, uh, not taking this situation seriously." Bethany held the phone away from her ear. They could all hear a man shouting. When there was a break in the noise, Bethany said, "Here's Dean Minton," and held out the phone. The dean eyed the phone as if it might bite her before accepting it.

Chief Dwight must have already been talking because she didn't say a word. Lily came around to stand behind Bethany. She read fear, then anger on Diana's face. Diana turned toward her and began nodding. For the first time she looked Lily in the eye. Her mouth set in the line that Lily had seen before when the dean solved problems. Lily took the other chair in front of the desk. Bob ambled over to join Constance.

"Let me see what I can put in motion here, Chief Dwight. I agree with you completely that something must be done immediately. I would appreciate it if you would send those phoned photos to me here." She gave him her email address. "I'll call you in about an hour? Excellent." She hung up and shook her head. "Well, this is a fine mess."

"Time for truth, Diana?" Lily said.

"I hated lying to you," she answered.

"No you didn't. And Jane Hardy didn't hate sleeping with my husband."

Minton's jaw dropped, just like in a novel.

"How's that lyric go?" Lily said, looking over Minton's head. "Manipulation is just another word for nothing left to lose? Or is it being manipulated? And by whom?" She shook her head in mock dismay. "Cut the crap, Diana. You report up the bureaucratic ladder," Lily said.

"I'm relieved you understand."

"I've always understood. Do not confuse that with condoning your behavior or the behavior of this college," Lily said. "Tell me what happened, please, from the beginning."

The dean looked pointedly at Bethany and Constance, but Lily would have none of it. "They're part of the story now. In fact, so are the police and FBI back in Connecticut. All of which might have been avoided had this place chosen the correct course rather than this song and dance."

"The FBI?" Minton's face cracked. "We just got rid of the son of a bitch because he was lying to donors. When their accountants pointed out that his interpretation of the tax law was wrong and cost them big bucks, they demanded he go."

"Did you happen to warn Lakeland U. about his, uh, habit?" Lily asked.

"No way. Jonas would have sued us."

There was silence in the office. "Typical," Lily said. "Collateral damage."

"You know Jane Hardy wanted that new administration position. Getting rid of you and replacing you at the same time. If she did it well, that job was hers."

"With Jonas' help. However, this sounds like the college president's reasoning," Lily said.

Minton nodded.

"It never occurred to anyone around here that I'd find out, did it?"

Minton shook her head.

From the back of the office, Constance said, "It never occurred to anyone around here that they were firing the best researcher on campus? That maybe why she was being fired would be something she might, oh, look into?" Silence. "You know, Lily, you're better off out of here. This is an institution run by idiots."

At that comment, Bethany started laughing. When she could get her breath, she said, "They all need to take your English 101 course, Dr. A. The one where you teach your students to think and analyze."

"You going to get this child into Lakeland, Lily?" Constance asked.

"How about Yale?"

"Sure," Constance said. "Has she the grades?"

"Straight A's," Minton said. Everyone looked at her. She shrugged. "She's on the Dean's List. That's this dean." She tapped her chest. "All right, here's what I suggest we do. Suggest, you understand. Let's discuss this. I tell the president that Jonas has been up to his old and some new tricks. He tells the vp for development to call his counterpart at Lakeland and warn him about Jonas Atwood. When the LU guy wants to know why we're all of the sudden being so open, we'll suggest he call a couple of police departments. That means, young lady, that you'll need to make out a complaint here."

"I already decided that," Bethany said.

Constance came up to stand next to Lily. "If the college does all this, it means Jonas will be cornered. Do we want that? An animal lashes out when cornered." Everyone looked at Bob, who'd followed Constance to the front of the office.

"How about we give him something to worry about, something to focus all that manipulative energy on?" Lily said. "Diana, can you arrange for the head of development here to have an off-the-record chat with Jonas' new boss?"

After Diana Minton stood up and came around the desk, Lily hugged her, which seemed to surprise her. She held onto Lily's hand and demanded, "Yale?"

It was Constance who answered. "That woman who got a promotion out of firing Lily?"

"Jane Hardy? What about her? What's that got to do with Yale?"

Lily smiled widely and nodded at Constance to tell the story.

"Even this place might reconsider when they find out she fired a professor with a $50,000 renewable grant from the National Endowment for the Humanities."

The dean seemed to trip backwards, rump landing on her desk and knocking books and papers to the floor. She ignored the fallout, staring at Lily. "It came through? The grant came through? Why didn't Jane know? Jane insisted that you'd never receive a dime."

"Jonas assured her that he'd torpedoed my grant applications. She believed him as long as he was shtupping her," Lily said. She waved her hand as if batting away a fly. "Doesn't matter now."

"But we'd have you back in a nanosecond," Minton protested.

"Diana, for the umpteenth time, don't you get it? I don't want to come back. I'm free of this place."

Constance clipped Bob's leash onto his collar. Lily found her bag before noticing that Bethany looked upset. "What's wrong?"

"What about me? I'm still here."

"Careful what you say, Lily," the dean said.

"Unnecessary." She put her arm around the student's shoulders. "Brave it out here for a bit. Then I'll make sure you're in a more sophisticated place."

"With more sophisticated bureaucratic maneuvering," Minton warned.

"No doubt." It was Constance who offered this parting shot.

Chapter 50

The next morning, Lily was sound asleep when the phone rang. She knocked over the alarm clock before waking up enough to grab for the telephone. "What? Hello?" She fished the clock off the floor: 6:30 am. "Who is this?"

"Cindy Adler. I am your husband's boss, director of development at Lakeland University."

Lily sat up and swung her feet over the side of the bed. She looked around and realized she was back in her own bed in Lakeland. That meant Constance and Bob were sleeping in the guest room. At that thought, a black nose nudged open the bedroom door. "Come in, Bob," Lily said.

"Bob?" Cindy said. "Where's Jonas?"

"Bob's a dog. I don't know where Jonas is."

There was a long silence on the line. Still not quite awake, Lily rubbed behind Bob's ears and had just about forgotten that she was holding the phone when she heard, "Son of a bitch."

"Technically, yes."

"What?"

"Bob is."

"Are you always this humorous in the morning?"

"Jonas never thought so."

"Jonas doesn't have a sense of humor."

"Ms. Adler, you called me. In fact, you woke me up."

"I heard late yesterday from the head of development at your college."

"I don't have a college."

"I thought you were at Prairie Shores. It would appear that I'm behind on my networking. I apologize. Would you be free for breakfast?"

If she was awake, Lily thought, she might as well get to it. "Breakfast at eight at the Main Cafe. You're buying."

"Of course."

"For three."

"This is just between you and me. We've got things to talk about beyond Jonas and Rule 27b."

"For three, eight o'clock," Lily repeated before ending the call. She headed into the bathroom to wash her face and teeth, then down the hall to wake up Constance. Bob followed her.

The next call was at 7:30. Constance poked her head out of the bathroom and asked if there was a Midwest etiquette rule about calling before nine o'clock. Since Lily couldn't remember any other time when the phone had rung this early, she said, "Not that I know of."

This time it was Diana Minton. According to Jane Hardy, Jonas had "bumped into her" on campus the previous November. That's when he told her that Lily had never submitted her grant application to the NEH or anywhere else. Jonas told her Lily was "too frightened, but give her time, she'll do it and I'll lose the paperwork." So when Jane received the new English department budget and saw she had to let someone go, Jonas said he'd help her lose the professor who would never pay her own way: Lily.

"Wonder why she came up with the November story? I know for a fact that she and Jonas were together in September," Lily told Diana. "Oh, and I have a video of the pair of them." Let Diana do with that tidbit what she may.

But it meant that Jonas knew in advance what he wanted for Lily. Just like his good old Dad: Joel Atwood arranged for his wife to lose her tenure-track professorship after getting her pregnant. Jonas following his father's blueprint. But Lily had lost the baby.

"Oh," said Diana, "and one more thing: Jane said she wants you back. I said maybe she should have done her homework before committing adultery with your husband and firing you. You know it won't be long before the president hears about this. One of Jane's enemies will be sure of that."

"Would you be that enemy?" Lily asked. All she heard was laughter from the other end of the line before the connection clicked off.

"Free at last, free at last, oh yes, I'm free at last," Lily sang.

Constance emerged from the guest bedroom, face still covered in sleep. "Coffee. Now. Before singing."

After coffee and getting dressed, Lily bundled Constance into the rental car. During the five-minute drive to the coffee shop, her exhilaration evaporated. She found a parking place two blocks away, turned off the engine and sat. There was something Adler wanted to let her know. Out loud, she said, "Put that together with what the doctor said, you idiot."

...

May

It was her annual gyne exam. The fluorescent lights were beginning to hurt her eyes, already tired from too many nights reading a computer screen. The doctor said, "Lily. We have to talk."

Bad news? This was supposed to be a routine doctor's visit. Her stomach clenched just above where she'd been trying to relax. "What did you find?"

"Unless I'm mistaken, there's evidence of an STD." He frowned at her, seeming to place more distance between them. "Sexually-transmitted disease."

She bent toward Dr. Maroney, clutching the paper sheet. "Did you say STD? How would I get that?"

"The usual way."

She shook her head, trying to clear the confusion. "The usual way? You mean unprotected sex? The only person I'm sleeping with is Jonas."

The doctor stood up and looked down at her thoughtfully. "You've never had intercourse with anyone else?"

"Never." She hid her face in her hands.

"It could be worse."

Worse? she thought. He's telling me my husband cheats on me enough to infect me. Aloud, she said, "How?"

"It looks like gonorrhea. I won't prescribe anything until I'm sure, but I'll have the results back by this afternoon. Completely curable. Unlike, say, HIV or HPV."

"God I hate acronyms," she said, voice too loud. "Sorry, sorry, I didn't mean to shout. What's HPV?"

"Human papilloma virus. In about forty percent of the cases, it causes cervical cancer. There's a vaccination for it now. Lily, get dressed and we'll talk."

To her surprise, she said, "We'll talk now. You're telling me Jonas has given me the clap."

"Haven't heard it called that in years, but yes, that's it. You'll be fine, but—" He broke off.

Jonas. The clap. Gonorrhea. STD. That son of a bitch. The doctor's words spun through her mind, but what she was trying not to pay attention to was that little voice from way inside, that tiny noise that reminded her that sex with her husband had been a duty for her for the last year or so. She could place a time on it but not a reason. After he left Prairie Shores, he'd smothered her with attention. She'd hated it, knew that there was some reason his attentions felt wrong, but felt guilty, too, feeling that way. Something had happened between them, something had died or evaporated and she'd stopped paying attention to the little voice because she didn't know what to do about Jonas. She'd turned her efforts to her research and her students, but mostly her research.

"Lily. Pay attention."

The doctor leaned down, looking directly into her face. "You'll be all right. I'll call in the prescription this afternoon."

"All right?" All right implied everything was the same as it was before the doctor had said "STD." "No." She couldn't remember the last time they'd had sex—a few days ago? Last week?—but that would also be the final time. "Does this have anything to do with losing the baby?"

He shook his head firmly. "You weren't infected then. We would have known from several of the routine tests. However, Lily, in my experience—well, I'm not sure you want to hear this right now."

Lily gathered the paper sheet around her and slid off the examination table. She felt drowned in white light, from the ceiling and the white-painted walls and the sheet. Spotlighted, when what she desperately wanted was to disappear. Standing as straight as she could while maintaining her modesty, she said, "Dr. Maroney, tell me everything. I hate secrets, lies, euphemisms. Let me have it." Then she smiled. "Please."

"I thought that might be the case." The doctor's eyes were dark, almost black, under thick salt and pepper brows. He must have been a lady-killer in his day, she thought, then blanched at the double entendre. He mistook her reaction to her thought for fear of what he was about to say, because he added, "Are you sure you want to hear it? This can wait. We can talk another time."

"No, no, no, no. Tell me. It's about time people start telling me what I need to know."

He crossed his arms, leaning against the sink. "In my experience, women who are faithful to their husbands and find they have a sexually-transmitted disease have to make some choices. Difficult choices. Love the husband? In that case, what happens? Can the wife ever trust the husband again? Maybe, after long months, maybe years, of psychotherapy. Not love the husband? That's another situation. Because then you have to decide what you want to do with your life."

Lily was nodding as he spoke.

"Because the STD is the symptom not only of a physical disease," he said.

"But of a diseased situation," she finished for him.

"Exactly, my dear."

"Thank you, Dr. Maroney."

. . .

August

In the passenger seat, Constance had been sitting quietly watching her. Her face looked more awake, the features more distinct, eyes wide open. "What did the doctor say?"

Lily started, not having realized that she'd spoken aloud. She didn't answer, couldn't decide whether she wanted to tell her new friend about the course of antibiotics necessary to clear up her last conjugal experience with Jonas. Or about how she'd tap-danced around his demands until she'd left for Yale. How he only wanted sex when she obviously didn't. She sat for a few minutes, mind fizzing. Finally she said softly, "It's a dirty story."

"Lily, we are far enough into friendship to share the occasional dirty story. Dirty how?"

"Last trip to the gynecologist ended with antibiotics. You know that Jonas is the only man I've ever slept with."

"Ah."

"You're not shocked?" Lily asked. She watched commuters dressed in as little as possible trudge toward the elevated and Metra train stations a few blocks away. She'd never wanted to join their ranks, an attitude probably instilled by her uncle, who'd once told her, "I was not cut out to be *The Man in the Gray Flannel Suit*." His words sent her off on one of her first literary researches to find out what he'd meant. At an impressionable age she'd read all of Sloan Wilson's books and watched the old Gregory Peck movie. Her career, such as it was, had never involved a daily commute.

"No. Rather, it fills in a bit of information, doesn't it?" Constance's words snapped Lily back to her current problem.

"The woman who asked us to breakfast—she's Jonas' boss, the LU director of development."

"Ah," Constance repeated. "Perhaps she, too, found herself on a course of antibiotics."

Lily turned toward her. "Would you be surprised that I don't want to know that?"

Constance shook her head. "However, I do think we should give her every opportunity to tell her story." She poked Lily's arm. "Remember Maureen's periodic table. Our hunt is for the missing elements. Let's go listen."

• • •

A few hours later, they were at Nate's workshop. He sanded a curving freeform coffee table while he listened. Lily watched his hands as he touched sandpaper to wood, put it aside to smooth the wood with fingers, feel a rough spot, then apply sandpaper. Gently, always gently. Izzy came downstairs, popping with familiarity onto Lily's chair to lean on her and purr. She scratched under his chin, feeling the rumble.

"Cara's very good with him," Nate said without looking up from his work. "Bethany loves him, too. She has stayed here several times, including, I understand, last night."

"Cara lives in the apartment upstairs," Lily told Constance while pointing with her chin toward the ceiling. "A long story. Tell you another time." She chewed the inside of her cheek for a moment, caught herself and stopped.

"Cara is Lily's first experience of going with her gut. A success. The child is happy, doing well in school and knows what she wants to do with her education." He waved the sandpaper in the cat's direction. "When Izzy here is seven or eight years older, he just might be the veterinarian's cat." Nate went back to his sanding. "What'd you find out from that woman Jonas works for?"

"Jonas was hired at Lakeland on the strong recommendation of Prairie Shores' head of development. He came with the specific portfolio of transforming upper middle-class alumni into large donors."

Constance said, "Lily is quoting the woman's words exactly."

Nate laughed. "She's not a bad mimic, my Lily. Go on."

Lily told them how Jonas had performed brilliantly at first, gaining a salary increase that he'd failed to tell her about. He was the bright new boy in the office. When Adler's twin sister died of breast cancer, he was there to console her. He went with her to the funeral and helped Cindy decide whether she should have a preventive mastectomy."

"I would guess he talked her out of it," Nate said.

"More like distracted her with sex," Lily said, watching her uncle carefully. He merely nodded. "As tax season accelerated, everything began to fall apart. Jonas' interpretation of a bit of the tax code concerning donations to nonprofit organizations such as universities turned out to be completely wrong. In fact, so wrong that several of the donors' lawyers called Adler, the director of development, and used the word 'fraud.' The alumni threatened to rescind their agreements for future donations. Adler called Jonas in. Jonas claimed he'd never made any promises."

"This next is the best part." Constance was watching Nate so intently she could have been referring to a rough spot on the wood.

"The director believed him. Adler continued sleeping with Jonas until, suddenly, he lost interest in her." Lily stopped talking. She turned toward Constance and shook her head.

Constance raised her brows, nodded toward Nate. Lily mouthed, "Please."

"What else?" Nate asked, not having missed this by-play.

Constance said, "It turned out that Adler had contracted an STD. What she wanted to know from Lily was whether Lily had it, too. This morning she asked."

"I did," Lily said to the cat. Izzy's ears flicked. He turned and butted his head against Lily's chin.

Nate dropped the sandpaper into his toolbox. He sat down next to Lily. "I'm so sorry that I wasn't more insistent about my objections when you wanted to marry Jonas."

"It wouldn't have changed anything, you know." Lily faced him. "I was in lust. Now I have learned the difference between love and lust."

"Anyway," Constance said, "when the Prairie Shores development vp called LU's counterpart and told her why Jonas had been fired, Adler dropped him."

"All hell break loose?" Nate asked.

"This is higher education," Lily chided. "They're trying to figure out how to cover their bad choices. Except for Cindy Adler. It turns out she'd warned the powers that be that donors were getting the wrong information from, well, her lover. She appears quite good at compartmentalizing her love life from her career. She might have wanted Jonas in her bed but she wasn't going to let him derail her career. Then he left her, she found out he'd given her the clap, and she started gunning for him."

She put Izzy down on the floor. He sashayed over to Nate, placing his paws carefully to avoid piles of wood shavings, and sat next to him. "Here's the problem now: no one seems to know where Jonas is. You know, he's got a Ph.D. in psychology, whether or not he's using it."

Constance asked, "Do you remember how scared Maureen was when you told her that Jonas' specialty was psychology?" She pulled herself out of the rocking chair and walked over to Nate.

Lily nodded.

"One of the things I learned from dealing with my husband's mental illness is how often doctors become shrinks because of their own problems."

"You're saying that Jonas knows he's doing something wrong," Nate said.

"No, that Jonas likes what he does and that he studied so he could learn how better to get away with it. It is probable that he also wanted to know how his father managed to control so many people for so long. "His father didn't have to leave town and pretend his mother was dead." Lily shook her head. "Let's assume that Jonas is back to his old tricks. That means he's left town. How do we find out where he's gone?"

"Thought you said you had some cop friends," Nate said. "Find out where he's spending money. Did he empty your accounts?"

"There was only a few hundred dollars in our joint account," Lily said. "But I'll find out." She marched toward the back of the shop, taking her cell phone out of her pocket. The back door slammed.

Nate leaned down to Constance. "How is she handling this?"

"This morning she was singing about freedom before her mood crashed. Up and down and up."

"Headaches?"

"Not since Kansas City, what, three days ago."

"Then she's okay." Nate handed Constance a piece of sandpaper and showed her how to barely touch the wood.

Chapter 51

Sunlight crept into the condominium across from Lakeland University where Jonas had moved the previous week. Usually by this time he'd be out the door, walking the two blocks to his office. He opened his eyes to find Harper perched on the far side of the bed, arms crossed. When she saw he was awake, she flipped that glorious strawberry blonde hair—why hadn't he gone for blondes before?—over her shoulder. She stood up, a full six-feet tall, and was around to his side of the bed in seconds.

"This has been fun, old man, but I'd like you out of here before I leave for class."

He jutted out an arm to pull her into bed but she stepped out of his grasp. "No, seriously. When you asked for a place to stay for a few days, that was good. But you're not moving in here. I need my space, you know?"

Ending her sentence with a question might have softened her demand except that the girl looked angry. Jonas felt rage welling up in him. "I'll do as I damn well please." He began to swing his legs over the side of the bed, realized he was naked, then went ahead. Old man? He looked between his legs.

"Out. I put your stuff by the front door and took this out of your pants." Harper opened her hand, revealing the condo key.

"How about one last hookup?" Jonas hoped he was using the lingo right.

But Harper had turned her back on him. His pants and underwear—yesterday's clothes, not laundered, what use was this woman?—came flying over to land on his head and shoulders.

"Dude, you just don't get it, do you?" She went into the other room.

Jonas didn't move. This was a new situation for him; he waited to see what buttons needed to be pushed. "Tell me, babe."

Returning with his shoes and socks, she slammed them onto the floor in front of him. One shoe bounced and hit him on his instep. He stifled a cry of pain.

"You're over the hill." She stood over him, hands on hips, glaring down at him. She was something, Jonas thought. Gorgeous and rich and smart. Blonde all the way down. He reached for her. "Jonas, pay attention. Go find someone your own age. No, older. I don't know what's happened to you in the last few weeks, but the old electricity is gone, you know? Lights out and all that."

Jonas froze. What the hell did she mean by "the electricity is gone"? No.

Way. He stood up, the clothes she'd slung at him falling to the bed, and grabbed her arms. She easily broke his hold.

"Jonas, you were a good fuck. Then you were a convenient fuck. Now you're just a dumb fuck." She looked at her watch. "You've got five minutes."

Never, ever had a woman thrown him out. He'd always been the one who left. But no way was he going to let Harper know that. Instead he dressed in slow motion, watching her irritation grow. Five minutes later he had on pants, socks and shoes and was thinking about shaving when there was a knock at the front door. He heard Harper open it and her conversation with a man as they approached the bedroom. In the doorway stood a cop, a real cop, not one of those campus security buffoons, telling him, "Sir, you're trespassing."

...

Sitting in the Lake Hotel over breakfast, Jonas took stock. He didn't blame Harper: he didn't have time to train her properly before he'd needed her. That might have been bad planning on his part, but really, Lily had no right to throw him out. She was his wife. It was that blasted uncle of hers who must be calling the shots. He knew it had been Nate Miller who had changed the apartment's locks. Jonas' own father had been smart, getting his wife her own place but keeping the deed in his name. She couldn't throw him out. Of course, she never wanted to, either. The question was why he kept her around.

Jonas ordered more coffee and seconds on English muffins from the hovering waiter. The waiter brought the coffee pot plus another pitcher of cream, topped up Jonas' cup and left him to his thoughts. When was the last time he lingered over breakfast by himself, planning? He ran his hand over his chin and was surprised at the roughness. Well, these days he'd be right in style, with a day's stubble and rumpled clothes. It made him look like some rich guy who didn't have to work in an office. Like Harper's father, most likely. What was that guy thinking, buying his daughter a huge apartment in Lakeland? He had to know she wasn't sleeping there by herself. Probably paid for her birth control, too.

His thoughts returned to Lily. Ever since he'd met her in graduate school, he'd planned her life. She was his. He'd known it the first time he'd seen her in the university's rare books library, buried in some Wharton book. He'd been there to study. The rare books library was a nice quiet place, decorated with old carved wood and portraits of a century of university patrons. He'd come to think of one of the scuffed brown leather chairs as his. Lily must have found the place conducive to study, too. She sat in the same place at one of the medieval-style wood trestle tables, work spread out around her. It was almost as if she'd purposely placed herself right in his line of sight.

One day after she'd left, he sat in her regular chair and looked over to his leather chair. That's when he'd discovered that she couldn't see him watching her. After several months, he could tell what she was thinking by the look on her face and the state of her hair. She'd start each study session by pulling her blue-black hair together, in a tail and looping an elastic band over it, then literally tying it into a knot on the top of her head. When she got excited about something she was looking at, her fingers would massage at her scalp, loosening the knot until it slid to the nape of her neck. Jonas longed to touch both knit and nape.

Instead, he found out about this woman. He laughed to himself, thinking about it, how he'd researched the researcher. She was absolutely not his physical type. In fact, as the school year moved into winter months, she became plumper and her complexion pastier. She didn't wear any makeup. He knew he was going to bed her. That she didn't know it wasn't an issue.

When he found out that she specialized in the late nineteenth and early twentieth century realists, particularly Edith Wharton and Henry James, he did a bit of reading about them so he could carry his end of a conversation if necessary. While he was sleeping his way through the English department grad women, he kept his eye on Lily. He got what he wanted. But then he always had.

Something, though, had gone wrong this past spring. Something that changed Lily's view of him. That's what he was trying to find out about when he followed her to Connecticut.

It was a mess, and just when his plans were gelling so well. She was out of her job, and let's face it, he smiled to himself, didn't have a future. She'd gotten pregnant right on schedule, too, though she'd lost his baby. His brilliant Lily was becoming the wife of his intentions, though it had taken years.

Now what? He poured himself more coffee, adding cream and sugar. He didn't want to start over again, though he could if necessary. No job—check. No wife—maybe she thought otherwise, but he didn't. So, wife—check. No money—now there was the problem. Lily had squirreled away that grant money somewhere. She'd sent her last paycheck to that same somewhere. He'd asked around at local banks but didn't get anything except strange looks from the tellers. One suggested that he ask his wife.

Money had never been a problem in his life. His mother had whatever funds his father put into her account. His father's estate provided money to send him to college. When he was ready for grad school, he chose a place that would pay his way. He and Lily had always had plenty of spending money, mostly because they didn't have to pay much in the way of rent when they settled in the apartment belonging to her parents.

That was a mistake.

He dismissed the thought.

If he had to up and move, where would he go that he could still keep and eye on Lily?

But why up and move?

Money, money, money. The refrain played in his mind until he found his fingers tapping out the rhythm on the white tablecloth.

The waiter brought his check. He handed over the Visa card that was billed to Lily.

Until Harper pulled that stunt, he'd been intending to get money from her. Now he needed another plan.

He signed the credit card slip, leaving a nice tip. The waiter surprised him by returning to announce that the credit card had been rejected. Jonas dug cash out of his pocked, canceling the tip. Then he found his car where he'd left it in the university parking garage across the street. Where to now? All that came to mind was the post office, to check his mail box.

And Lily. Lily, Lily, Lily. Could it possibly be that he loved her?

Had his father loved his mother? He thought about that, sitting at one of Lakeland's interminable stoplights.

The car behind him honked. He accelerated, circling the post office twice before finding a parking space.

Yes, perhaps his father had loved his mother. But he hated her more.

Jonas didn't hate Lily. He admitted to himself that he didn't know what love might feel like. But he knew he needed Lily, that he needed to own her. He'd never analyzed why Lily, why this particular woman. The similarities to his mother were obvious. It didn't require his doctorate in psychology to see those.

He wondered if Lily ever felt she'd needed him. He would have loved to analyze his wife. Face it, guy, he told himself, she would never have put up with it. Early on she talked to him all the time, about everything. He really should have paid more attention. None of it seemed important at the time. Who cared about her unreliable family and her ambitions? He was going to be her family and all that she needed.

It was really quite a simple equation. He shook his head, got out of the car and went into the post office.

His phone buzzed with another text message. He checked though he knew it would be Audrey again. This time the message echoed his thoughts. "Get home to P for your money. Now."

He went into the post office. He didn't bother to look at his mail before jamming it into a pocket. He stopped at a laundromat before driving to Midway and a cheap flight to Kansas City. He promised himself that he'd come back for Lily.

...

While Lily was on the phone with Ed Sharply, the cop mentioned that he'd received another call from Parthenon. "This one was strange. It wasn't from my cop connection there. It was some woman from one of the local banks, looking for your husband."

"Why would she want to find Jonas?" Lily was sitting in the hot sun behind Nate's workshop. Inside the building she'd felt cold. The sun wasn't helping. She still felt cold.

"Seems that his disappearing act caused some sort of glitch in settling his father's estate."

"I thought his mother inherited it all since there wasn't a will. That's what someone told me while we were in Parthenon, anyway."

"Well, if I got this right," Ed said, "Kansas law would split the father's estate between mother and son. The son was gone according to his mother, but her word wouldn't have been good enough, no death certificate, so the state put his half of the money into an account and it's still there. It's the other half that the mother's been living on."

"One of the banks set up a trust for her. Not that she spends anything." Lily thought of the tee shirt and shorts her mother-in-law had been wearing when they visited her house, clothes that had belonged to Jonas and probably worn out while he was in high school.

"Anyway," Ed said, "Your showing up back there and saying your husband is alive? Well, that bit of information worked its way to the bank."

"So there's money in Parthenon if Jonas shows up?"

"I'll bet a month of Maria's sweet rolls that there's a letter on its way to him."

"I've just about had it with bureaucracies," Lily said.

"They have their good points," Ed put in. "Like tracking that the next-to-last last place your husband used your Visa card was this morning at the Lake Hotel. That mean something to you?"

"It's across the street from his office. What was the last place he used the card? Which I thought I'd canceled."

"Lake Hotel picked up on the cancelation. But he used another card at Midway Airport. Southwest Airlines to Kansas City."

"Ed, I've got to get off the phone. I've got a bad feeling. I think I'd better call a couple of people from Jonas' past."

...

With the school year starting the following week, Maureen, a.k.a. Vice Principal Copeland, had three to-do lists. When her cell phone rang, she briefly considered letting it go to voicemail before heeding that back-of-the-mind simmering worry about Peter. She answered on the third ring.

"Maureen? It's Lily. Have you got a minute?"

Not Peter. She settled into her desk chair. Around her the school ticked with preparatory sounds of the janitor waxing the front hall floor, secretaries in the outer office clicking computer keys and, from the open window, shouts from outside of football coaches hectoring their players. "Lily. Are you coming back?"

"Not at the moment."

"Peter is talking about Thanksgiving."

"How would he like to see Connecticut about then?" Lily sounded rushed.

"What's wrong?"

"Maureen, did you know that Jonas' father had money?"

She didn't, but she wasn't surprised. From what she'd heard in Parthenon about Joel Atwood, he had his hands in multiple pots. "I assume, then, that that's what Lillian has been living on."

Lily explained about the trust that Betty and the others had arranged for the woman who had fooled them into thinking she'd lost her grip on reality. "By the time they arranged it, Jonas had disappeared, and of course Lillian had spread the word that he'd died in a car accident. But I've just learned that under Kansas law, half of his father's estate is being held in his name, just in case he turns up. That was maybe half a million dollars in 2000."

"You're kidding. I would have thought Joel would have spent every dime on himself."

"Maybe he would have if he'd lived longer. Now that Parthenon knows Jonas is alive, word will reach him any moment about his inheritance. My cop friend says Jonas is booked on a flight to K.C. Jonas was fired yesterday. My gut tells me Jonas is on his way home to Parthenon to collect. That and the fact that there's only a few hundred dollars in our joint bank account."

"Lillian."

"Exactly. Oh, Mo, what have I done, raking up all this history?"

"Stop it. We both know that it had to happen sometime. Knowing is better than not knowing." Maureen pictured Lillian hiding behind her closed door, reading her books. "Maybe it's time for Lillian to grow up. That's not our call. But we can warn her. I'll call Dorothy. She'll go see Lillian, put the word out for everyone to be on alert."

"Thank you. Maureen, do you think Jonas knows about Peter?"

Maureen's worry came to a rolling boil. She caught her breath. "Hang on." Maureen put down the cell. On her desk phone, she punched out her home number. After a half-dozen rings, Peter answered. She breathed again. "Peter, has anyone been to the house today?"

"No. I mean the post lady, but that's it. What's wrong, Mom?"

"There's an off-chance your father might show up. In his current frame of mind, I'd prefer to keep the two of you apart. Can you understand that?"

"What's wrong with my father?"

"He's been fired from his job, among other things."

"Did Aunt Lily have anything to do with this?"

"Some, but mostly it's your father's doing."

"You mean his actions have caught up with him."

"Peter, when did you grow up? Since I went to work this morning?"

"I wish. I won't open the door to anyone, okay?"

"Thanks. I'll see you soon." Maureen went back to the cell phone. "Peter's all right. He's home, probably reading."

"Sorry to worry you."

"Lily, are you going to talk to a lawyer?"

"I think so. I'm sitting on the loading dock of my uncle's workshop right now. When I go inside, I'll ask him to find me a lawyer. Knowing him, he may already have done that. How about you? You going to talk to a lawyer?"

"For what?"

"Protect Peter from Jonas? If word's around Parthenon that Jonas is alive, it's a certainty that word's around that he's got a son, too."

"Oh, shit. Gotta go, Lily."

Maureen shot out the door, found her car in the blazing sun, and started it, air conditioner blasting. The driver's seat was so hot she could hardly put her weight on it. Her foot landed hard on the accelerator, sending her spinning into the street. "Careful, careful," she chanted. She drove towards her house, circling the park, looking for the police patrol car that was usually in the neighborhood. She finally spotted it on the southeast corner of the park. When she pulled up next to it, she saw that it was unoccupied. She ran out of her car, yelling, "Marty, where are you?"

A young cop in the uniform of the Kansas City, Missouri, police department emerged from some trees about a hundred feet away and jogged toward her. "Mrs. Copeland, what's wrong?"

She stopped, bent over and leaned against a tree to catch her breath. He caught up with her. Thank goodness for being a schoolteacher, she thought, or I wouldn't know anyone except Peter. After a couple of decades teaching, she knew cops and nurses and young doctors and, come to think of it, a couple of lawyers. "Marty, I need your help to protect Peter."

Marty stood up straight. She thought he might salute her. "Yes, ma'am. From what?"

"From whom. His father."

Marty opened his mouth to object, but found himself looking at Maureen's raised palm. "Peter's biological father has never had any contact with him. Now he might want to, but for the wrong reasons. If you see a man who looks like Peter only in his thirties, please keep him away from my son. I'm getting an order of protection just in case."

The young policeman cocked his head and frowned at his former teacher. "Mrs. Copeland, is this man dangerous?"

Define dangerous, she thought but didn't say. "Yes. He scares me, especially since Peter is just too young to handle him."

"Got it. Well, you got me through chemistry class, I'll get you through this." He reached out and shook her hand.

She squinted at him in the bright sun. "Didn't you get an A in chem?"

"Like I said."

Chapter 52

Jonas found Audrey at his father's house, just as he'd expected. She was waiting up in the loft. He climbed the ladder, expecting to find her stretched out on the bed. That's where she was supposed to have been that night fifteen years before. Everyone was where they were supposed to have been—his father meeting him at the track, Audrey waiting for them back here—except for his mother. What had prompted the damn woman to leave home and follow him to the high school track? Everything would have been perfect if his mother had stayed home. If she'd just stayed home. Damn her.

Audrey stood looking out the tall window his father had installed. Her figure was silhouetted against the dying light. Thin. He remembered her as what could only be described as voluptuous. His father had described her as the Venus di Milo with arms still attached. He wouldn't explain what he meant, and Jonas had to look it up in the encyclopedia.

"That better be you, Jonas." The woman turned around. With the light behind her, Jonas couldn't see her face clearly until she'd crossed the huge loft. He met her halfway. Her face was ordinary, he thought, little nose, thin lips, pale eyes. Though some of the wonderful flesh he remembered seemed to have dissolved, the woman who faced him was still stacked. "Jonas," she repeated, "pay attention to something besides my breasts, will you? We have to talk."

"Not here." Without waiting for her, he went back down the ladder, cut across the bedroom and down another floor into his father's study. The loft was for sex, the bedroom for sleeping. He could hear his father's voice clearly across the years.

He started to sit down behind the desk but found that she'd gotten there before him. It forced him to take the only other chair, an uncomfortable one. His father discouraged company in his study.

"Your father died intestate." She sat at the desk, hands clasped before her, looking every bit the judge. "That means he never bothered to draft a will."

"Audrey," he warned. "Tell me something I don't know."

"In good time."

He started to get up, to go around behind her and lift her out of that chair. He'd done that before and she'd arched against him. He felt that reassuring stir between his legs.

"Jonas, did you know that your father was worth millions?" She had his attention. "No, I didn't think so. The two of you never talked about money, did you?"

"You become a feminist after you left town?"

She laughed. "You mean after the cops found me here waiting for you two the night your father was killed? After my husband divorced me?" She laughed again.

He was surprised at how happy she sounded. He studied her face. There were lines bracketing her eyes. The skin under her chin was beginning to sag. She looked every bit her age, which was halfway between his and his father's ages. That made her about fifty. She'd been the oldest woman he'd slept with. She and his father taught him. That had served him well with Maureen. Served her well, for that matter. Wasn't the same without his father, though.

"I went to law school. That's how I spent my alimony. My ex paid my way. Delicious, yes?" She didn't wait for any comment. "Then I came back to Parthenon County and put myself in line to be probate judge. I was the one that made sure that half of Joel's money went into an account for you. Want to know how much you're worth?"

"Absolutely." What had prompted her to look out for his interests? Somehow she hadn't seemed the type. He looked at her suspiciously but remained silent. She wanted his attention. Sure, he knew how to give that.

"About three million dollars."

"I'm a millionaire?"

"You could be. Do you want to be?"

"Could be? I thought you said the money was in an account for me."

"Listen carefully, Joel Jonas Atwood the Third," she said slowly, as if to a child. "I'm the district court judge. You disappeared, remember? Did you know your mother put word around town that you'd died?"

"No, but so what? Who cares?"

"Your mother's trust petitioned that you be officially declared deceased ten years after your father died so that your inheritance would go to her. She probably didn't know about that. By then, I was district court judge. In charge of declaring missing persons dead. Are you still with me on this?"

"I'm worth three million. You're telling me how brilliant you are. Can we cut to the chase? It's been a long day."

She looked at him with, he could swear, pity. No, not pity. Something else. Something that made her eyes shine. A look he'd seen on his father's face but never directed towards him, a look reserved for his mother. "You're worth three million, unless, of course, you killed your father."

"I didn't." He said that in the certainty that only his mother was there that night.

"That, my dear, is arguable."

He stood up. "What bank's the money in? Let's go there and ask them."

"Absolutely. First I'll be handing copies of these to the cops. If you want me to, that is." She seemed highly entertained by something.

He stared at the photographs that Audrey fanned out onto the surface of his father's desk.

They showed him pushing his mother away from his father. Him pulling the tourniquet that she'd made out of her dress off his father's leg. God, had she gotten that far? He had no clear memory of that night. He thought she was jumping his father's bones. Tourniquet? He looked at the next photo. It showed him throwing his mother onto the ground. Then there was the photo that showed him carrying his mother's limp body. Another caught him slinging her into the back seat of his car.

"What's missing here, Jonas?" Audrey was sitting behind that desk again. He'd been right. She acted like a judge. Prosecutor, too.

"Audrey, who took these photos?"

Her smile widened. "That's my Jonas. Your father said you were the brightest thing going, that there was a brain in you, too."

"You took these photos."

"Doesn't really matter, does it? The photos are of you, letting your father die."

"My mother killed him."

"Really." She drawled the word. Pushing the photo toward him of his younger self pulling off the tourniquet, she added, "Your word won't hold up in court."

Why would it have to hold up in court? Jonas felt no guilt over his father's death, though he missed him terribly. He looked at Audrey, paying attention finally to her expression. Her satisfied smile. Her, yes, her sexuality. This was a woman in full bloom. Was this what his father had seen in her? Joel would never have dared used that combat flick knife on this woman. No, there was something else going on. "What?" he demanded. "What's with the photos? This would never get to court."

"It will if you go after the three million. Before, that is."

"Before what?"

"Before we're married."

"You're crazy. I'm married now."

"From what I hear around town, not for long." She pulled another folder out from somewhere. Without hurry she flipped through its papers. Then she handed a paper-clipped set over to him.

He read the papers. In them, one Dr. Joel Jonas Atwood III petitioned a divorce from Dr. Lily Miller Atwood. In exchange for the prompt execution of said request, Dr. Atwood would transfer $435,000 to the soon-to-be former Mrs. Atwood. Divorce Lily? "Audrey, you really are crazy. This isn't going to happen."

She pulled one last photo from another folder and slapped it down in front of him. "Sure about that? Absolutely, positively certain?"

He stood up, leaned over the desk and said, "Sure," without glancing at the photo.

She reached for Joel's old phone. There couldn't be service. She dialed. He thought she was faking it. His glance fell on the picture. His mind went blank.

She asked for the police chief. He yanked her hand away from the phone, which she hung up without fuss.

"This picture isn't real."

"Actually, it is. I have the negatives to prove it."

In the picture, a teen-age boy in running clothes has his hand on a knife. A knife sticking out of his father's thigh.

She pushed one more picture toward him. He fell back onto that hard wooden chair. In this one, the boy looked like his hand is holding the older man's over the knife hilt. "It explains why only Joel's fingerprints were on the knife," Audrey said helpfully.

That wasn't what happened. His father's hand had been trying to pull the knife out of his leg. Jonas had closed his hand over his father's, trying to help him. "Forget the money." Jonas got up to leave. He'd figure something out. He always did. He just had to get out of here.

"No can do, my love. You get the money and me and your life. Or I call the cops, hand them this evidence and they go after you. There's at least one Parthenon detective who'll spend every waking moment on your tail. I can guarantee it."

"Why?" he asked.

"Because I can," was all she answered. "Your father taught me quite well, you know."

Chapter 53

September

They had stopped at Constance's house to wash some clothes. With Bob ensconced in the back seat of her Subaru, Constance drove from New Haven to the Massachusetts line, then turned the driving over to Lily. Lily took that as a signal that her friend thought she'd straightened out enough not to risk their lives.

It was Labor Day weekend, which pretty much defined high season for the Berkshires. The area's bed and breakfasts, inns and motels were booked to capacity, what with end of summer and the Tanglewood music festival. On such short notice, Lily thought they'd have to camp out or sleep in the car, but Constance said, "The family business, remember? Land? Houses?"

Lily pulled her gaze from the road for a fraction of a second, catching Constance's withering look.

"My great-grandfather kept to the area he knew when he began buying property. New York, Connecticut, New Jersey, New England. Our first property up here was a summer house. The Cordrey family rule is to buy and hold, never sell. That summer house is now an inn. Turn right at the next driveway."

"Does that include jets?"

"Chance is a cousin from my father's mother's side. His last name is not Cordrey."

Constance steered the car onto a narrow two-lane road that wound its way up a hill into a thicket of old trees. Once they got through the little forest, there was a sprawling white two-story house with columns guarding the front. She pulled the car onto the gravel drive. A woman about Constance's age came through one side of the wide double-doored entrance and up to the passenger side. Constance climbed out to hug her. "Isabel, it has been too long. How are you?" She held the woman at arm's length. "You look wonderful." In fact, she looked like a slightly larger and blonder version of Constance.

"We're full so I put you both in grandpa's old room, if that's acceptable. Otherwise I'll lose someone else's booking."

By this time Lily had turned off the engine and walked around the car to stand next to Constance. "That will be fine," Constance said. "We really appreciate your making room for us. I doubt we shall be here for more than a day or two." She looked at Lily for confirmation.

"It's either here or it's not," she shrugged, leaving any explanation to Isabel's look-alike.

Constance frowned at her. "And you either know where it is or not?"

Lily nodded. Constance looked surprised. Lily gave herself points for being ahead of the librarian, for once. "It's still early. We could go over to The Mount now." Lily wasn't sure that she wanted to do that, to find out right now, today, if her quest would pay off.

Constance consulted with Isabel, who instantly conjured up a teenager to take care of their bags and Bob. Then they were back in the car, Constance navigating.

"You have visited Edith Wharton's mansion before?" Lily said, winding back down the driveway and onto the brief main drag of Lenox.

"Right before the Edith Wharton Restoration group began its renovation. I haven't seen it since."

They parked the Subaru in the lot outside of the ticket kiosk at The Mount. Lily bought them both tickets, pocketing the receipt. While they were walking up the cinder drive under the shade of massive old trees, Lily asked whether Constance wanted to see the ground floor first or to follow Lily up to the second floor. Now that they were at the home Wharton helped design and decorate for herself and Teddy, Lily found herself not in such a hurry. It was here or it wasn't. If it wasn't here, then she had months or years more research ahead of her.

"Upstairs first." Constance led the way through the front door, threaded around a tour guide and her group, and aimed at the center staircase. She looked as though she knew where she was going, which was why, Lily thought, that the tour guide let her pass unchallenged. That and her shabby chic clothes: perfectly-fitting faded khakis, starched white tailored linen shirt, worn boat shoes over bare feet. Her emerald pendant was her only jewelry. Constance Cordrey looked and acted as though she could be living at The Mount in the twenty-first century. Lily followed, her worn Birkenstocks slapping against the stone steps as they had that first morning at the Beinecke.

When they reached the upper floor, Lily took charge. "This way." She walked as quickly as she could without running, past the second floor living room to the corner occupied by Edith Wharton's bedroom suite and Teddy Wharton's dressing room. By the time Constance caught up to her, Lily stood poised in the center of Wharton's bedroom.

"Here's the story," she said, Constance her only audience. "It's autumn

1908, six years almost to the day since the Whartons first moved into The Mount. Edith is forty-six years old and a successful author. *The House of Mirth* had been published three years previously and become a bestseller. She's close friends with Henry James; she and Teddy and James have spent several seasons traveling through Europe together. But Teddy is showing signs of the same manic-depression his father had, not only with mercurial mood changes but in his handling of money. The money, remember, is largely from Edith's side of the family and from sales of her books. Teddy Wharton never worked. Theirs has been long a marriage of convenience, perhaps from their wedding day."

"Word in the family was that the marriage was never consummated," Constance said. She was looking out the windows at the formal gardens originally designed by Edith Wharton's niece.

"It would make sense, though we'll never know for sure." Lily's laugh was mirthless. "No one knows what the inside of another's marriage really looks like. As we know too well."

Constance crossed the room to her. "Just educated guesses."

"Anyway, while they'd been in Paris that winter, James stood guard while Edith began her love affair with Morton Fullerton, a journalist. Rumor has it that years before James had had an affair with the same man, but again, who knows? The important point is that Edith Wharton was beginning to pull up anchor. Her allegiance had always been split between family and her literary world, between America and Europe.

"Now Wharton's ship was pointing distinctly in the literary direction, to people who were as well-read and as cultured as she herself. Teddy Wharton was not one of those people. Henry James was central. By most reports, Edith didn't bother to try to include her husband in her interests. Teddy couldn't keep up with the wit and conversation that animated this house. I wouldn't be surprised if Teddy showed his resentment toward Edith's literary friends, particularly James. And I wouldn't be surprised if she arranged to keep her correspondence with James from Teddy's sight.

"James' most recent book is *The Golden Bowl*, published four years previously. He's moved seriously into his experimentation with narrative structure. This is the man, mind you, who pretty much invented the novel in the form that we now know it, or certainly perfected it. But nothing's really happening for him. Edith is worried that he's on the path toward another embarrassment like his play *Guy Domville*. When it opened in London in 1895, James came out at the end to take a playwright's bow and the audience booed him off the stage.

"So she begins to experiment with writing in the voice of Henry James.

She's always been able to mimic his syntax and word choices perfectly. She writes enough of a short story to send a query letter to her publisher."

"But she cannot have actually had the story published, you know," Constance said. She was leaning against the deep gray marble fireplace mantel. "He would never have spoken to her again."

"Don't be so sure he'd know what she was up to," Lily said. "There's solid evidence that three times during her friendship with James she tried to divert money to him without his knowledge. Twice she succeeded brilliantly. This would be one more way of not only enriching James but helping him toward some of the public acclaim that he now missed. The story would be her way of thanking the man who had taught her so much, who took her seriously at a time when female writers were regarded as second class. But she wouldn't actually discuss her experiment with Teddy.

"It's the last summer that Edith will spend at The Mount. After years of wrangling, she and Teddy will finally sell it. Edith will settle permanently in France. She doesn't realize the permanency, of course. When she packs up her papers, she hides a few things that she doesn't want Teddy to see. Perhaps some letters from Fullerton. Perhaps a letter or two from James that obliquely mention Fullerton. But certainly anything concerning her Jamesian experiment in voice and narrative structure. Perhaps Teddy hides things from her as well." When Lily realized that Constance was staring at her, she turned and added, "What?"

"Suddenly you sound like an English professor."

"What's that mean?"

"In charge. On top of your subject. As if you crawled into Edith Wharton's brain." Constance went to stand next to Lily, to look in the same direction Lily was looking. "Do you see all this, I mean, right now?"

"Stop it, Constance."

Constance poked her shoulder. "It's a serious question. Because you've known exactly where you wanted to go in the house. How long have you known?"

"Ever since I looked into that last box of Wharton correspondence at the Beinecke. I knew. Call it an intuitive leap or something. But I had to feel safe before I could come here." She turned to her friend. "Do you understand that? Being here—it has to be clean. Pure." Her fingers attacked her scalp, dislodging hairpins. "I'm not making sense, am I?"

"You make perfect sense. This—" she gestured at the not-quite-furnished room, at the Italianate bedstead—"is your new life. You had to make sense of the old one before moving on."

"Though we both know I'll never understand the old life."

"In my experience, that depends on your husband, whether his next move tells you something you need to know." Constance turned slowly, checking out Wharton's bedroom. "Is that Teddy's dressing room, right next door?" She pointed to a pocket door.

Lily ignored her. "There's a secret hiding place in this room. Something that doesn't have anything to do with furniture or with anything that could be removed. It must be a structural hiding place, in the very skeleton of this house. The Mount *is* Edith Wharton." Lily tapped her chin. Her gaze kept returning to the marble fireplace. "According to information published about The Mount, that fireplace is the original. So is the chair rail." Now she moved over to stand next to the edge of the fireplace, crouching to examine the chair rail. "As are the pocket doors."

While Lily examined fireplace marble, Constance began knocking gently on the wainscoting that surrounded the door pocket. When she got to a place about five feet up, the wall sounded hollow. Leaning around the wall, she caught Lily's attention. "Listen." She knocked lower down, producing a muted sound, then higher up. Her knuckles brought a small echo.

"Do that again, would you? In the hollow-sounding place. Not so loud that you'll bring any of the house managers or tour guides, though."

Constance drummed softly. Lily laid her fingers against the chair rail, walking them to follow the vibrations. Her fingers were stopped by the mantle. "Hold on." She slipped over to Constance and placed her open hand over the space she'd been hitting. Then Lily knocked on the marble mantle.

"No vibrations," Constance said.

Lily slapped her open hand down hard on top of the mantle, right near the edge.

"Ow!" Constance alternately flapped her hand and sucked at a bloody scratch.

Lily whipped around the corner into Teddy Wharton's sitting room to dive for the tiny opening in the wallboard. Her fingertips sought to expand the crack. Nothing. She hopped back into Wharton's bedroom to slam her hand down again on the fireplace mantel. This time a tiny drawer showed itself in the doorway between Wharton's room and Teddy's. The square placement of molding on the wall panel turned out to be the edges of the drawer. She pulled at the underside of the drawer, sliding it gently outward. By this time Constance had stepped out into the hallway to stand guard.

A few minutes later, Lily joined her, tucking something into her shoulder bag. In Constance's ear, she whispered, "I'm trying not to run for it."

Loudly, the little librarian said, "Ready for dinner?"

"Perfect," Lily said, leading the way down the hall. "Let's see if we can buy tickets for tomorrow."

Just after they left the ticket kiosk, Lily's cell phone rang. "Oh, hell, I forgot to turn it off." She checked caller ID. It was her uncle.

...

Phone to her ear, Lily wound her way through the parking lot to the car. When Constance caught up to her, Lily tossed her the keys. Constance propped herself against the car door, looking off into the trees, wondering what Nate was calling about. Lily's uncle didn't chatter. His few words held weight. Lily's expression was grave, her gaze somewhere over Constance's head.

Timing is everything, she mused. Here Lily had found what she'd been looking for—or at least she seemed to have, judging by her body language. Now her personal life loomed again.

If there were men out there like Nate Miller, then there might be hope. Too bad he didn't have a son.

Suddenly Lily was beside her. "Jonas has filed for divorce."

In one respect, that was a relief, since it took the decision away from Lily. But still, "Odd, somehow," Constance said.

"Let's walk." Lily pointed toward the stand of sky-high trees skirting the parking lot and front drive. Once under their canopy, which blocked the sun's heat, Lily slowed. "I know I haven't spoken much about what Jonas has been up to. It's because I can't seem to correlate the Jonas I thought I'd married with the Jonas of this summer." She held up a hand to stop Constance's comment. "I've come to the conclusion that it's because there's another Jonas, the one behind both personas.

"I learned how his father needed to control, to own, his mother. How Jonas needed to control Maureen. He must have wanted to control me from the moment he laid eyes on me. Why me is another question, one I'll leave alone for now. But here's the man who persisted until I married him, managed to lose me the one good job I could get in an impossible job market, discouraged me from my research. The key was that weird list of wifely chores he left for me the day after I'd been fired. At the time it pissed me off, but now I realize that was Jonas showing his hand. I was to be his good little wife, dependent on him alone, catering to him alone." She shook her head. "Now he's filing for divorce? Something has changed."

"Leave it," Constance advised, knowing fully that she'd be ignored.

"Can't. I have some more finding out to do." They'd walked from parking lot to driveway. Lily turned and grasped Constance's hands. "I have to know. Otherwise," she dropped her hands, put them in her jeans pockets and kicked at the gravel. A stone lodged in her sandal. She shook it off, found the stone and threw it into the trees. She slid her foot back into the well-worn shoe. "Otherwise, I won't have learned anything." She smiled wanly at Constance. "Not surprisingly, I'd like avoid that. Though you know, I wouldn't mind getting married again, some day."

"After a thorough investigation of the man in question." Constance knelt down to pick a tiny blue wildflower growing at the base of a tree. If those trees were planted when the Whartons built The Mount, then they were over a hundred years old. She patted the tree.

"Yes." Lily pointed to the car. "Let's go back to your cousin's. I want to make some phone calls."

"Are we going back to Parthenon?"

Lily looked up at an oak tree. She picked up an acorn, held it in her hand, her eyes following the tree all the way up. Then her fingers closed around the acorn, holding it loosely until she slipped it into a pocket. "Not unless I have to. Going there at all changed too many lives—Lillian's, Maureen and Peter's, Betty and Jane's, mine. I'm going to find out why it changed Jonas'."

"Money is usually the answer there." Constance was following Lily to the car. Lily stopped long enough to tighten the elastic around her hair and retie her topknot. Without looking at Constance, she said, "Maybe. But there's something else. I know it. What I don't know is if it has anything to do with me, besides divorce papers."

During the drive back to their inn, Lily didn't say a word. Constance left her to her thoughts.

Chapter 54

After returning to Chicago, Lily had gone shopping. She'd actually ventured into a North Shore department store. When she'd asked Cara for a suggestion, the younger woman had wanted to accompany her. Lily demurred, declaring that she might like to pick out her own clothes. Cara had looked doubtful but sent her off alone nevertheless.

At the store, Lily had discovered that there was actually a department with clothes for short women, even some styles designed for those possessed of distinct waist, hips and breasts. A tiny young clerk tucked her into a dressing room along with a dozen dresses. Lily wanted to buy a pretty dress. She wanted to own something besides jeans and teaching suits and the old black knit dress. She didn't know what she wanted to look like so much as how she'd like to feel once dressed. Not something explainable to Cara or the salesclerk.

It was the eighth dress she tried on that did it. She looked in the mirror. There she saw a shapely youngish woman, black hair neatly pinned to the top of her head, looking smart and, yes, attractive in a pewter gray silk jersey knit. It wrapped across under her bust and cinched over at the side, accentuating her small waist. She looked grown-up. Sophisticated. In charge.

Lily directed the saleswoman to find the same dress in other colors, and to have some shoes sent up. The woman started to say something. But off she went, coming back with the same dress in a blue the color of the Kansas sky, so deep it was almost violet. "It also comes in tomato, but we're out of your size. I could have it sent to you."

Lily agreed. Then another young woman came up with a selection of heeled black sandals. Finally the original saleswoman shyly proffered a wide silver and gold filigreed hair clip. When Lily tried it, the clip held her hair in place firmly while seeming to throw light onto her face. She bought that, too.

That was earlier in the day. Now she stood in front of the mirror in her bedroom, the one she'd always shared with Jonas. The dress made her feel prepared to meet Jonas. She saw herself smile. She, Lily Miller Atwood, was developing a persona. "How about that," she said aloud. Then her smile faded.

After receiving Jonas' petition for divorce, Lily had found out as much as she could about the why of it without going back to Parthenon. She'd go there eventually, to see her mother-in-law, just as she'd see Maureen and Peter in Kansas City. However, this time she had called Dorothy Cranmer, the high school principal, and then called her new best friend, the aging Parthenon police detective originally assigned to Joel Atwood's murder. If she went to Parthenon, these were the people she'd talk to.

Then Maureen's former student who edited the newspaper called with the information that Judge Audrey King was being squired around town by a man a decade younger than her who was rumored to be Jonas Atwood. She emailed their photo with the question, "Do you know this man?" It was Jonas, dressed in his khaki suit. His hair was longer, but that wasn't the only thing that made him look different. She'd printed out a copy of the photo. There was something odd about his face and posture. What was it?

According to Dorothy, it turned out that Jonas was something of an heir. His half of his father's money had been invested profitably, taking much more risk and reaping higher returns than was normally the case for money being held for a missing son. Dorothy had asked the newspaper editor about why that might be. The two of them conducted interviews at the bank and with a few local estate lawyers to find out how this had transpired. It had been Dorothy who had called Lily. "It's a little hard to tell, since Jonas' money was caught in the state bureaucratic web. So what I'm telling you is partly based on fact and partly on surmise. First, did you know that the woman who was waiting for Joel Atwood on the night of his murder was Audrey King?"

"No, her name was never mentioned. Just that her husband had divorced her and she'd left Parthenon."

"All true," Dorothy said, voice brisk. "While she was away she finished law school—she'd already completed a year or so of it before quitting to marry. When she came back here, she worked her way into county government. She ran for circuit court judge maybe three years after the murder. Took on the probate stuff. Been there ever since. I mean, who wants to be probate judge for little old Parthenon County? If Audrey King wants it, everyone's been willing to let her."

"Fine," Lily interrupted, "but how does she know Jonas?"

"Honey, she was his father's last lover. That'd do it. But—wait for it—what's maybe more interesting is that somehow his money came under her purview. Oh, not so directly that she could be accused of anything. But it was her court that stopped the bank from declaring Jonas dead, which would have shoved his half of Joel's estate in with his mother's. It was her court that said maybe the money could be invested for a little better return than in the usual Treasury notes."

"I've got a photo your editor pal sent of the pair of them."

"My former student, you mean? She can't wait to write about all this. Said you promised, once everything was settled. Until then she's bound to off-the-record, she says. Don't know how we managed to instill ethics in the child, but I'm glad she's an old-fashioned journalist that way."

Lily had thanked her, telling her she owed her dinner in Parthenon. Or Chicago, for that matter. Dorothy had surprised her, saying, "How about Kansas City? I'm going over to see Maureen and that boy of hers next month."

...

Armed with information and protective coloring—the gray dress, hair clip, new sandals, all gleaming—Lily stepped off the elevator outside her lawyer's offices. Her divorce lawyer had come recommended by her uncle's friend Walter as "a gracious shark." Lily actually liked the woman.

Jonas, it appeared, was already there, waiting for her in one of the firm's conference rooms. Lily straightened her back and walked through the door. The picture of the last time she'd seen Jonas alone in a room at the Guilford police department flashed across her mind.

This Jonas sat at the table, hands spread palms down in front of him. When the door clicked shut behind Lily, he looked up. For a moment he didn't move. Then he stood up and crossed the room to her. He didn't try to touch her. Instead, he held out his hands to her, palms up. "Lily, I'm sorry about all this."

Her husband stood in front of her, hands still held out. She grasped them lightly for a moment before stepping back to look at him. Yes, his hair was longer, as it had been in the photograph. He didn't look like an up-and-coming money man now. His suit was one she'd never seen. Though it hung perfectly, it seemed to own him.

Then she had it. Jonas looked defeated. It was that simple. She'd never seen Jonas defeated until now.

Lily gestured toward the table. Jonas pulled back a chair and waited until she had seated herself near the head of the oval before sitting down. He was acting like such a gentleman, but also as if he'd recently learned the moves. Lily knew for a fact that he'd never done this for her before.

"Jonas, talk to me."

He nodded. "You're owed that, at the very least." There were lines radiating from his eyes, she noticed. Also the skin under the eyes looked loose.

"Are you feeling all right?" she asked.

He smiled, but in a way that turned the corners of his mouth down. "Yes. According to a Parthenon doctor, I boast perfect health."

"Why would you go to a doctor?"

He ran a hand over his face. He placed both hands on the table, in the position he'd held when she walked in. His eyes watched his fingers, then moved to her face. "You know, I think I loved you all along."

Lily bit the inside of her cheek, fighting back tears. She managed to say, "There must have been some reason you stuck it out for those two years going after me. Why were you so intent on marrying me? Was it me or would anyone have done?"

His eyes were back on his spread hands. "You. From the moment I saw you, over in Holding Library. Old Holding, up in the rare books section. I used to watch you."

A chill passed down her back. He watched her? "For how long? Before we met, I mean."

"Months. I found out all about you."

Without realizing it, she'd pushed back her chair. "Did you stalk me? The way you stalked Bethany?"

"No, no, not at all. I wanted to find out who you were, what you liked, what interested you."

"Oh, Jonas, why make it so difficult?"

"That's what I'd always done. With Audrey. With Maureen. But it was like they were for practice. You were for real. Then once I had you…" His voice trailed off.

"I wasn't what you thought."

He nodded.

"Well, that makes two of us. I think, though, that that's what marriage is, actually finding out about the other person. You never let me see you, did you?"

He shook his head.

"Why?"

Now he looked up at her. His eyes were haunted. "Who would you see?"

Her Jonas had always been absolutely certain of himself. Everything he did was the right thing, even if it turned out wrong. Then the next thing would be right. This Jonas had lost that certainty.

"Jonas, what happened?"

"You got that grant, went to Connecticut, left me behind."

She waved her hand, as if to wash his words out of the air. "What about Bethany?"

He smiled and shook his head. "That was lunacy. I was trying to get your attention."

"Was Cindy Adler lunacy, too? And whoever gave you gonorrhea to share with both of us? Did your doctor discover that?"

His face dissolved. Behind the mask of a man was a young boy. His lips pursed as if he might cry. Then he laughed. Guffawed. Hooted. When he finally caught his breath, he only said, "Oh, that's perfect. Now she'll get everything and what she deserves, too."

"Jonas, what are you talking about?"

He didn't answer. From the inside breast pocket of that perfect suit he brought out a slip of paper and handed it to her. She unfolded it. It was a check made out to Lily Miller Atwood for $700,000. "What's this?"

"It's a hundred thousand dollars for each year we've been together. You deserve more than that. There's more if you ever need it."

She pushed the check back to him. "I don't need this. This is money from your father."

"Please take it, Lily. Please. The seed money came from my father. The rest came from, well, my actions."

She pushed further away from him. "From the night your father died."

His nod was brief but definite.

"Your mother says she killed him by accident. That your father was trying to kill her. That you removed the tourniquet around his thigh."

"Sounds about right. Perhaps one day my mother and I will actually talk. So much else is changing, why not that?" The edge of his hand cut the air like a knife. "Will you sign the divorce papers? Audrey wants to marry me."

What an odd way to put it. "Do you want to marry her?"

He studied the inside of his wrists. Then he shot his cuffs. His shirt was the palest sage green, a color which made his eyes appear more green than they were. "I have a new life. Did you hear I'll be teaching psychology again?"

He hadn't responded to her question. But Lily knew Jonas well enough to understand that he didn't want to answer.

He abruptly stood, slid the check toward her, and left the room, closing the door behind him.

She fingered the light blue check. Sadness overwhelmed her, weighed her down. Not regret so much as a sort of mourning. Jonas was alive but he wasn't.

The afternoon light drew her to the window. She looked down at the street. From this height she could see the university across the street. In the sorority quadrangle, young women were going to and fro around the cars. School would start in another week. The students were coming back.

She had a week to file her grant report. The irony of that struck her. She would mourn her marriage to Jonas in her own way.

On the way out of the conference room, she saw the check. It stopped her for a moment. She considered walking away. Then she had an idea. The weight on her shoulders shifted slightly. Lily tucked the check into the pocket on the inside flap of her shoulder bag, carefully zipping the pocket closed.

Lily signed the divorce papers. Her lawyer handed her a note in Jonas' handwriting. "Is there a male Venus di Milo?" was all it said. She zipped the note into the pocket with his check.

Jonas had told her what he could. She would find out the rest, in time. Now she had a flight to catch. Boston. Her bag was in the car.

Chapter 55

Two days later, a tired but relaxed Lily showed up on Constance's front step in New Haven. Before she could ring the bell, Bob came bounding around the side of the house. Lily instantly sat down on the step, holding out her arms. The dog did some broken-field running in her direction. What was he up to? When he finally stopped in front of her, he pulled what looked like a tiny ball of his own fur out from behind him and presented it in his mouth to Lily.

That's how she met Oz. The tiny puppy bounced on her lap, jumping up to lick Lily's cheek. Lily hugged her. "Your name is Oz. That means brave. Are you ready to be my brave dog?"

From behind her came Constance's voice. "The question is actually whether you are ready to be her brave owner. A pistol, this one. If she is the runt of the litter, it is hard to imagine the biggest." She reached over and ruffled Oz's gold curls.

"Constance?"

The tiny woman turned in the doorway of her house. "What?"

"I found the short story."

Constance marched back out and softly whacked Lily on the back of her head.

"Why do you keep hitting me?"

"When the hell were you going to tell me?"

"Now." Lily put Oz down on the lawn. The puppy instantly went over to Bob, who knocked her over and tucked her against him. "Remember where we found the letter, at The Mount?"

"In Wharton's bedroom."

"Ah, ah, never assume." Lily wagged her finger. "It was in the wall between Edith's bedroom and Teddy's dressing room."

Constance began shaking her head. "No way."

"Just think about it. The story was actually published. I checked. It was sold to a magazine in which Wharton rarely published, one that was ecstatic to publish something by the famous authoress. They'd never seen her handwriting. The editors didn't know that they were actually dealing with Teddy Wharton. He sent them the typewritten story. They sent the check. He deposited the check. After their divorce, Teddy landed in the same mental institution as his father and my ex-husband. But you know that. Anyway, he left his papers to his alma mater."

"Harvard. The enemy."

"Only in Yale football games. Well, no one much cared about the later papers of the loony ex-husband of the famous author."

"But rare book libraries are loathe to get rid of anything that might potentially be worth something." Constance nodded.

"It took two days to find the right box. I never even checked into a hotel, just stopped long enough to eat. Of course, Harvard didn't let me make away with what I found. I had to sign more papers in order to get photocopies. But they signed things, too, saying what I'd found was authentic."

"Accession dates?"

"The whole shebang."

Constance hugged Lily. "You're going to be famous."

But Lily was watching the two dogs, stretched out in the late-day sun. "Not yet. There's more to this story. I have some research to do in Paris. Then more in Rye, at Lamb House—James' house on the English coast. Probably back to Harvard."

"You're taking on Henry James?"

"His part of the story. Edith Wharton thought him a great man to have on your side."

Constance picked up Oz and deposited her in Lily's arms. "Now, how are you going to train your puppy? I will not allow you to become one of those Wheaten owners whose dogs run them."

Constance had tried to get Lily to take time off to stay with her and take Oz to Bob's trainer. But Lily had work to do. She had some writing to do. She caught Oz's attention, peering into those deep brown eyes. "Get used to this," she told the puppy. "I'm in charge. Let's get that straight." Oz stretched out with her head on Lily's shoulder and promptly fell asleep.

"I signed the divorce papers." Lily told Constance about seeing Jonas, his check and his note. "I can repay you for travel expenses now," Lily said.

"Thanks for the offer, but I'd rather you used the money on something else."

"It's expensive money, that $700,000 Jonas handed me. Do you know what I mean?"

"The cost of innocence," Constance said. "Always high."

"When I was at the lawyer's office in the conference room after Jonas had gone, I almost left the check on the table. But then I had an idea. Let me run it past you."

"Of course."

"Remember the Maine coon cat, Izzy?"

Constance peered at her as if to check to see that Lily hadn't gone crazy, sat back and crossed her arms. "The one who lives at your father's workshop?"

"Actually, Izzy belongs to my dad's lodger, Cara, whom you met that day at Prairie Shores when Bethany took on Jonas." Lily told Constance how she'd met Cara in her spring quarter writing class and why and how she'd brought Nate into her student's life. "Cara's been living upstairs at his workshop ever since. She's still at Prairie Shores and she's working at the local pet shelter. Cara has decided she wants to be a veterinarian. In the meantime, she's qualified as a dog trainer. Our baby Oz here is going to be her first paying client."

"I was impressed with Cara. Still, she has her work cut out for her with this one. So, how much does she charge to civilize a Wheaten?"

The four of them sat in the September sun—two women, one puppy and one watchful adult dog.

"Oh, we haven't set a price. I'm thinking in the neighborhood of a hundred thousand dollars, though."

Constance merely nodded. "Vet school?"

"As you said, the cost of innocence. It doesn't come cheap."

"My grandmother used to say cheap is dear." Constance stood up. "Want some dinner? I have salads and subs from Mario's. Ed and the others are on their way over. You owe them a story. Oh, and we have a surprise visitor on her way, thanks to Chance."

Epilogue

After the Guilford friends had left, the three women sat on Constance's patio, sipping Nestea and watching Bob and Oz. Cara was the surprise. She arrived halfway through dinner, chauffeured by Chance, and had been introduced to the Guilford trio and New Haven Italian food. Chance stayed for a quick meal before heading back to Westchester and his jet, returning to the oil fields. Constance noted Chance's interest in Cara, Chance could just have easily put her in a cab to New Haven. She was thinking that that was interesting when Cara asked her how she understood Jonas so well before she had even met him.

"Your turn," Lily said. "Tell us."

Constance looked up at the stars which were just appearing in the night sky. "Alden. A man chosen for me by my mother, approved by my family. I was so young. No, make that so naive. It was a big wedding. If you do your research," she pointed at Lily, "you'll find an article about our wedding in *The New York Times*. Alden wasn't anything special, but his family is equal to mine in, oh, you know, economic status."

When Constance was quiet for a long while, Cara reminded her, "Tell us."

Constance was quiet for a moment before standing up. "I'll be right back. This requires knitting."

Lily and Cara looked at each other. Cara asked, "Does she mean like with yarn and needles? Have you ever seen her knit?"

Lily shook her head. "Must be part of the story."

Constance returned with needles and yarn. "It is part of the story. Knitters saved my life so of course I learned."

"The wall hanging in your front hall? You made that?" Lily asked. Constance nodded. "That's amazing. The colors, all those blues and greys and pinks, and the textures. Like a modern tapestry. When I saw it that first time I thought it was a work of art. I still think so."

Constance's eyes were on her knitting; she seemed embarrassed by the praise.

"Tell us," Cara reminded her.

"I could have stopped him so many times," Constance said. "When I said yes to a date. Or after he walked two miles to bring me a single rose, his mouth still numb from having his wisdom teeth pulled.

"Or when I told a college classmate what he had done and she asked, her voice filled with a level of skepticism I can still hear, 'And you believed him?

That he'd walked miles to bring you a rose after dental surgery? Sure he didn't take a bus? I mean, we're talking Manhattan here, right?' Instead of considering her skepticism sufficiently valid to think over I registered it as unfair criticism of a romantic gesture.

"Yes, I believed him. We will believe, women like us. Until we don't. What was I thinking?"

Lily responded, "Here I sit, living proof that thinking doesn't enter into it. Which, may I remind you, had to be pointed out to me before it was too late."

Cara, the youngest of the trio by nearly a decade and far more skeptical than Constance's long-ago roommate, said, "Wow, Constance, you must have been a completely different person back then, buying into that crap. A red rose? I mean, he couldn't be more inventive? How about a tea rose? Or maybe something that showed he understood you."

"For example?" Constance asked.

"Like a book. An old book. Hell, any book." Cara shook her head. "It's like these men cast us in the play of their lives, write the whole script, then we recite the lines they assign us. We don't know it's not a play until the pain begins."

"I married him." Constance seemed to be reminding herself. "His script was exactly what I had been brought up to do and be. Until the script changed."

Lily said, "We play by their rules. Until we don't. It just takes some of us longer to begin to write our own rules."

www.ingramcontent.com/pod-product-compliance
Lightning Source LLC
Chambersburg PA
CBHW071153300426
44113CB00009B/1196